BOOM AND BUST

Why do stock and housing markets sometimes experience amazing booms followed by massive busts and why is this happening more and more frequently? In order to answer these questions, William Quinn and John D. Turner take us on a riveting ride through the history of financial bubbles, visiting, among other places, Paris and London in 1720, Latin America in the 1820s, Melbourne in the 1880s, New York in the 1920s, Tokyo in the 1980s, Silicon Valley in the 1990s and Shanghai in the 2000s. As they do so, they help us understand why bubbles happen, and why some have catastrophic economic, social and political consequences whilst others have actually benefited society. They reveal that bubbles start when investors and speculators react to new technology or political initiatives, showing that our ability to predict future bubbles will ultimately come down to being able to predict these sparks.

William Quinn is a Lecturer in Finance at Queen's University Belfast, where he conducts research on market manipulation, stock markets and, above all, bubbles.

John D. Turner is a Professor of Finance and Financial History at Queen's University Belfast. He is a Fellow of the Academy of Social Sciences and an editor of *The Economic History Review*. His book *Banking in Crisis* (2014) won the Wadsworth Prize in 2015.

William Quinn
John D. Turner

BOOM AND BUST

A Global History of
Financial Bubbles

CAMBRIDGE
UNIVERSITY PRESS

CAMBRIDGE
UNIVERSITY PRESS

University Printing House, Cambridge CB2 8BS, United Kingdom

One Liberty Plaza, 20th Floor, New York, NY 10006, USA

477 Williamstown Road, Port Melbourne, VIC 3207, Australia

314–321, 3rd Floor, Plot 3, Splendor Forum, Jasola District Centre,
New Delhi – 110025, India

79 Anson Road, #06–04/06, Singapore 079906

Cambridge University Press is part of the University of Cambridge.

It furthers the University's mission by disseminating knowledge in the pursuit of
education, learning, and research at the highest international levels of excellence.

www.cambridge.org
Information on this title: www.cambridge.org/9781108421256
DOI: 10.1017/9781108367677

First published 2020
Reprinted 2020

Printed in the United Kingdom by TJ International Ltd, Padstow Cornwall

A catalogue record for this publication is available from the British Library.

Library of Congress Cataloging-in-Publication Data
Names: Quinn, William, 1990– author. | Turner, John D., 1971– author.
Title: Boom and bust : a global history of financial bubbles / William Quinn, Queen's
University Belfast, John D. Turner, Queen's University Belfast.
Description: New York : Cambridge University Press, 2020. | Includes bibliographical
references and index.
Identifiers: LCCN 2019048274 (print) | LCCN 2019048275 (ebook) | ISBN
9781108421256 (hardback) | ISBN 9781108367677 (ebook)
Subjects: LCSH: Business cycles – History. | Financial crises – History. | Business
forecasting.
Classification: LCC HB3716 .Q56 2020 (print) | LCC HB3716 (ebook) | DDC 338.5/
4209–dc23
LC record available at https://lccn.loc.gov/2019048274
LC ebook record available at https://lccn.loc.gov/2019048275

ISBN 978-1-108-42125-6 Hardback

Contents

Figures

LIST OF FIGURES

Tables

CHAPTER 1

The Bubble Triangle

The definition of a bubble we take to be an undertaking which is blown up into an appearance of splendour and solidity, without any probability of permanence, and the name, we take it, is derived from the specious products of puffing and soapy water, with which the most of the ingenious youth of this realm have been long familiar.[1]

Anon.

We have to turn the page on the bubble-and-bust mentality that created this mess.[2]

President Barack Obama

WHAT IS THE DIFFERENCE BETWEEN THE GREAT COMPOSER George Frideric Handel and Shane Filan, the lead singer of Irish boyband Westlife? To those of a musical bent, the answer is obvious: Handel is one of the most respected classical musicians of all time, having composed several famous operas. Filan, on the other hand, largely specialised in saccharine cover versions of 1970's pop songs. The difference that interests us, however, is that while one lost all of their wealth in a bubble, the other got out before a bubble burst, making a handsome profit as a result.

By the time he was 30 years old, Handel's musical compositions had already made him a very wealthy man, and his patron, Queen Anne, provided him with a considerable annual income. In 1715 he invested some of his wealth in five shares of the South Sea Company, which would have cost about £440. Handel sold his shares before the end of June 1719 for a profit of about £145 – just before the huge bubble in the company's shares.[3] By the time Shane Filan was 30, Westlife was one of the most successful pop groups of all time and the net worth of the group's four members was over £32 million. Along with his brother, Filan decided to become a property developer in the midst of the Irish housing bubble. In order to purchase as much housing as possible, he supplemented his own funds by borrowing large sums of money from banks. In 2012 he was declared bankrupt, owing his creditors £18 million.

Shane Filan was not the only loser when the housing bubble collapsed. In Northern Ireland, where we both live, house prices more than trebled between 2002 and 2007; by 2012, they had collapsed to less than half their peak.[4] We thus observed at close quarters the economic destruction that a bubble can wreak. Bubbles can encourage overinvestment, overemployment and overbuilding, which ends up being inefficient for both businesses and society.[5] In other words, bubbles waste resources, as clearly illustrated by the half-built houses and ghost housing estates that stood across Ireland when the housing bubble burst. Other inefficiencies are in the realm of labour markets, as people train or retrain for a bubble industry. When the bubble bursts, they become unemployed and part of their investment in education has been wasted. After the collapse of the housing bubble, many of our friends, neighbours and students who had trained as architects, property developers, builders, plumbers and lawyers were either unemployed, in a new industry, or travelling overseas to find work.

The most severe economic effects usually occur when the bursting of a bubble reduces the value of collateral backing bank loans. This, coupled with the inability of bubble investors to repay loans, can result in a banking crisis. The collapse in house prices after 2007 was followed by the global financial crisis and we witnessed the downfall of American, British, Irish and other European banks. This resulted in major long-lasting damage to the economy. Financial crises are astonishingly economically destructive: estimates of the losses in economic output for post-1970 banking crises range from 15 to 25 per cent of annual GDP.[6] These estimates, however, conceal the large costs that financial crises have on psychological and human well-being.[7] They also ignore the human costs associated with the imposition of austerity measures once the crisis is over. We both experienced and witnessed cuts in real pay, decreased levels of public service provision and cuts in welfare payments to family members.

Not all bubbles, however, are as economically destructive as the housing bubble of the 2000s, and some may even have positive social consequences.[8] There are at least three ways in which bubbles can be useful. First, the bubble may facilitate innovation and encourage more people to become entrepreneurs, which ultimately feeds into future economic growth.[9] Second, the new technology developed by bubble companies may help stimulate future innovations, and bubble companies may themselves use the technology developed during the bubble to move into a different industry. Third, bubbles may provide capital for technological projects that would not be financed to the same extent in a fully efficient financial market. Many historical bubbles have been associated with transformative technologies, such as railways, bicycles, automobiles, fibre optics and the Internet. William Janeway, who was a highly successful venture capitalist during the Dot-Com Bubble, argues that several economically beneficial technologies would not have been developed without the assistance of bubbles.[10]

Why do we refer to a boom and bust in asset prices as a bubble? The word 'bubble', in its present spelling, appears to have originated with William Shakespeare at the beginning of the seventeenth century. In the famous 'All the world's a stage' speech from his comedy *As You Like It*, he uses the word bubble as an adjective meaning fragile, empty or worthless, just like a soap bubble. Over the following century, 'bubble' was widely used as a verb, meaning 'to deceive'. The application of the term to financial markets began in 1719 with writers such as Daniel Defoe and Jonathan Swift, who viewed many of the new companies being incorporated as not only worthless and empty, but deceptive.[11] The bubble metaphor stuck, but over time its use has become somewhat less pejorative.

Nowadays the word 'bubble' is used by commentators and news media to describe any instance in which the price of an asset appears to be slightly too high. Among academic economists, however, using the word at all can be deeply controversial. One school of thought sees a bubble as a non-explanation of a financial phenomenon, a label applied only to episodes for which we have no better explanation.[12] Eugene Fama, the father of modern empirical finance, goes further than this, calling the term 'treacherous' and complaining that 'the word "bubble" drives me nuts'.[13] In Fama's view the word 'bubble' is devoid of meaning, having never been formally defined.[14]

In this book, we borrow the definition of Charles Kindleberger, the MIT economic historian and bubble scholar, who describes a bubble as an 'upward price movement over an extended range that then implodes'. In other words, a bubble is a steep increase in the price of an asset such as a share over a period of time, followed by a steep decrease in its price.[15] Others have suggested that, for an episode to constitute a bubble, prices must have become disconnected from the 'fundamental value' of the asset.[16] However, this definition makes bubbles much more difficult to identify with any certainty, which can lead to lengthy discussions about whether a particular episode was a 'real' bubble or not. It is also divorced from the historical usage of the term. The beauty of Kindleberger's definition for us is that, because the definition makes no claims about the underlying causes of bubbles, we can investigate these causes for ourselves. One implication of this definition is that a bubble can only be identified with 100 per cent certainty after the event. However, this does not mean that bubbles are wholly unpredictable and random events. In this book, we propose a new metaphor and analytical framework which describes their causes, explains what determines their consequences, and – we hope – will help predict them in the future.

THE BUBBLE TRIANGLE

The starting point of our metaphor is to think of a financial bubble as a fire: tangible and destructive, self-perpetuating and difficult to control once it begins. While fires can cause serious damage, they can also be useful in certain ecosystems, contributing, for example, to the renewal of savannas, prairies and coniferous forests. The same is true of bubbles. Taking this metaphor further, the formation of a fire can be described in simple terms using the fire triangle, which consists of oxygen, fuel and heat. Given sufficient levels of these three components, a fire can be started by a simple spark. Once

POLITICS AND/OR TECHNOLOGY

Figure 1.1 The bubble triangle

the fire has begun, it can then be extinguished by the removal of any one of the components. We propose that an analogous structure can be used to describe how bubbles are formed: the bubble triangle, summarised in Figure 1.1.

The first side of our bubble triangle, the oxygen for the boom, is marketability: the ease with which an asset can be freely bought and sold. Marketability has many dimensions. The legality of an asset fundamentally affects its marketability. Banning the trading of an asset does not always make it wholly unmarketable, as demonstrated by the abundance of black markets around the world. But it does usually make buying and selling it more difficult, and bubbles are often preceded by the legalisation of certain types of financial assets. Another factor is divisibility: if it is possible to buy only a small proportion of the asset, that makes it more marketable. Public companies, for example, are more marketable than houses, because it is possible to trade tiny proportions of the public company by buying and selling its shares. Bubbles sometimes follow financial innovations, such as mortgage-backed securities, that make previously indivisible assets – in this case, mortgage loans – divisible.

Another dimension of marketability is the ease of finding a buyer or seller. One of the least marketable investment assets is art, for example, because the pool of potential buyers is very small in comparison to assets like gold and government bonds. Bubbles are often characterised by increased participation in the market for the bubble asset, expanding the potential pool of buyers and sellers. Finally, it matters how easily the asset can be transported. Assets which can be transferred digitally can now be bought and sold multiple times a day without the buyer or seller leaving home, whereas more tangible assets like cars or books need to be moved to a new location. Some bubbles are made possible by financial innovations that allow transportable assets to be used in lieu of immobile ones – trading the deeds to a house, for example, instead of the house itself. Like oxygen, marketability is always present to some extent, and is essential for an economy to function. However, just as one would not keep oxygen tanks beside an open fire, there are times and places where too much marketability can be dangerous.[17]

The fuel for the bubble is money and credit. A bubble can form only when the public has sufficient capital to invest in the asset, and is therefore much more likely to occur when there is abundant money and credit in the economy. Low interest rates and loose credit conditions stimulate the growth of bubbles in two ways. First, the bubble assets themselves may be purchased with borrowed money, driving up their prices. Because banks are lending other people's money and borrowers are borrowing other people's money, neither are fully on the hook for losses if an investment in a bubble asset fails.[18] The greater the expansion of bank lending, the greater the amount of funds available to invest in the bubble, and the higher the price of bubble assets will rise. When investors start selling their bubble assets in order to repay loans, the price of these assets is likely to collapse. Financial bubbles can thus be directly connected to banking crises.[19]

Second, low interest rates on traditionally safe assets, such as government debt or bank deposits, can push investors to 'reach for yield' by investing in risky assets instead. As a result, funds flow into riskier assets, where a bubble is much more likely to occur. The propensity of investors to reach for yield has a long history. Walter Bagehot, the famous editor of *The Economist*, observed in 1852 that 'John Bull can stand a great deal, but he cannot stand two per cent ... Instead of that dreadful event, they invest their careful savings in something impossible – a canal to Kamchatka, a railway to Watchet, a plan for animating the Dead Sea.'[20] In Bagehot's experience, investors would often rather invest in something ridiculous than accept a low interest rate on a safe asset.

The third side of our bubble triangle, analogous to heat, is speculation. Speculation is the purchase (or sale) of an asset with a view to selling (or repurchasing) the asset at a later date with the sole motivation of generating a capital gain.[21] Speculation is always present to an extent; there are always some investors who buy assets in the expectation of future price increases. However, during bubbles, large numbers of novices become speculators, many of whom trade purely on momentum, buying when prices are rising and selling when prices are falling. Just as a fire produces its own heat once it starts, speculative investment is self-perpetuating: early speculators make large profits, attracting more speculative money, which in turn results in further price increases and higher returns to speculators. The amount of speculation required to start the process is only a small fraction of that which occurs at its peak.

Once a bubble is under way, professional speculators may purchase an asset they know to be overpriced, planning to re-sell the asset to 'a greater fool' to make a capital gain.[22] This practice is commonly referred to as 'riding the bubble'.[23] However, it is often difficult to distinguish investors who rode the bubble from those who were lucky enough to sell at the right time. Speculation is also much more widespread when many investors have limited exposure to downside risk. This may be the case when defaulting on debts incurs few costs, when institutional investors are faced with poorly designed incentive structures or when bank owners have limited liability. In these circumstances, the prospect of buying a risky asset in the hope of short-term gains is much more appealing.

Of course, investors can also speculate 'for the fall': selling assets in the hope of buying them back later for a lower price. If the speculator does not own the asset, they can speculate for the fall by short selling: borrowing the asset, selling it, buying it back later for a lower price, then returning it to the lender. The short seller is hoping that the asset's price will fall in the intervening period so that they can make a profit from the trade. In practice, however, short selling is often much more difficult and risky than simply buying an asset. When an investor buys a stock, the potential losses are limited, but the potential gains are unlimited; when an investor short sells a stock, the opposite is true. Short selling even the most clearly overvalued asset can thus completely ruin an investor if its price continues to rise. Often there are legal or regulatory restrictions on short selling, coupled with social opprobrium against short sellers. At other times it can be extremely expensive to borrow the asset in the first instance.[24] In less regulated markets, short selling can leave investors exposed to market manipulators who engineer corners on the short-sold stock.[25]

What is the spark that sets the bubble fire ablaze? Economic models of bubbles struggle to explain when and why bubbles start – according to Vernon Smith, a Nobel Laureate, the sparks that initiate bubbles are a mystery.[26] In this book, we argue that the spark can come from two sources: technological innovation, or government policy.

Technological innovation can spark a bubble by generating abnormal profits at firms that use the new technology, leading to large capital gains in their shares. These capital gains then attract the attention of momentum traders, who begin to buy shares in the firms *because* their price has risen. At this stage, many new companies that use (or purport to use) the new technology often go public to take advantage of the high valuations. While valuations may appear unreasonably high to experienced observers, they often persist for two reasons. First, the technology is new, and its economic impact is highly uncertain. This means that there is limited information with which to value the shares accurately. Second, excitement surrounding technology leads to high levels of media attention, drawing in further investors. This is often accompanied by the emergence of a 'new era' narrative, in which the world-changing magic of the new technology renders old valuation metrics obsolete, justifying very high prices.[27]

Alternatively, the spark can be provided by government policies that cause asset prices to rise.[28] Usually, but not always, the rise in asset prices is engineered deliberately in the pursuit of a particular goal. This goal could be the enrichment of a politically important group, or of politicians themselves. It might be part of an attempt to reshape society in a way that the government deems desirable – several housing bubbles, for example, have been sparked by the desire of governments to increase levels of homeownership. The first major financial bubbles, described in

Chapter 2, were engineered as part of elaborate schemes to reduce the public debt.

As well as creating the spark through their policy decisions, governments can pull other policy levers which affect one or more of the sides of the bubble triangle. For example, governments can lower interest rates or increase the money supply, thus ensuring that the public have sufficient funds to invest in the bubble. They may pursue financial deregulation, allowing banks to lend more money on less restrictive terms, thereby increasing the amount of credit. An extension of credit can allow more investors to buy into the bubble on leverage, encouraging them to engage in more speculation. Financial deregulation may also make it easier to buy and sell the assets involved in the bubble, increasing their marketability.

Why do bubbles end? One obvious reason is that they run out of fuel. There is a finite amount of money and credit to be invested in the bubble asset, and increases in the market interest rate or central bank tightening can cause the amount of credit to fall. This makes borrowing to invest in an asset more difficult for speculators, which can in turn trigger a sell-off in the bubble asset as investors look to raise capital. Alternatively, the tightening of credit markets can make it impossible for those who invested in the bubble with borrowed money to extend the duration of their loans, forcing them to sell the asset.

The number of speculators is also finite, and can eventually reach an upper limit. Speculators may be spooked and exit the market when new information arrives which changes their expectations about future prices. For example, a bubble might burst in response to news announcements suggesting that the future cash flows associated with the bubble assets will be lower than expected. Since speculative investors typically buy an asset because its price is rising, even a slight reversal can dramatically reduce the asset's appeal. The effect of momentum trading is reversed: investors sell the asset because its price is falling, and the belief that prices will continue to fall becomes self-fulfilling.

Why do some bubbles cause widespread economic damage, whereas others have little effect on the macroeconomy? There are two important variables: the size of the bubble and its centrality within the wider economy. The most damaging bubbles are those where substantial wealth is invested in an asset that is deeply integrated with the rest of the economy. This integration may be in the form of supply chains; for example, the failure of a bubble company may also bankrupt its suppliers, who in turn default on payments to another firm. However, a more common route for the damage to spread is via the banking system. To extend the fire metaphor, banks are the equivalent of a combustible oil rig in the middle of a busy town. When banks fail, often as a result of the bank or its borrowers holding too much of a bubble asset, it can set off a chain of bankruptcies and defaults that destroys businesses, jobs and livelihoods. In the worst-case scenario, the failure of one bank exposes several others, with similarly devastating effects. Banks also tend to service a wide array of customers, many of whom would otherwise have no connection to the bubble. The exposure of banks to a crash can thus cause a regional or industry-specific bust to develop into an economy-wide recession.

In summary, our bubble triangle describes the necessary conditions for a bubble – marketability, money and credit, and speculation. They become sufficient conditions for a bubble only with the addition of a suitable technological or political spark. We believe the bubble triangle is a powerful framework for understanding why bubbles happen when they do, as well as their severity or societal usefulness. Since it describes the circumstances in which a bubble is likely to occur, it is also useful as a predictive tool. However, since the various elements of the framework cannot be reduced to a neat set of metrics, the application of the framework for predictive purposes requires the use of judgement.

The most long-standing existing explanation for bubbles is irrationality (or madness) on the part of individuals and concomitant mania on the part of society. One of the earliest expressions of this explanation came from Charles Mackay, a Scottish journalist and writer, who first published his *Memoirs of Extraordinary Popular Delusions and the Madness of Crowds* in 1841. This book has been so popular that it is still in print today. Mackay was a great storyteller, and his theory was supported by a series of colourful anecdotes that supposedly illustrated how insane societies could become. His tales covered witches, relics, the Crusades, fortune telling, pseudoscience, alchemy, hairstyles and even facial hair. Having demonstrated the near universality of madness, he then had chapters on the South Sea

Bubble, the Mississippi Bubble, and the Dutch Tulipmania, all of which argued that bubbles occur because of the psychological failings of investors.

Mackay was not the first to associate bubbles with madness and irrationality. Sir Isaac Newton, one of the most brilliant and influential scientists in all of history, lost a fortune by investing in the South Sea Bubble. When questioned about his losses, he is reputed to have said 'that he could not calculate the madness of the people'.[29]

This madness-of-crowds hypothesis has been refined and expanded by the likes of Kindleberger, John Kenneth Galbraith and, most recently, Nobel Laureate Robert Shiller.[30] Shiller and other economists argue that bubbles can largely be explained by behavioural economics, with cognitive failings and psychological biases on the part of investors causing prices to rise beyond their objective value.[31] A subset of investors, for example, may suffer from an overconfidence bias, whereby they overestimate the future performance of a company stock, or they may have a representativeness bias, whereby they incorrectly extrapolate from a series of good news announcements and overreact.[32] Other investors may simply follow or emulate this subset of investors simply because of herd behaviour and naivety on their part.[33]

The view that bubbles are largely a product of irrationality has been contradicted by economists who, like Nobel Laureate Eugene Fama, believe investors to be rational and markets to be efficient.[34] Much recent research on the subject has thus focused on establishing whether a particular bubble was 'rational' or not.[35] This is unfortunate, because the rational/irrational framework is almost useless for understanding bubbles. Partly this is because the word 'rational' is so loosely defined that many common investor behaviours can be classed as either 'rational' or 'irrational', depending on the preferences of the economist.[36] But more fundamentally, the framework is too reductive. Asset prices in a bubble are determined by the actions of a wide range of investors with different information, different worldviews and investment philosophies and different personalities. They often also face different incentives. Simply dividing these investors into categories labelled 'rational' and 'irrational' does not do justice to the complexity of the phenomenon, and as a result, we try to avoid these terms altogether.

HISTORICAL BUBBLES

We approach the historical bubbles in this book as if we were fire scene investigators, sifting through the ashes of historical bubbles in an effort to understand their causes. We then attempt to use this knowledge to become like fire-safety advisers, devising policies which may prevent bubbles from happening or being socially destructive in the future. First, however, we need to decide which fires to investigate. We have two selection criteria. Consistent with our definition of a bubble, we are interested only in bubbles where there was a large rise and then fall in asset prices. How large is large? We require a rise in asset prices of at least 100 per cent over less than 3 years, followed by at least a 50 per cent collapse in prices over a 3-year period or less.[37] For stock market bubbles, we do not require the entire market to have experienced a reversal; rather, the reversal may have taken place in specific sectors or industries.[38] This set of criteria means that those bubbles included in our catalogue are major ones. However, it also means that we may have overlooked some bubbles simply because we or previous scholars have been unable to find and collate price data.

The second criterion is that the asset price reversal must have been accompanied by a promotional boom, with new companies or financial securities being floated on financial markets. This ensures that the bubbles we select are those which had an impact on the economy beyond the effects of the price reversal. One implication of this criterion is that we exclude bubbles in commodities or collectables, such as comics, beany babies and baseball cards. Real estate or property bubbles are excluded unless they were accompanied by bubbles in stocks or facilitated by the issuance of newly created financial securities.

Table 1.1 contains a list of the major historical bubbles which meet these criteria, and which are studied in detail in this book. This list is by no means exhaustive. However, there are at least five things about our bubble catalogue which are of note. First, our selection of bubbles extends from the birth of stock markets through to the present day. Second, our catalogue is global in scope, covering four continents and nine countries. Third, although Table 1.1 contains many famous bubbles, there are also some which are less well known: the first emerging

TABLE 1.1 *Major financial bubbles*

Bubble	Country	Years	Asset	Post-bubble financial crisis
Mississippi Bubble	France	1719–20	Mississippi Company stocks	No
South Sea Bubble	UK	1719–20	Company stocks (including stocks of the South Sea Company)	No
Windhandel Bubble	Netherlands	1720	Company stocks	No
First emerging market bubble	UK	1824–6	Company and mining stocks	Yes
Railway Mania	UK	1844–6	Railway stocks	Yes
Australian Land Boom	Australia	1886–93	Company stocks and real estate	Yes
Bicycle Mania	UK	1895–8	Stocks of bicycle companies	No
Roaring Twenties	USA	1920–31	Stocks of new technology companies	Yes
Japanese Bubble	Japan	1985–92	Company stocks and real estate	Yes
Dot-Com Bubble	USA	1995–2001	New technology stocks	No
Subprime Bubble	USA, UK, Ireland, Spain,	2003–10	Real estate and houses	Yes
Chinese bubbles	China	2007, 2015	Stocks	No

market bubble of 1824–6; the Australian Land Boom, which burst in the 1890s; the British Bicycle Mania of the 1890s; and the Chinese bubbles in 2007 and 2015. Fourth, six of our twelve bubbles were followed by financial crises, and at least five were followed by severe economic downturns. Fifth, several of the bubbles listed in Table 1.1 were explicitly connected to the development of new technology – railways in the 1840s, bicycles in the 1890s, automobiles, radio, aeroplanes and electrification in the 1920s and the Internet and telecommunications in the 1990s.

Probably the most famous absentee from our study is the Dutch Tulipmania of 1636–7, which witnessed the rapid price appreciation of rare tulip bulbs in late 1636, followed by a 90 per cent depreciation in bulb prices in February 1637.[39] This is excluded for the simple reason that the price reversal was exclusively confined to a thinly traded commodity, with no associated promotion boom and negligible economic impact.[40] In other words, the Tulipmania was too unremarkable to merit inclusion. Although the wild fluctuations in price are striking, they are not unusual for markets in rare and unusual goods, particularly those predominantly used to signal status.[41] In the case of the Tulipmania these fluctuations were compounded by legal ambiguity over the status of futures contracts, suggesting that the price movements may have had a somewhat mundane explanation.[42]

The infamy of the Tulipmania is largely the fault of Charles Mackay.[43] Mackay painted the picture of a society overcome with collective insanity on the subject of tulips, where the value of some bulbs exceeded the value of luxury Amsterdam houses. He also stressed the universality of the trade, with the general populace of Amsterdam 'investing' in tulip bulbs at the various taverns dotted around the city. But Mackay's work is unreliable. His sources are based on second-hand accounts, which are in turn based on contemporary pieces of propaganda criticising the trade in tulips.[44] Very few of the claims Mackay makes can be substantiated. The popular narrative of the Tulipmania is thus largely fictional, 'based almost solely on propaganda, cited as if it were fact'.[45] Indeed, for several episodes in this book we can see a similar process of myth-making, whereby bubble anecdotes that were originally satire or propaganda are repeated years later as if they really happened.

Another notable set of absentees from our list are the property bubbles which occurred in Scandinavia in the 1980s and in South-East Asia in the 1990s.[46] In both cases major credit booms had their roots in financial liberalisation, and in both cases the crash was followed by a banking crisis. Capital account liberalisation exacerbated the credit boom in South-East Asia, where substantial amounts of international capital flowed into the region, resulting in twin banking and currency crises.[47] However, the only one of these housing bubbles that was accompanied by a major stock market boom was in Thailand. The scale of the Thai stock market bubble does not meet our criterion for inclusion, and there appears to have been no promotional boom.[48]

Having chosen our fires, how do we go about investigating them? A good place to start is usually the findings of previous investigators. We thus make extensive use of existing literature, much of which comes from fields far beyond history or economics.[49] However, the memory of an event and the experience of an event are often very different, and we also want to understand the thoughts and actions of those who were on the scene at the time. We therefore also investigate the writings and speeches of contemporary journalists, politicians and commentators during each bubble. What were they saying while the fire was going on? Were they calling the fire brigade or fanning the flames? We do not want to focus exclusively on the powerful – we are also interested in so-called ordinary people who were caught up in the fire. Who suffered, and who, if anyone, benefited from it? Finally, as financial economists, we do not want our analyses to be purely descriptive – we want to be able to quantify the size of each fire and the scale of the damage it caused. For famous bubbles this was straightforward, but for lesser-known bubbles it involved painstakingly compiling our own data from old records in dusty archives. The overall result, we hope, is a comprehensive overview of the subject told over three centuries. Our story begins in 1720 with a seminal moment in financial history: the invention of the bubble.

CHAPTER 2

1720 and the Invention of the Bubble

The nation then too late will find,
Computing all their cost and trouble,
Directors' promises but wind,
South Sea at best a mighty bubble.
Jonathan Swift[1]

FEW MOVIES HAVE BEEN MADE ABOUT KING CARLOS II OF Spain. His life does not make for a satisfying story: he suffered tremendously for 38 years, and in the end his death started a war. The Habsburg family to which he belonged had almost exclusively married other family members in order to consolidate its wealth and power. This end was achieved, but at a severe physical and mental cost to Carlos, who inherited a range of deformities as a consequence of five generations of inbreeding. His bone structure made it difficult for him to eat, speak or walk, and he suffered frequent seizures; his learning difficulties were so severe that no attempt was ever made to educate him formally. He ascended to the throne at the age of 3, but even in adulthood, ruling the country in his own right was effectively impossible.[2]

Carlos was probably also infertile, and neither of his two marriages produced any children. His death in 1700 thus sparked a succession crisis. As his heir, Carlos had named a grandson of Louis XIV of France, Philip, Duke of Anjou. As Carlos's grand-nephew, Philip had the strongest genealogical claim to the throne, but his accession would have unified the French and Spanish empires. This threatened the British, Dutch, Portuguese and Holy Roman empires, who instead proposed Archduke Charles of Austria as king. By 1702 their attempts to solve the crisis through diplomacy had failed, and Britain, the Netherlands and Austria declared war on Spain.

The resulting conflict, the War of the Spanish Succession, lasted for 13 years and was resolved in 1715 by the Treaties of Utrecht and Rastatt. The resolution was straightforward: Philip could remain king of Spain as long as he renounced any claim to the French throne. The war, however, had been extraordinarily expensive. In order to fund it, governments had relied on a relatively new method of war finance: borrowing money from the general public by issuing debt securities. This resulted in unprecedented levels of French, British and Dutch public debt. In France the public debt in 1715 stood at over 2 billion livres: between 83 and 167 per cent of GDP, depending on the estimate used. In Britain the public debt rose from £5.4 million pre-war to £40.3 million, around 44 to 52 per cent of GDP.[3] Holland's public debt nearly doubled as a direct result of the war, and the cost of financing it was just over two-thirds of Holland's total fiscal revenue.[4]

These debt levels represented an existential threat, because if creditors doubted a nation's ability to repay its debts, it would struggle to finance future wars. The French and British governments were both acutely aware of this. After the death of Louis XIV in 1715, several of the new French Regent's counsellors proposed recalling the French Parliament (the *Estates General)* to deal with the disastrous state of the public finances. Britain was withdrawn from the war by a Tory government that campaigned heavily for the reduction of the public debt.[5] For each country the challenge was reducing the debt in a way which minimised both the risk of revolution and the cost of future borrowing. It was therefore crucial to prevent the cost of additional taxation from landing too heavily on those with political power. In addition, defaults, which were normally only partial, must somehow be portrayed as justified and/or unlikely to be repeated. Ideally, creditors would readily accept them.

France, where the problem was most acute, recycled numerous debt reduction methods that it had used before. The new finance minister, the Duc de Noailles, imposed a non-negotiable write-down on creditors, with some short-term debt being unilaterally devalued by two-thirds. Financiers were charged with profiteering, and around 110 million livres were confiscated. The currency was repeatedly debased, with coins restamped with a lower gold and silver content in 1701, 1704, 1715 and 1718. In combination with a substantial austerity programme, this meant that, excluding interest payments, France had moved from a deficit of over 60 million livres in 1710 to a surplus of 48 million livres in 1715. However, the problem was that the interest payments on its debt were around 90 million livres per year.[6] And that was just to finance the debt – reducing it would have cost substantially more. New tricks were required.

The French demand for financial innovation was met, almost single-handedly, by a Scottish financial theorist called John Law. Describing Law as a 'Scottish financial theorist' invokes exactly the wrong image; his life was sufficiently fascinating to have inspired not only an extensive historical literature of its own, but at least one lowbrow romantic novel.[7] In 1694, at the age of 22, a Scottish court sentenced him to death for killing a man in a duel, but he escaped prison and fled to the Continent, growing rich through a combination of professional gambling, financial services and networking. At the same time, he wrote several treatises on economics, most notably *Money and Trade Considered*, which was published in 1705. Virtually every serious work about Law has emphasised both his reckless character and his genius: the famous Harvard economist Joseph Schumpeter placed him 'in the front rank of monetary theorists of all times'.[8]

Law arrived in Paris in 1715, and immediately met with the Regent to propose the establishment of a 'General Bank' as a branch of government. The General Bank foreshadowed the emergence of the modern central bank, and was more ambitious than the Bank of England, which had been around since 1694. Its remit was to collect all of the king's revenues, issuing in their place bank notes that were exchangeable for coins. Once the bank was established, it only needed to hold coins worth a fraction of the value of all outstanding bank notes, since it was unlikely that a large number of bank notes would be presented for redemption at the same time. The government could then increase the money supply by lowering the fraction of bank notes backed with coins. Law argued that giving the Bank control of monetary policy would encourage economic growth, thus increasing tax revenues and helping the government to pay off its debt. Although the scheme was initially rejected, a privately owned version of the scheme was allowed to proceed a year later.[9]

Despite the fact that the Bank was nominally a private company, Law understood that its success depended on the backing of the political authorities. He therefore ensured that a large proportion of its shares were distributed to influential noblemen. This gave the government a vested interest in the success of the scheme, which was compounded when the Regent deposited large sums of money in it at a very early stage.[10] This political support proved invaluable to the scheme, as it led the government to introduce legislation that virtually guaranteed its success. From October 1716 onwards, tax collectors were required to redeem bank notes for cash, and from April 1717 the bank's notes were accepted as payment for taxes. At the end of 1718, when the bank was nationalised, its initial subscribers had gained an impressive annualised return of 35 per cent, providing Law with a track record that lent credibility to his promises of spectacular capital gains from subsequent ventures.[11] Furthermore, the bank's nationalisation gave the French government the power to print money, dramatically increasing its control of one side of the bubble triangle.

In 1717, Law was granted a charter for the establishment of the Mississippi Company, whose original remit was to develop land near the Mississippi River.[12] As soon as the first shares were issued, Law set about expanding its operations through a series of mergers and acquisitions. The initial capital was spent in December 1718 on acquiring the Senegal Company and the French monopoly on tobacco production. Additional share issues were made in the June, July and September/October of 1719, raising 27.5 million, 50 million and 1.5 billion livres respectively. These funds were used to purchase the right to conduct almost all French overseas trade, the right to mint coins, and tax collection rights equivalent to about 85 per cent of French revenues. In February 1720, the Mississippi Company took over the General Bank.[13]

The Company's largest operation, however, was a scheme for the reduction of the public debt. The essence of this scheme was as follows. When the final Mississippi share issue of 1.5 billion livres took place, payment was only accepted in the form of government bonds. The average yield on these bonds was around 4.5 per cent. The Mississippi Company then lent money to the government, which used the loan to buy out its debt. Since the interest rate on the loan was only 3 per cent, this substantially reduced the government's debt burden. But the public needed to be convinced to exchange government debt for shares in a company whose main asset was government debt with a much lower yield: a self-evidently bad deal.[14] Law's solution was to create the self-fulfilling belief that the price of the shares would rise after they were issued. Even if debt holders noticed that they were getting a raw deal in terms of future cash flows, the prospect of spectacular capital gains on the shares in the short run would be likely to prove too tempting to resist.

In short, Law solved the government's debt problem by inventing the bubble. First, he made sure Mississippi shares were much more marketable than the debt used to purchase them. Whereas most of the debt had been highly illiquid, Mississippi shares traded freely on a vibrant secondary market. Liquid assets are more desirable, so this added some real value – though not nearly enough to justify the large reduction in future interest payments. Second, he used the General Bank to expand the money supply, ensuring that an abundance of funds were available to purchase the shares. The total note issue was expanded from 200 million livres in June 1719 to 1 billion livres by the end of the year. Third, he made the shares highly leveraged by allowing them to be purchased for an initial down payment of 10 per cent: a massive extension of credit.[15]

Finally, Law attracted the attention of speculators by using an array of 'market management' tricks to engineer a series of rapid increases in the Mississippi share price. For example, each successive share issue required the subscriber to hold existing shares, which increased the demand for these shares on secondary markets. The rising price of existing shares then made the current issue look like a much more attractive investment. When the price started to flag, Law propped it up by publicly committing to buying derivatives that would allow investors to limit their potential losses.[16] He was also able to use the news media, which was at that time subject to strict political control, to stimulate demand. Sometimes this simply amounted to widely broadcasting his commitments: his offer to buy call options in 1718 was published in the *Gazette d'Amsterdam*. At other times the news media was used to spread propaganda. A defence of his policies was published in several newspapers in February 1720, and he repeatedly attempted to portray the Company's assets as far more profitable than they really were.[17] Law's popularity with the government, coupled with the government's control over the newspapers, meant that favourable narratives about the scheme went unquestioned.

The scale of the resulting bubble can be seen from Figure 2.1, which tracks the price of Mississippi shares from 1718 through to the end of

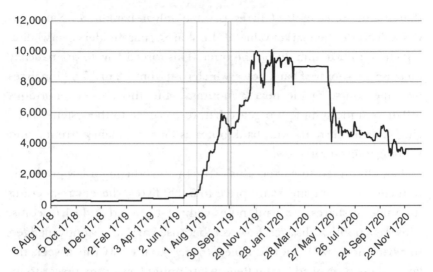

Figure 2.1 Mississippi Company share price (livres) and subscription dates[18]

1720. The potential profit from getting involved early was enormous: a share costing 140 to 160 livres in 1717 was worth over 10,000 livres two years later. Even subscribers to the later issues could have doubled their money in the space of a few months by correctly timing their exit from the market.

Law's power over the French economy reached its apex in January 1720, when he was appointed Minister of Finance. He soon discovered, however, that he could not sustain prices indefinitely, and his attempts to do so became increasingly unsubtle. In an effort to prevent Mississippi shareholders from converting their gains back into gold and silver coins, a compulsory re-coinage devalued coins relative to bank notes. Laws were passed banning the export of gold or silver, and on 27 February it became illegal to hold more than 500 livres in coins or to use coins for transactions above 100 livres in value. The French state, however, did not have the capacity to enforce such draconian measures. Many members of the public simply ignored the new laws; others converted Mississippi holdings into diamonds instead. Law responded by placing similar restrictions on diamonds.[19]

On 5 March, after a 25 per cent decline in the price of Mississippi Company shares, Law committed to having the General Bank buy any shares at the price of 9,000 livres, payable only in bank notes. Since this was well above the market value of the shares, shareholders overwhelming chose to take him up on the offer. This forced Law to dramatically increase the supply of bank notes, which rose from 1.2 to 2.7 billion livres over the course of the next 3 months.[20] But this created enormous inflation, undermining two goals that were crucial to the system: replacing metallic currency with bank notes as France's main currency, and keeping interest rates low.

Law attempted to correct this error by introducing a law gradually reducing the Company share price to 5,000 livres, thereby re-aligning the value of shares and bank notes with that of gold and silver coins. This was a political disaster, however, because Law had recently pledged that bank notes would not be subject to any variation. Within a week, the law had been revoked by the Regent, stripping Law of the power to fix perceived flaws in his system and demonstrating his sudden loss of political influence. Law was dismissed as Minister of Finance on 29 May, and the Company's share price fell to just over 4,000 livres on 31 May.[21]

Law was swiftly reinstated as a *de facto* Minister of Finance and the market temporarily recovered. But it was clear that the scheme had failed, and his role thereafter consisted of managing its decline. The General Bank was closed, and it was announced that bank notes would no longer be accepted for the payment of taxes. Against Law's wishes, a series of punitive measures were visited upon Mississippi investors: capital was called up, the nominal share price was reduced and subscribers who had sold their shares were forced to buy them back at a penalty rate. The Mississippi Company's tax collection and minting rights were removed. On 8 December 1720, the marketability revolution was reversed when the king abolished the trading of Mississippi shares. Nine days later, Law was sent into exile to protect him from angry investors.[22]

The government then attempted to rebuild some kind of monetary and financial system from the ruins of Law's regime. An instrument called the 'Visa' was set up, to which all assets relating to Law's regime were submitted, accompanied by a statement outlining how the assets were obtained. The purpose of the Visa was ostensibly to convert these assets into a public debt 'based on the realm's abilities and on the rules of fairness', which in practice meant favouring those with small holdings. The political environment was by then so toxic, however, that the government was forced to reverse the reduction of its debt repayments that Law's system had enabled. When the Visa finally concluded in 1724, debt servicing cost the state 87 million livres per annum – almost exactly the same as it had in 1717.[23] The French government's ambitious efforts to reform its finances had comprehensively failed.

The South Sea Bubble similarly arose from the British government's desperation to get its debt under control. In the years following the War of Spanish Succession, a series of Acts of Parliament attempted to reduce the government's interest payments. However, the representative nature of Parliament, coupled with the political power of debt holders, made it difficult to tackle the most expensive tranches of the public debt. By the beginning of 1720 the government was still crippled by substantial sums of expensive debt: £13.3 million of long-dated annuities paying 7 per cent interest for almost 100 years and £1.7 million of short-dated annuities paying 9 per cent interest until 1742.[24] The more lucrative the debt was for its holders, the more of an incentive they had to mobilise politically in opposition to any effort to reduce its value. The government's previous attempt to tackle the annuities, in 1717, failed as a result of an effective lobbying operation by annuity holders.[25]

The prospect of John Law's system succeeding in France, however, elevated the debt burden to the status of a national emergency. In January 1720 the directors of the South Sea Company, a slave-trade firm that had helped the government refinance its debt in the past, presented a potential solution to Parliament. The essence of the proposal, which borrowed heavily from Law's ideas, was that the Company would offer its equity to the public in exchange for government debt. The Company would then receive a reduced interest rate on this debt, substantially reducing the government's financing costs. Furthermore, it would pay the government a fee of £4 million for the privilege of conducting the scheme, plus an additional fee of up to £3.6 million, depending on how much debt was converted. Following the payment of several strategic bribes to wavering MPs, this offer was accepted by Parliament.[26] Debt subscriptions, whereby creditors could submit debt for South Sea shares, were arranged for late April, mid-July and early August 1720. These were accompanied by money subscriptions in April, May, June and September, which simply involved the purchase of shares at a price determined by the company.[27]

The benefit to the government was clear: it received a cash payment and reduced the costs of financing its debt. If anything, it was surprising that the measure required so much politicking to pass Parliament. The benefits to the South Sea directors are less clear and have in the past been the subject of some debate. Adam Anderson's influential account suggested that directors could have kept cash from the sales of 'surplus' stock, i.e. shares in excess of the amount needed to clear the public debt.[28] Since the mechanics of the scheme were such that a higher market price meant greater sales of surplus stock, the directors (according to Anderson) could profit substantially by generating a bubble. However, this theory does not add up. Selling surplus stock meant undertaking additional liabilities which offset the additional assets, leaving nothing for the directors to pocket.[29] Alternatively, the directors could have used inside information to ride the bubble, as was alleged by the 1721 Commons committee.[30] But, surprisingly, this rarely occurred, and certainly was not widespread enough to have been the motivation underpinning the whole scheme. The only explanation we are left with is that the directors genuinely intended to establish a profitable company to rival the Bank of England.[31]

Even more puzzling is why so many debt holders agreed to the deal. The Mississippi Company had at least held significant wealth-generating assets, even if they were not sufficient to justify the price of the shares being offered. The South Sea Company's wealth-generating assets were trivial. It could in theory trade slaves to South America, but its right to do so was disputed by Spain; historians have debated whether this asset was literally worthless or just very close to being worthless.[32] Debt holders were supposed to exchange government debt for shares in a company that held (virtually) nothing but the promise of a reduced rate of interest on this debt, and that had incurred significant additional liabilities in the form of promised cash payments to the government. Before John Law, one would have thought it impossible to convince them to agree to such a deal. But the Mississippi Bubble had demonstrated how the prospect of capital gains could lure investors into accepting an apparently bad bargain.

The South Sea directors thus set about creating a bubble. First, South Sea shares were made extremely marketable, especially in comparison to the illiquid debt that could be used for their purchase. Not only were the shares freely transferable, but the secondary market for them was very active, so it was generally easy to find a buyer or seller. The directors then expanded credit in several ways. Money was lent directly to those who wished to invest: 2,300 people borrowed from the South Sea Company during 1720. The shares were highly leveraged, with only a small proportion of capital on each share called up. Calls on the remainder of the capital were scheduled over long periods of time, so investors had ample opportunity to re-sell the shares before they had to make any further payments. Furthermore, the calls themselves were allowed to be paid on credit. This not only made the shares appealing to risk-seeking investors, but freed their remaining cash, which in many cases was used to purchase yet more shares.[33]

The ability to buy shares for relatively small down payments opened up the market to elements of society that could not previously have afforded to invest. This later proved deeply controversial: critics in the aftermath of the bubble reacted with horror to a perceived increase in social mobility, with the undeserving poor said to have made great sums of money at the expense of the rightfully well-off elites.[34] In truth, however, the vast majority of investment still came from the super-rich. The average subscriber bought £4,600 worth of shares in the first subscription, £3,400 in the second, £8,600 in the third and £4,600 in the fourth, with no long tail of small subscribers. This was well outside the capacity of the middle classes; the typical annual income of an army officer, for example, was around £60. Politicians were deeply engaged in the scheme, with three-quarters of MPs and peers subscribing to at least one of the issues. This group alone accounted for 14 per cent of the investors in the first two subscriptions. Interestingly, when it came to the highly unprofitable third and fourth issues, this group accounted for only 9 and 5 per cent respectively of the subscriptions, suggesting that they may have been better informed than the average investor.[35]

Having increased marketability and expanded credit, the directors then needed to encourage speculation. As with the Mississippi Company, subscriptions were divided into 'tranches', and in the first instance only a small proportion of shares was issued. This created a market which was large enough to remain liquid, but small enough for the directors to manipulate at a relatively small cost. Early subscribers could thus be provided with spectacular capital gains, encouraging subscriptions for future tranches. As subscriptions proceeded, some scarcity was maintained by delaying the issue of tradeable receipts, reducing the supply of shares on secondary markets.[36]

Unlike Law, the South Sea directors had to reckon with a free and vibrant press. The expiration of the *London Gazette* monopoly in 1695 had led to the publication of several competing newspapers, such as the *Weekly Journal, London Journal, Daily Courant* and *Evening Post*.[37] These newspapers devoted substantial coverage to financial matters and were widely read in local coffee houses that doubled as stock exchanges.

Why did these newspapers not alert investors to the nature of the scheme? Part of the problem was that they were not entirely reliable. Daniel Defoe warned his readers against 'false news' spread with the intention of manipulating share prices.[38] At other times, made-up news was simply sold to investors. Small boats would reportedly leave English ports pretending to visit Amsterdam, take a turn around the harbour while making up plausible gossip, then return to the port to sell fake news to speculators. However, when it came to dispelling outright misinformation, the financial news appears to have functioned reasonably effectively. Defoe claimed that false rumours were almost always dispelled by the end of the day, and there is very little evidence that the rumours were a significant factor in pushing up prices.[39]

Perhaps the greater problem was that most journalists and writers did not fully understand the scheme. The debt conversion scheme was somewhat arcane; few had the necessary numeracy to properly value South Sea shares, particularly when the Company was misrepresenting the potential value of its slave-trading rights. As a result, an incredibly wide range of valuations was published. Lord Hutcheson, using cash-flow analysis, correctly ascertained that the shares in the final subscriptions were being offered at a price well above their true value.[40] At the other end of the

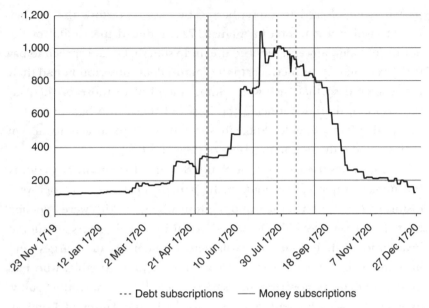

Figure 2.2 South Sea Company share price (£) and subscription dates[41]

spectrum, one infamous article in the *Flying Post* argued that the higher the price investors paid for South Sea shares at subscription, the better the deal they were getting.[42] In the absence of established financial analysts, uninformed investors were unsure whose valuation was correct.

The success of the South Sea scheme in engineering a bubble can be seen from Figure 2.2. The price of South Sea stock rose from £126 at the beginning of 1720 to a peak of £1,100 in mid-July. The crash was just as dramatic, accelerating in October to end the year, symmetrically, at a price of £126. By then, however, the government's primary goal had already been achieved: 80 per cent of non-callable annuities had been converted into South Sea shares. Tellingly, one of Parliament's first actions when it reconvened in December 1720 was to exclude the possibility of rescinding this conversion.[43]

The fallout from angry investors then had to be managed without provoking adverse political consequences. These consequences were potentially serious; P. G. M. Dickson argues that the public mood in late 1720 was foul enough to pose a genuine risk of revolution.[44] The government's solution was a combination of carrot and stick. The carrot was partial relief offered to subscribers. The 'Act to restore the publick Credit', which was passed in August 1721, reduced the capital of the South Sea Company and reduced the lump sum that it had agreed to pay the government.[45] Subscribers to the August debt subscription had their terms altered so that they were almost identical to those of the May subscription, thereby reducing the losses of those who had bought at the peak of the bubble. Still, all subscribers were forced to accept a substantial reduction in the value of their stock.[46]

The stick was used against the South Sea directors, in order to satisfy the public's thirst for retribution. In January 1721, six directors were dismissed from public office, and the four who were MPs were expelled from Parliament. A bill was passed requiring all directors to submit inventories of their estates to Parliament, and corruption charges were brought against members of the government. John Aislabie, who had masterminded the government's side of the scheme, was found guilty, expelled from Parliament, and imprisoned in the Tower of London. A bill confiscating the assets of all the directors was passed in July.[47]

This scapegoating of the previous administration did more than channel public rage towards a convenient target. By imposing a personal cost on those who had implemented the scheme, the British government could credibly reassure investors that it would not be repeated, as any politician who tried could expect to be punished and disgraced. This preserved the government's ability to issue bonds at reasonable interest rates. However, the main benefit of the South Sea scheme to the government was also preserved, since the reduced debt payments remained in place. Parliament had performed an impressive feat: a partial default on existing debt with no corresponding increase in the future cost of its borrowing.

A feature of the South Sea Bubble that had not occurred in France was a concurrent boom in the establishment of new companies. Julian Hoppit estimates that around 190 British joint-stock companies were established in 1719 and 1720, with a subscribed capital of anywhere between £90 million and £300 million.[48] Almost all of these companies quickly vanished, largely due to regulatory opposition in the form of the 1720 Bubble Act and a series of writs issued against the firms. Only two of the new companies, London Assurance and Royal Exchange Assurance,

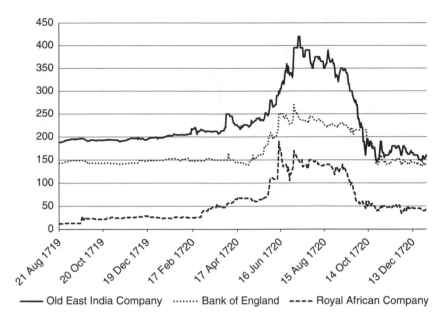

Figure 2.3 Share prices (£) of the Bank of England, Royal Africa Company and Old East India Company[49]

were long-term successes, largely as a result of the monopolies granted to them by Parliament.[50] As Figure 2.3 shows, existing firms also experienced a boom and bust at the same time as the South Sea Company. Between September 1719 and June 1720, Royal African Company shares rose from £13 in September 1719 to a peak of £180, while Old East India Company shares rose from £189 to £420.

The Netherlands, despite also having run up significant public debt, did not experience a debt conversion like the Mississippi or South Sea schemes. Similar proposals were suggested but deemed unnecessary; the government could borrow much more cheaply than in France or Britain, partly because Dutch debt already traded extensively on secondary markets.[51] The 1720 bubble in the Netherlands consisted entirely of a promotion boom and stock price reversal. Between June and October 1720, 40 joint-stock companies were projected, with a proposed nominal capital of 800 million guilders, about three times the Dutch Republic's GDP. Almost all of these companies were designed to encourage speculation, having a very low proportion of paid-up capital. Most were either

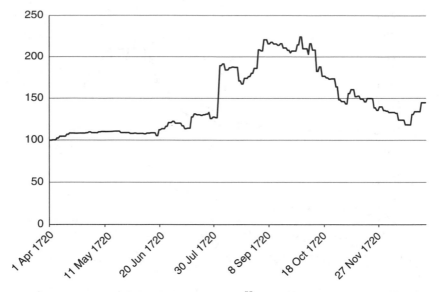

Figure 2.4 Share price index for the Netherlands[52]

pure insurance companies or insurance was a large proportion of their business. Of the 40 companies, only 6 ever became fully operational, and only one, Stad Rotterdam, was a long-term success.[53]

An index of Dutch share prices, as reported in *Leydse Courant,* is shown in Figure 2.4. This data is presented with the caveat that the source is not entirely reliable. Prices were sometimes listed before any shares had been issued, and it is unclear whether the price is that of certificates entitling the holder to purchase a share, unofficial pre-subscription trading or simply fabricated by company directors.[54] The reported prices nevertheless represent the best available estimate of the amount by which Dutch shares rose and fell, doubling in the spring and summer to a peak on 1 October 1720, before losing half their peak value by December.

The promotion and share price boom has been attributed to the flow of speculation into the Netherlands as the Mississippi and South Sea schemes burned out.[55] Although movements of exchange rates indicate that this did occur, it is probably less of a factor than it might appear: much of the share price movements can be attributed to market manipulation, falsified or misleading price reports and concerns about the regulatory response to Stad Rotterdam's proposed business model. It is also notable how few of the proposed companies achieved full subscription, which seems inconsistent with an abundance of speculative money. Oscar Gelderblom and Joost Jonker hence describe the bubble in the Netherlands as a 'damp squib', lacking the economic, political or cultural impact of those in France and Britain.

There were also a series of Mississippi-inspired schemes in other European countries. Debt-to-equity swaps were considered in Spain, Portugal, Piedmont, Denmark and Sweden, and proposals to set up colonial trading companies reached Russia, Vienna and Sicily. The motivation in each was broadly similar: a Spanish conversion scheme was sold to the king as a means to 'imperceptibly pay off' his debts, and a proposal to create a Russian land bank argued that it would enable the Tsar to raise funds for warfare. Hamburg, Venice, Spain and Portugal also experienced minor financial booms.[56] However, the level of marketability in financial markets was generally too low for any significant bubble to develop outside of England and France.

CAUSES

As well as being the first documented financial bubbles, the 1720 bubbles were notable for having been explicitly and deliberately created by a small number of people. Both John Law and the South Sea directors had an intuitive understanding of the bubble triangle, expertly cultivating all three sides with the specific goal of alleviating the government's debt burden. Their first and most fundamental move was to increase marketability by swapping very illiquid debt for highly liquid equity. A financial asset that was very difficult to buy and sell was thus replaced by one that could be bought and sold easily. This created the potential for frequent price changes on a secondary market, which in turn allowed the assets to become instruments of speculation. Without this initial increase in marketability, which required the endorsement of the French and British governments, neither bubble would have been possible.

Credit and leverage were then rapidly expanded to help investors buy shares in the bubble companies. The South Sea Company used part-paid shares with payments by instalment, also lending money to individuals to help them buy shares in the company. Similar methods were used in France, where they were supplemented by a substantial expansion of the money supply. Law's control of the General Bank meant that he could direct France's entire monetary policy towards generating the bubble.

Stimulating speculative investment was a cornerstone of both schemes, as the prospect of quick capital gains was what induced debt holders to accept a conversion on inferior terms. This was deliberately stoked through what Hutcheson called 'the artful management of the spirit of gaming'.[57] Some investors, particularly foreigners, were very good at speculating and managed to reap large profits; others were essentially gambling and suffered heavy losses.[58] None of this mattered to the engineers of the bubbles, who simply needed speculative investment to keep prices rising.

Technically, investors could have speculated in the opposite direction, betting on the bubble bursting. There were no particular legal restrictions on forward contracts, so investors could simply enter an agreement to sell shares at today's price in a few months and wait for the price to fall before buying those shares. However, it seems unlikely for two reasons that short selling South Sea shares was a viable alternative for informed investors. First, there was a risk of share prices rising further before the contract became due. The *Whitehall Evening Post* reported, in March 1720, of a Jewish stockbroker who lost £100,000 in this way.[59] Second, as previously noted, the Mississippi Company and South Sea Company both had some control over the supply of their own shares. Short selling on a scale significant enough to affect prices would probably have been seen as an attack on the company, which could respond with a corner – buying large numbers of their own shares to drive up prices, possibly even forcing the short seller to purchase shares from the company to fulfil the forward contract. The losses for short sellers in such a scenario could have been extremely high. Perhaps as a result of these two factors, contemporary sources rarely recommended short selling. Hutcheson, for all his scepticism of the scheme, did not even mention the possibility, and strategies incorporating short positions do not seem to have been used by a significant number of investors.[60]

With all three sides of the bubble triangle in place, the emergence of a bubble only required a spark: an initial burst of price increases that could kick off the self-perpetuating process of speculation. This was provided, in the case of Law, through a combination of propaganda, the temporary restriction of supply, and commitments to buy shares at prices above market value. Once early purchasers of shares had experienced spectacular capital gains, such measures became less necessary. As for the South Sea scheme, propaganda was augmented by the issuing of shares in tranches at successively higher prices, which communicated an expectation that the price of the shares would rise. Its chief engineers probably had no intention of prices rising as high as they did in the summer of 1720: a less dramatic bubble would still have converted most of the government debt, but with fewer personal consequences for the directors.[61] But once the fire had spread beyond a certain level, it became impossible to control.

The level of speculation was the most striking aspect of the bubbles, and has driven most popular accounts of the episodes. The most influential of these is Charles Mackay's *Extraordinary Popular Delusions and the Madness of Crowds*, which was first published in 1841. Mackay weaves a compelling narrative in which foolish and greedy investors were swept up in a gambling mania, and were ruined as a result of their own folly. The Victorian middle classes loved the neat moral message about fiscal responsibility, and the book sold exceptionally well.[62] Its continuing popularity owes a lot to a series of colourful anecdotes that supposedly illustrate the extent of investor stupidity. The most enduring of these anecdotes concerned a million-pound undertaking entitled 'A Company for Carrying on an Undertaking of Great Advantage, but Nobody to Know What It Is', for which subscriptions were supposedly filled in one day, after which the proprietors disappeared. The exceptionally well-written critical accounts of the bubble by Daniel Defoe and Jonathan Swift were used to support the narrative, and elements of the abundant satire of the period were reprinted.[63]

There are two major problems with Mackay's account. First, it does not provide a convincing causal explanation for the bubbles, treating them instead as spontaneous outbursts of madness. Second, it is mostly fictional. Almost none of the anecdotes can be substantiated. The satirical pieces were, of course, not supposed to be taken literally, but Mackay also failed to place them within their cultural context. From 1720 onwards a growing religious movement concerned with moral decay seized upon the South Sea Bubble as the embodiment of society's problems. To further the goals of this movement, it made sense to exaggerate the extent to which the bubble was a consequence of greed.[64] This spread a popular conception of the bubble that ignored its political nature in favour of a simple narrative of an 'extraordinary popular delusion'.

We also reject the hypothesis, most famously advanced by Peter Garber, that the prices seen during the bubbles can be fully explained by unforeseeable changes to the prospects of the Mississippi and South Sea Companies, with price-distorting speculation playing little role at all. In Garber's hypothesis, the high price of Mississippi shares reflected a potential increase in economic activity resulting from Law's financial reforms. The South Sea Company, meanwhile, is characterised by Garber as 'finance-first': having accumulated a large fund of credit and the backing of Parliament, it was conceivable that the company would have found profitable investment outlets.[65]

The problem with this argument is that it is unfalsifiable: there is no theoretical price level for which it could not be made. A more conventional way of valuing an asset is to compare its price to its associated discounted cash flows, making allowances for uncertainty and liquidity. This was the method used by John Law himself, whose calculations showed that the peak share price of the Mississippi Company was only consistent with his estimates of future cash flows if he could reduce the discount rate to a wildly optimistic 2 per cent. François Velde, after working through various possible scenarios, finds that it is 'difficult to avoid the conclusion that the company was overvalued several times over'.[66] Hutcheson's contemporary analysis of the South Sea Company's assets implied a price of £557 per share, well below the peak share price of £1,100, and even this valuation was based on unrealistically optimistic assumptions.[67] Despite Garber's contention, there is no evidence to suggest that the South Sea directors made any effort to find new profitable outlets for its excess capital.[68] The peak share prices of the Mississippi and South Sea Companies are simply not explicable without the presence of substantial price-distorting speculation.

CONSEQUENCES

The Mississippi Bubble had three notable negative consequences for France. The first of these was a short but severe recession. Although its effect on GDP has not been reliably estimated, the available economic data supports the abundant qualitative accounts of economic ruin. For example, the price level in Paris fell by 38 per cent in 1721, a more severe deflation than the United States experienced during the Great Depression.[69] The second negative consequence was that potentially beneficial financial reforms were delayed or rejected on account of their association with Law's regime. Paper money, for example, became a pejorative term, and attempts to re-introduce it during a liquidity crisis in 1789 failed to sustain the confidence of the public. Finally and most significantly, the experiment cemented France's failure to reform the public debt, and its interest rates thus remained high for the rest of the century. As well as restricting the country's economic development, this represented a serious handicap in future conflicts. It has therefore been linked, albeit indirectly, to both the French Revolution and the ultimate failure of Napoleon.[70]

The South Sea Bubble, too, was long thought to have been accompanied by a recession, because qualitative sources from 1721 suggest that the country was in severe economic turmoil. Contemporary newspapers and pamphlets were full of opinion pieces, satire and poetry condemning the scheme. Attempts were made to organise collective action by those who had lost money, and losses in the bubble were blamed for several suicides.[71] The 1721 Commons committee investigating the bubble received numerous petitions reporting, in somewhat hysterical terms, that the economy had ground to a halt.[72]

These sources, however, had a transparent agenda. Newspapers and pamphlets faced the usual incentive to be hyperbolic in order to increase sales, and were often participating in a moral crusade against the perceived greed and excess of the bubble. The petitions, meanwhile, were submitted when Walpole's government was in the process of resolving the scheme, and appear to have been a part of an organised campaign on behalf of those who had lost money. In fact, the economic effect of the bubble was small and localised; its most tangible impact was an increase in bankruptcies in the Greater London area. Export levels were almost unchanged, agricultural price fluctuations were within normal bounds and exchange rate movements typically did not indicate an economic or financial crisis. Estimates of industrial production and GDP also suggest very little effect.[73]

Much has been written about the misery of those who lost money in the South Sea scheme, but there was another side to those transactions. Many investors made a great deal of money out of the scheme, though they typically had the good sense to keep quiet about it. These gains were not limited to insiders: there is evidence to suggest that outgroups performed very well, their detachment from mainstream financial circles perhaps granting them a more sober view of the schemes. Women, who typically accounted for around 20 per cent of investors, were significantly more likely than men to speculate successfully in Bank of England and Royal African Company shares. Jewish investors also appear to have performed better than average, generally by purchasing shares cheaply after the crash, and Huguenots performed relatively well.[74]

It is difficult to find any silver lining for France in the Mississippi Bubble. Improvements in the public finances were reversed and any of Law's financial innovations that could have improved the economic situation were thrown out with the bathwater. The South Sea scheme, however, was arguably a net positive for Britain, significantly reducing its debt burden and only having a manageable and short-lived economic impact. The bubble in the Netherlands, insofar as it even existed, had few economic consequences beyond the emergence of some new and innovative insurance business models.[75]

Most histories of the first financial bubble have been framed by the assumption that its consequences were negative. Typical topics for discussion include how blame should be apportioned and how modern policymakers might prevent something similar from happening again. A more insightful approach might be to compare the bubble across the three main countries to determine why the economic consequences were severe in France, but not elsewhere. The key features of each bubble episode are summarised in Table 2.1. Britain undertook a large debt conversion scheme while experiencing a concurrent boom and bust in existing company shares; the Netherlands experienced only the latter.

TABLE 2.1 *Comparing the first financial bubble across France, Britain and the Netherlands*

	France	Britain	Netherlands
Debt conversion scheme	Yes	Yes	No
Promotion boom and bubble pattern in existing company shares	No	Yes	Yes
Part-paid shares and margin loans	Yes	Yes	Yes
Banking system involved in bubble	Yes	No	No
Sustained reduction of financing cost of public debt	No	Yes	No
Substantial negative economic consequences	Yes	No	No

Private debt, in the form of both part-paid shares and margin loans, increased in all three countries. Nevertheless, only France experienced a severe economic downturn.

There are two reasons why the economic impact was so much more severe in France. First, the Mississippi Bubble involved a direct effort to overhaul the country's currency, and thereby drew in a much greater proportion of the population. In 1720, simply holding gold, silver, jewellery or bank notes was enough to expose any individual to the whims of John Law's scheme. The South Sea Bubble was much less ambitious and had almost no effect on the vast majority of the population, who were too poor to invest in stocks. Participation in the Netherlands joint-stock boom was even narrower. In both cases, most of those who lost money could afford to do so and the scale of bankruptcies was not enough to cause a chain of defaults that could have led to a full-blown financial crisis.

Second, the banking system was much more deeply involved in the manufacture and maintenance of the Mississippi Bubble. As a result, the bursting of the bubble and Law's attempts to manage it led to an over-issue of bank notes and high inflation, followed by sharp deflation and a contraction of credit. These major problems in the financial sector created a severe economic fallout that affected every class in French society. In contrast, the Bank of England and Bank of Scotland were largely detached from the bubble, and in 1721 both institutions actively worked to sustain credit flows and to maintain monetary stability.[76]

A final consequence of the bubbles, common to all three affected countries, was the decline of the joint-stock company form. Such a device was out of the question in France, which was so scarred by the experience that it reverted to its prior financial system characterised by strict adherence to religious directives on money lending. French financial institutions and markets thus remained stagnant and inefficient for over a century.[77] Britain, under pressure from the South Sea Company, passed the Bubble Act in 1720, which forbade the formation of any joint-stock companies in the absence of parliamentary approval. The importance of this Act may have been overstated – joint-stock companies were already illegal under the common law – but in any case, very few formed after the South Sea scheme collapsed.[78] The Netherlands passed no equivalent law but, curiously, the joint-stock format almost disappeared anyway.[79] This resulted in a widespread absence of companies with transferable shares, removing the marketability side of the bubble triangle. As a result, no major bubbles occurred for over a century after 1720.

CHAPTER 3

Marketability Revived: The First Emerging Market Bubble

The mania for mining concerns, which raged in London and the empire generally in 1824 and 1825, after the opening of Mexico and other parts of Spanish America to our intercourse, forms a remarkable and, we are sorry to add, disgraceful era in our commercial history.

John R. McCulloch[1]

> Come with me, and we will blow
> Lots of bubbles, as we go;
> Bubbles, bright as ever Hope
> Drew from fancy – or from soap;
> Bright as e'er the South Sea sent
> From its frothy element!
> Come with me, and we will blow
> Lots of Bubbles as we go.
> The Bubble Spirit[2]

WHILE THE ADVENT OF MASS MARKETABILITY HELPED THE British government restructure its debt in 1720, the accompanying bubble led to a cultural and regulatory backlash. Over the next century, share marketability was successfully suppressed. The Bubble Act, which had been passed in 1720, forbade any company with marketable shares from establishing without explicit government approval. In addition, common law judges, who were by nature very conservative, were hostile to companies attempting to operate with even a semblance of share tradability. Even the authorisation of 51 canal companies with tradeable shares by Parliament between 1790 and 1794 did not result in a bubble because canal shares all had very high share denominations and, as a result, the market for them was very thin.[3]

In 1807–8, marketability threatened to come back when there was a small promotion boom. However, most promotions were so-called unincorporated companies: enterprises which did not have parliamentary authorisation to act as a company. This meant that their shares were not freely transferable, and trading in their shares was illegal. Consequently, these companies attracted the ire of the Attorney General, and the Bubble Act was invoked for only the second time in its history.[4] When the next wave of new companies began to form in 1824, however, politicians did not step in, having rediscovered how they could use marketability to further their own interests. The result was the first emerging market bubble, and, unlike after 1720, the marketability genie could not be put back in its bottle afterwards.

The poet calling himself the Bubble Spirit highlights one of the key ingredients of this bubble – an avaricious and dishonest politician. The politician targeted in the poem is John Wilks, elected MP for Sudbury (or Sudsbury as the Bubble Spirit called it), who earned the moniker 'Bubble Wilks' because of the various far-fetched companies he was associated with and helped promote.[5] One of his earliest (and ultimately unsuccessful attempts) to float a company was in 1822, when he published a prospectus for a company to enforce Tudor laws on Sabbath observance.[6] During 1824 and 1825, however, the mining, gas-light, annuity and railway companies that he helped promote met with varying degrees of success. One of his main ploys was to give these companies an air of respectability by persuading MPs and peers to become directors. But he had not lost his penchant for ludicrous schemes, such as a wood condensing company to transform soft wood into hard wood by passing it mechanically between two giant rollers. As *The Times* sarcastically observed, 'perhaps it was discovered that the same process which compressed the fibres of soft wood, also broke them, and thereby somewhat diminished their strength'.[7] His fraudulent manipulation of the Devon and Cornwall Mining Company then led to his arrest, bankruptcy, resignation from Parliament and banishment by his family to Paris. Even in exile, Wilks was unable to resist financial chicanery, and his rumour-mongering on the *bourse* resulted in him being banned from its vicinity and eventually expelled from France.[8]

The years leading up to the first emerging market boom were marked by the Napoleonic Wars. Britain's victory over Napoleon came at a huge cost. By the time of Waterloo in June 1815, the National Debt stood at £778.3 million, having risen by nearly £536 million over the previous 22 years of war.[9] Unlike in 1720, the government did not need an elaborate scheme to reduce the cost of servicing this huge debt burden. The development of the market for government debt and financial engineering meant that it was simply able to retire debt and refinance it at a lower cost. This refinancing, plus a growth in surplus savings arising from a recovering economy, led investors to look for more remunerative homes for their funds, particularly after 1822.[10] Into this void came Latin American loans, first; Latin American mines, second; and third, a plethora of joint-stock companies.

The Napoleonic Wars had loosened the grip of the Iberian powers on Latin America, with the result that, from about 1810 onwards, armed struggles for independence succeeded one another. By the early 1820s, many Latin American countries had declared their independence from Spain and Portugal, while British foreign policy had moved from trying to mediate between Spain and its rebellious colonies to preparing to recognise the independence of the latter as nations.[11]

These newly independent countries came to London to raise funds for their military, possibly at the active solicitation of British financiers.[12] The first batch of Latin American loans was issued in 1822 to Colombia, Chile, Peru and the mythical country of Poyais in Central America. Poyais was 'ruled' by the infamous General Gregor MacGregor, a Scottish adventurer, mercenary and narcissistic fraudster. As well as inducing investors to give him £200,000, he also convinced many Scots that they should emigrate to Poyais. Most of the first two shiploads (about 250 people) died soon after reaching the malaria-infested fake country. His con was eventually exposed, and by 23 January 1824, the Poyais bonds were worthless. Still the Poyais scam did not deter investors, and Brazil, Colombia and Mexico issued bonds in 1824 and 1825.

The Latin American loan boom prepared the way for the bubble in Latin American mining shares in 1824 and 1825, because the bonds were high yielding and they raised the profile of the region in the minds of investors. Investor interest in Latin American mines was further stimulated by British travellers who came back from the newly liberated countries to educate the British public about the economic potential of the new states. One such person was William Bullock, who was among the first British travellers to visit Mexico after it became independent in 1821. On his return to Britain, he published an account of his travels, and in 1824 staged in London a major exhibition of Mexican artefacts and fauna, which was visited by 50,000 paying customers.[13] In his book, Bullock emphasised the potential of the abandoned silver mines and possibility of a vast market for British products in Mexico.

The first of these mines to list on the stock market were the Anglo-Mexican and United Mexican, both established in early 1824 and listed in *Wetenhall's Course of the Exchange* by July 1824. Thereafter, until the end of 1825 (see Table 3.1), prospectuses were issued for 74 Latin American mining companies, 44 of which were still operating at the end of 1826.

The narrative that developed around the Latin American mines, which was used *ad nauseam* in their prospectuses, went as follows. First, the abandonment of the silver mines in 1810 was due to political upheaval rather than exhaustion, meaning that they held untold riches for those who could resurrect them. Second, the Spanish court had enjoyed much prosperity thanks to the mines, despite working them

TABLE 3.1 *Joint-stock companies formed in 1824 and 1825*[14]

	Number of companies	Nominal capital (£m)	Shares ('000)
Surviving companies	127	102.8	1,618.3
Abandoned companies	118	56.6	848.6
Projected companies	379	212.7	3,494.4
Total	624	372.1	5,961.3
Surviving mines	44	27	359
Abandoned mines	16	6	98
Projected mines	14	6	80
Total	74	39	537

Notes: Surviving companies (mines) are those still in existence at December 1826; abandoned companies (mines) are those which had issued shares but had been abandoned by December 1826; and projected refers to companies (mines) which had issued prospectuses or announced their projection in the press, but which have left no evidence about their actual formation.

inefficiently – they had never been fully exploited. The somewhat hubristic implication was that 'by the introduction of English capital, skill, experience and machinery, the expenses of working these mines may be greatly reduced, and their produce much augmented'.[15] Third, there was an explicit belief that precious metals were abundant in Latin America. For example, the prospectus of the Imperial Brazilian Mining Association referred to large lumps of virgin gold being found, and that of the General South American Mining Association talked of inexhaustible resources of gold, silver, quicksilver and copper.

As well as the promotional boom in Latin American mining companies, there was a boom in the promotion of other companies. As can be seen from Table 3.1, 624 companies were promoted in 1824 and 1825. But by the end of 1826, only 127 of these were still in existence – the remainder had either been abandoned, failed or had never got far beyond publishing a prospectus. The total nominal capital of the 624 companies was a staggering £372.1 million, but of this, only £17.6 million was actually raised.[16]

Table 3.2 reveals how the trickle of company promotions during the early part of 1824 grew in the latter part of the year and had become

TABLE 3.2 *Major companies projected from February 1824 to January 1825*[17]

	Number of companies	Number of companies with MP or peer as leading director	Capital (£'000s)	Shares ('000s)
Feb 1824	5	1	6,360	38
Mar 1824	4	0	6,630	69
Apr 1824	10	7	11,220	197
May 1824	4	3	9,250	188
Jun 1824	4	2	2,330	28
Jul 1824	8	3	5,000	65
Aug 1824	9	3	4,670	69
Sep 1824	4	1	2,000	41
Oct 1824	4	0	3,425	54
Nov 1824	15	2	14,711	167
Dec 1824	16	6	14,015	153
Jan 1825	65	15	56,551	873
Total	148	43	136,162	19,421

a deluge by January 1825, with 65 major companies being promoted in that month alone. January 1825 was to be the peak of the promotion boom. In addition to the Latin American mines, there were companies which provided local public goods, such as gas-light companies and waterworks, infrastructure companies such as bridges, canals, docks and railroads, and numerous insurance and annuity companies. The companies established in these sectors were more likely to survive, and their share prices did not experience a run-up and subsequent crash.[18]

Two hundred and three companies promoted during the boom were put into a miscellaneous category by Henry English in his 1827 study of the boom – this catch-all group included shipping, agricultural, commercial, land development, manufacturing, trading and textile companies, around half of which had foreign operations. The business models of these companies, like those of the mines, were often based on the assumption that the intellectually superior British could exploit profit opportunities currently being missed by primitive locals. Somewhat inevitably, many such companies failed due to their disregard for local knowledge. Captain Francis Head, a travel writer and eyewitness of events in Argentina, described the experience of The Churning Company, which was set up to supply the people of Buenos Aires with butter for their bread. Having discovered this gap in the market, it promptly dispatched a shipload of Scottish milkmaids to Buenos Aires. Head concludes his account as follows:

> But the difficulties which they experienced were very great: instead of leaning their heads against patient domestic animals, they were introduced to a set of lawless wild creatures, who looked so fierce that no young woman who ever sat upon a three-legged stool could dare to approach, much less to milk them! But the Gauchos attacked the cows, tied their legs with strips of hide, and as soon as they became quiet, the shops of Buenos Aires were literally full of butter. But now for the sad moral of the story: after the difficulties had been all conquered, it was discovered, first, that the butter would not keep! – and secondly, that, somehow or other, the Gauchos and natives of Buenos Aires liked oil better![19]

Satirists at the time were quick to draw up mock company prospectuses that poked fun at the promotional mania. *John Bull*, a weekly periodical, showed a prospectus for a company for raising iron cannon-balls from the seabed around the scenes of great naval encounters.[20] *The London Magazine* told of a Mr Hop-the-twig forming the Aeronautical Swine-shearing Lunarian Joint Stock Commercial and Agricultural Company (or Lunarian A. S. S.) to develop swine wool commerce with the moon.[21] Another satirical prospectus, which appears to have emanated from a wag on the Stock Exchange, was for a company to drain the Red Sea to recover the gold and jewels left by the Egyptians in their pursuit of the Israelites.[22]

Figure 3.1 shows the classic bubble pattern in foreign mining stocks and new miscellaneous companies. Remarkably, the index of blue-chip stocks does not show this pattern at all. If an investor had invested £100 in the foreign mining index in August 1824, it would have been worth an impressive £511 by February 1825, the peak of the bubble.

At the start of February 1825, Lord Eldon, the Lord Chancellor, stood up and delivered the King's speech at the opening of Parliament. This soaring speech reflected and reinforced the mood of optimism about the economy.[24] It followed the largest 1-month increase in the two stock indexes in Figure 3.1, and coincided with

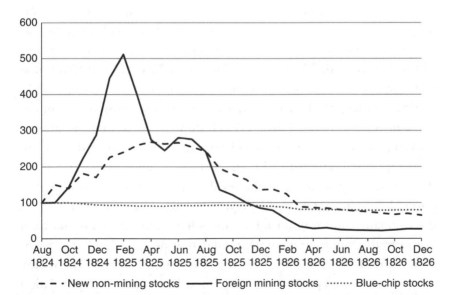

Figure 3.1 Stock return indexes, 1824–6[23]

the month when the largest number of company promotions had taken place. There was a lot to boast and be optimistic about. Then, immediately following his delivery of the King's speech, Lord Eldon did a complete about turn and delivered a speech which tried to prick the growing stock market bubble. Eldon stated that he would bring legislation before Parliament which would check dealing in the shares of unincorporated companies, i.e. those companies which had not been authorised by the Crown or Parliament. This intervention by the Lord Chancellor caused great panic in the stock market.[25] *The Times* reported that in the days following the Lord Chancellor's remarks, sales were very difficult and large price falls were sustained when holders insisted on selling.[26]

A further dampener on the stock market and company promotions came the very next day, when Chief Justice Abbott invoked the Bubble Act to rule that the Equitable Bank Loan Company (which had John 'Bubble' Wilks as a promoter and company solicitor) was illegal because it had transferable shares. Moreover, it had a mischievous intent because it charged a usurious interest rate of 8 per cent, which was 3 per cent above the maximum interest which could be charged.[27] This ruling, in combination with Eldon's speech, triggered a rush of bills to Parliament seeking either full incorporation or the lesser right for owners to be able to sue and be sued collectively. In total, 439 petitions for private bills came before Parliament in the 1825 session, 206 of which were passed.[28] However, at the end of March, Lord Eldon dramatically intervened once more by his judgment in the case of *Kinder v. Taylor*, which, on the face of it, was a minor legal dispute about the company constitution of the Real del Monte, one of the first mining ventures in Mexico. The Real del Monte had been operating as an unincorporated company, i.e. it had not been incorporated by Parliament yet had most of the legal features of a company. Eldon astounded both parties to the dispute by using the case to argue that the company, and by implication others like it, was illegal under both statutory and common law. One implication of his judgment was that even if the Bubble Act was to be removed from the statute book, the common law would prevent any 'slide towards uncontrolled speculation and chaos'.[29]

The combined effect of these interventions was that the prices of foreign mining stocks fell 50 per cent by the end of April and the prices of new miscellaneous companies stalled (see Figure 3.1). Although these interventions acted as a brake on trading activity and prices, they did nothing to slacken the promotion of new schemes coming to market or seeking parliamentary approval.[30]

The attempts to burst the bubble produced an active pamphlet literature opposing them as legislative interference and supporting, in particular, Latin American mining companies. Among the pamphleteers was a 21-year-old solicitor's clerk by the name of Benjamin Disraeli, who 43 years later would become Prime Minister. Disraeli wrote two pamphlets in March and April 1825 and edited a third later that year. His main aim was to refute what he saw as the erroneous parallel being drawn between the Latin American mining boom and the South Sea Bubble. He also puffed the benefits of Latin American mining companies by means of the following strategy. He first spent considerable time giving a detailed, somewhat mundane and seemingly measured overview of each Latin American mining company. He then moved on to deal with the 'very prevalent opinion that the property of the whole civilized globe is about to be depreciated by the sudden and immense increase of the circulating medium' because of the abundant silver and gold in the Latin American mines.[31] Disraeli showed unconcern at this, arguing that Mexico would require all the gold and silver coins which her own mines would afford. The final part of his strategy was to cast aspersions on the domestic joint-stock enterprises which were being established, suggesting that Parliament might need to act to restrain them.

Lord Eldon never brought his promised legislation to Parliament, but on the very day he made the ruling in Chancery on the Real del Monte, an MP moved in Parliament to repeal the Bubble Act. This was accomplished in July 1825, but Eldon's ruling in the Real del Monte case meant that the common law courts were still hostile to the unincorporated company form.[32]

The repeal of the Bubble Act failed to resuscitate the stock market and company promotion boom. In June, the rate on first-class discount bills rose from 3.5 to 4 per cent, making it difficult for speculators to pay instalments on their shares, having relied on rising prices to help pay previous calls.[33] In addition, investors had discovered 'that while the calls for payments were immediate and pressing, the prospect of returns was become more remote and uncertain; doubts too began soon to arise as to there being sufficient security for any income'.[34] From June onwards, trading became thin and there was a rapid decline in stock prices for the rest of the summer.

In September, the deterioration of the market in foreign mines and new miscellaneous companies had become acute. Information regarding the poor state of many Latin American mines had got back to the London market, and it had also become all too clear that the Latin American market for British manufactured goods was nowhere near as large as had been anticipated. Many shareholders refused to pay calls and had begun to sell out, while in London coffee houses, shareholders met to dissolve their companies before they lost any more money.[35] The panic on the stock market continued into November, and by December had spilled over into the money market. The banking system experienced a major crisis, which abated only in January 1826 after extraordinary intervention by the Bank of England.

News then started to spread about the costs of getting Mexican mines up and running, together with reports on the extent to which flooding hindered their operations. In May 1826, *The Times* reported that shares in mining companies were unsalable – no broker or jobber was willing to buy them.[36] By the end of 1826, most Latin American mining companies had folded. The index of foreign mining stocks in Figure 3.1, having been at 511 in February 1825, had fallen to 27 by the end of 1826. Even those that survived beyond 1826 produced little in the way of returns for investors.[37]

Captain Francis Head, an officer in the Royal Engineers and former manager of the Rio Plata Mining Association, published a devastating account of their failure in the autumn of 1826. He attributed their failure to three factors.[38] First, the physical difficulties of getting machinery, men, provisions and materials to remote mines – roads were poor, rivers often impassable and mines were usually miles from the nearest port. The Colombian Mining Association's chief engineer, the young Robert Stephenson (of Rocket fame) found that the steam engines and other machinery were too bulky to transport on mules over primitive roads and mountain paths.

Second, there were major personnel difficulties. Locals were unwilling to work and to adhere to contracts, most Cornish workers were permanently inebriated and mines were so difficult to inspect that a mine manager could easily steal the proceeds. Major disputes over pay broke out in Mexico, where the local workforce demanded their traditional payment method – the *partido*, which was a fixed daily wage plus a piece rate. The resulting strikes were prolonged and violent.

Third, the newly independent Latin American nations were subject to political instability, suffering from expropriation by politicians and weak contract enforcement. Reports by other travellers and officials also emphasised the instability and corruption of the new countries, as well as their economic difficulties.[39] Indeed, the political instability was such that bondholders quickly realised that they had little hope of repayment and by the end of 1827 all Latin American bonds, apart from those of Brazil, were in default.[40]

Newspapers played a key role in this first emerging market bubble. On the one hand, their editorials were sceptical: many company promotions were branded by the press as 'bubbles' or 'schemes'.[41] *The Times* warned its readers about the new fanciful company promotions and advised them 'not to become dupes of their own imaginations'.[42] It is perhaps not surprising that *The Times* opposed new schemes because it had a long history of opposing joint-stock enterprise and speculation in shares. From early in 1824, *The Times* was warning its readers to be circumspect and cautious about new schemes that were being projected, drawing parallels with what they called the South Sea tragedy or mania of 1720.[43] Indeed, after the bubble had burst one gentleman praised the paper for exposing all 'humbug speculations' and several readers wrote letters to the editor of *The Times* thanking the paper for their prescient warnings about the 'mania' for joint-stock companies.[44]

On the other hand, newspapers in a variety of ways might have helped inflate the bubble. Some journalists were paid to puff new schemes, with the editor of the *Morning Chronicle* questioning the integrity of fellow editors who permitted this to happen.[45] However, the role of newspapers during the bubble may have been more subtle.

They began for the first time to publish daily articles on the condition of the stock exchange, thus reflecting and probably magnifying the boom psychology which was gripping the market.[46] They also printed (for a fee) prospectuses of new schemes – on the 23 and 24 January 1825, *The Times* and *Morning Chronicle* contained prospectuses of 35 new companies. In addition, both *The Times* and *Morning Chronicle*, then the two main daily newspapers, devoted many column inches to Latin American issues, highlighting the investment possibilities and fabled precious metals of Mexico. It was even suggested that editorials and opinion pieces were bought in newspapers to laud any Latin American country that was about to about to issue bonds.[47] The newspapers thus helped to develop and shape the narrative which encouraged people to invest in Latin American enterprises.

CAUSES

Chief Justice Abbott's attempts to prick the bubble were partly motivated by what he saw as gaming and rash speculation – investors buying shares simply in the hope of a quick profit when they resold. Many other contemporaries also highlighted the increased spirit of speculation during the boom. *The Times* warned its readers at an early stage about 'the spirit of gambling' and the 'community of gamesters' who bought shares simply in the hope of making money by selling them.[48] This view was echoed in the pamphlet literature of the time. For instance, the contention of one pamphleteer was that 'too many people engaged in schemes of all kinds, not with any consideration of what the undertaking was likely to produce, not with an intention of contributing their share of the capital, but as a game on the prices of shares'.[49]

Joseph Parkes was an experienced company solicitor who, as well as experiencing the events of 1824 to 1825, made a careful study of the period. He presented his evidence before a parliamentary select committee in 1844. He describes as a national epidemic the extraordinary quantity of speculation which occurred in 1824 and 1825, and he told the committee how police officers had been employed to keep order in places where shares were being traded.[50] John McCulloch, the first economics professor at University College London, writing in 1832 of the events of 1824–5, maintained that 'many who were most eager in the pursuit of shares, intended only to hold them for a few days or weeks, to profit by the rise which they anticipated would take place, by selling them to others more credulous or bold than themselves'.[51]

John Francis, a director of the Bank of England, was also an eyewitness of this national epidemic of speculation. He described the scene around the entrance to the Stock Exchange during the boom months as follows: 'some lads . . . whose miscellaneous finery was finely emblematical of rag fair, passed in and out; and besides these, there attended a strangely varied rabble, exhibiting in all sorts of forms and ages, dirty habiliments, calamitous poverty, and grim-faced villainy'.[52] Francis recalled that it took a £5 fine for those who blocked the entrance to disperse the nuisance. One young speculator, who fits Francis' description, was Benjamin Disraeli. Having only £52 to his name in 1824, he had borrowed heavily to make his fortune by speculating in mining stocks.[53] In the spring of 1825, he found himself holding shares in all the great mining companies. It took him years to pay off his debts – as late as 1849, his stockbroker was still trying to obtain £1,200 plus interest from him.

The Times argued that this 'gigantic speculation' had no parallel but the South Sea Bubble.[54] One major similarity to the South Sea episode was the widespread use of part-paid shares by new companies. This feature enabled a moderate rise in share prices to produce a large profit because only a small instalment (about £5 or less) had been paid on the shares when they were sold. The possibility of making an enormous profit while only risking a small sum was 'a bait too tempting to be resisted', and opened up share speculation to the masses.[55] As a nineteenth-century chronicler of commercial crises put it, 'the old and young, men and women, rich and poor, noble and simple, one and all, were drawn into the throng'.[56]

Short selling was a well-known practice on the London Stock Exchange in the 1820s, but its usefulness in preventing the escalation of stock prices during the bubble was stymied by the presence of corners and rigs, whereby directors of a new company bought up its shares, making it very costly for short sellers to deliver on their contracts.[57] This had also been the case in 1720. Short selling was viewed as morally suspect and financial markets were happy for this market manipulation to be used to thwart the pessimistic and opportunistic short sellers.

During the first emerging market bubble, marketability, the second side of the bubble triangle, increased substantially thanks to entrepreneurs pushing for their enterprises to be incorporated and have free transferability of shares. These shares were usually much more marketable than those of established companies because they were issued in much smaller denominations. The average cost of one share in a canal company in 1825 was £271, compared to £10 for new miscellaneous companies.[58] To put these figures in context, the average labourer at this time would have been doing well to earn £50 per annum, and the average teacher £70. Furthermore, unlike the established sectors, unpaid capital was commonplace in both mining and new miscellaneous companies, with the result that shares with apparently high denominations of £50 or £100 were accessible even to people who had £10 or less to invest. The increased marketability of securities in 1825 is reflected in the overall liquidity of the stock and bond markets, which reached an all-time high that would not be surpassed until the next bubble arrived in 1844.[59]

The final side of the bubble triangle was a major monetary stimulus and expansion of credit. The government continually injected money into the economy by buying out its long-term debt, and in 1823 and 1824 it used debt conversion schemes to lower the long-term interest rate.[60] Under pressure from the government, the Bank of England reduced its discount rate for the first time ever, from 5 to 4 per cent in June 1822.[61] Furthermore, the Bank engaged in open market operations by purchasing the Dead Weight Annuity, which had been created by the government to pay for naval and military pensions and which they had failed to sell to investors.[62] As a result of these actions, the Bank's note issue in the 3 years before February 1825 increased by 25 per cent. The English country banks also increased their note issue by around 50 per cent between 1823 and 1825.[63]

After 1825, this monetary expansion was seen as a key misstep that allowed the bubble to occur. The economist Thomas Tooke, anticipating our fire triangle metaphor, argued that 'the Bank [of England] had not kindled the fire, but, instead of attempting to stop the progress of the flames, it supplied fuel for maintaining and extending the conflagration'.[64]

According to Tooke, the fire had been kindled by the government's debt-refinancing scheme, and the Bank should have reduced its note issue in 1824 to counteract this effect, but instead increased it.[65] Furthermore, he judged that the Bank's acquisition of government securities added to the spirit of speculation.[66] Others blamed the Bank and government equally for the monetary and credit easing, but the Bank, naturally, took a different view.[67] The majority view among the witnesses at the 1832 Committee of Secrecy on Bank of England Charter was that the blame for generating the stock market speculation and rise in asset prices lay with the country banks.[68]

The effect of the monetary and credit easing on stocks was exacerbated by the increased leverage available to investors through the unpaid capital of many new shares. In addition, many investors appear to have, like Benjamin Disraeli, borrowed heavily to invest in shares which required only a small down payment.[69] This double dose of leverage meant that individuals with small sums of money to their name could access the stock market.

The spark which set the fire alight was a change in government policy towards Latin America and the corporation. Once the Latin American states had gained their independence from Spain, the policy stance of Britain was to foster rapprochement between the two sides. However, in 1823, merchant groups from London, Liverpool and Manchester started to petition Parliament for the formal recognition of the states in order to protect the infant markets for their goods. George Canning, the Foreign Secretary from 1822 to 1827, sympathised with the merchants in this, but faced opposition from the king and fellow politicians. In 1823 Canning dispatched commissioners to Buenos Aires, Colombia and Mexico and increasingly his speeches in the Commons pushed for the recognition of these new nations. Many of the prospectuses of mining companies launched in 1824 stated that the political stability of the new countries was almost assured because their independence was shortly to be recognised by the British government.[70] Canning's formal recognition of the independence of the Latin American countries in December 1824 thus represented an enormous boost for company promoters. This policy change was immediately followed by the frenzied promotion boom and the rapid appreciation of stock prices, as investors focused their attention on Latin American mines and other companies which could take advantage of the resulting plentiful trade opportunities.[71] The ideology underlying Canning's move was used as a marketing tool, with investors encouraged to play their role in 'patronising infant liberty and liberal principles' by financing the reestablishment of mines in newly independent colonies.[72]

None of this would have resulted in a bubble, however, were it not for a second policy change: a more permissive attitude towards incorporation and the trading of shares. During 1824 and 1825, active MPs were supporting an unprecedented number of incorporation bills and requests from unincorporated companies to have the right to sue and be sued collectively. These bills passed easily because of a series of huge conflicts of interest facing MPs.[73] First, MPs were shareholders in companies and yet were able to sit on the committee that examined incorporation bills. In one case, 16 members of a committee held shares in the company whose incorporation bill was about to come before them. Second, MPs were often recruited to be directors of these new companies to give them an air of respectability. Many MPs were induced by the likes of John 'Bubble' Wilks to become directors by the gift of shares in the company, which they were free to sell for a large profit once the company had been incorporated. Of the 278 directors in Latin American mining companies listed by Henry English, 45 were MPs, and about one-third of the major companies promoted had MPs or peers as a lead or founding director. Thirty-one MPs were directors in three or more of the newly established companies.[74] The Lord Mayor of London, who was also on the list, later claimed to have received as many as five or six requests per day to become a director of a company.[75]

CONSEQUENCES

The boom was well and truly over by the early summer of 1825. Banks had lent considerable sums of money to investors and merchants who had been tempted by the rising stock and commodity prices, and were therefore extremely vulnerable to a downturn.[76] By the autumn, several banks in the west of England had collapsed, unsettling the money markets and the Bank of England. Then, at the beginning of December 1825, a major

London bank, Pole, Thornton and Company, which had been investing in risky securities, failed after experiencing a run. This collapse was followed by a series of bank runs and failures of English country banks. The panic peaked on 14 December 1825, the notorious 'day of terror', in which many London and country banks closed their doors; there were few towns in England where the 'stoppage of local banks had not occurred or was not feared hourly'.[77] According to *The Times*, in the week after the day of terror, banks all over England and Wales faced severe runs.[78]

Many of the banks which closed during December eventually reopened. But 30 English banks entered bankruptcy in December 1825 and a further 33 did so in the first quarter of 1826.[79] In total, almost 18 per cent of the English banking system failed.[80] But this failure rate does not fully capture the severity of the crisis. Nearly every English country bank approached the Bank of England for liquidity because money could not be borrowed from elsewhere, even on the security of government bonds.[81] According to William Huskisson, the President of the Board of Trade, England 'was within four-and-twenty hours of a state of barter'.[82] This is corroborated by witnesses before an 1832 parliamentary committee, who judged the entire banking and credit system in December 1825 to have been within a few days of completely collapsing.[83] Ultimately, the Bank of England brought the panic to an end by acting as a lender of last resort (i.e. lending to banks when no one else would) from 14 December onwards. The Bank 'did all in their power to relieve the distress, and they discounted as liberally as any body of men could do, and they deserve the greatest credit from the country for what they did'.[84]

Why was the banking system so vulnerable to the collapse of the 1825 boom? Regulation at the time meant that English banks were restricted to the partnership form of organisation and, if they wanted to issue notes (which most banks of the time did), they could have no more than six partners.[85] As a result, English partnership banks were very small, making them vulnerable in three ways. First, shocks to partner wealth gave them the incentive to invest the bank's money in risky assets in an effort to recover losses. Second, the small number of partners meant that banks had small equity cushions to absorb the losses arising from non-performing assets. Third, the restrictions on growth effectively forced banks to restrict their operations to one narrow geographical location, meaning that they could not adequately diversify their assets and liabilities.

The vulnerability of the banking system was caused by its regulatory structure, and hence the 1825 collapse of the English banking system ultimately had political roots. As a *quid pro quo* for providing finance to the government, the charter of the Bank of England meant that other banks could only operate as partnerships. The aristocracy and landed gentry, the political elite at the time, supported this regulation because it restricted the credit extended to small farmers, enabling landlords to maintain power and social control over them.

The economic effect of the bursting of the first emerging market bubble and the subsequent banking crisis was substantial. First, the money supply fell, due to the closure of so many banks. Second, merchants and entrepreneurs found it nearly impossible to obtain finance because many surviving banks reduced their lending and refused to discount bills of exchange.[86] Bankruptcies increased significantly, and in 1826 the United Kingdom's real GDP contracted by 5.3 per cent. To put this into perspective, between 1800 and 2010, only 3 years experienced a larger fall in GDP than 1826. The damage was not restricted to the United Kingdom, however, as the bubble also left a negative mark on Latin America. It would be nearly 50 years before British investors would once again take an interest in Latin American ventures. Although we can only speculate, it is likely that the bubble, by hamstringing finances and discouraging investment, contributed to the post-independence instability of Latin America throughout the rest of the century.

On the other hand, the first emerging market bubble brought two major beneficial changes to the financial system. The first change was the liberalisation of the banking system, started by an Act passed by Parliament in 1826, which allowed banks to form freely as joint-stock companies with unlimited liability. The banking system which was to emerge from this reform was a paragon of stability, while simultaneously meeting the monetary and credit needs of the country.[87] The second change was the abolition of the Bubble Act, which marked the move towards the liberalisation of incorporation law in the United Kingdom.

This made it easier for business people to aggregate their capital and build the large business enterprises which would transform Britain. However, it also made it much easier for companies to issue shares which could be traded in public markets: a substantial increase in fundamental marketability. Partly as a consequence, bubbles would be much more common in the nineteenth century than they had been in the eighteenth.

Another important legacy of the first emerging market bubble was the birth of financial journalism.[88] After 1825, newspapers began to publish city columns, cover company annual general meetings (AGMs) and comment on movements in and the state of the market. The new specialised financial press provided an independent and authoritative source of information and advice for investors. The events of 1824 and 1825 were therefore largely responsible for the rise of the press as a watchdog of the financial system, barking whenever things did not appear right. But how effective would the press be at preventing bubbles in the future? In Chapter 4, we will see that a major set of negative editorials in the UK financial press was instrumental in popping – but not preventing – the bubble in UK railway shares.

CHAPTER 4

Democratising Speculation: The Great Railway Mania

'Bless railroads everywhere,'
I said, 'and the world's advance;
Bless every railroad share
In Italy, Ireland, France,

For never a beggar need now despair,
And every rogue has a chance.'
William Makepeace Thackeray[1]

London is as flat as it can be. There is nothing to talk about, but Railroad shares. And as I am not a Capitalist, I don't find anything interesting in that.

Charles Dickens[2]

WHILE THE 1825 BUBBLE LED TO THE LEGALISATION OF companies with tradeable shares, marketability was still somewhat limited because only Parliament could grant the right for a business to incorporate with limited liability. Parliament, however, now had the power to substantially increase marketability at any time simply by granting large numbers of charters. In the mid-1840s they did exactly that, granting charters to hundreds of railway companies during what became known as the Railway Mania. *The Economist*, in 2008, described the Railway Mania as 'arguably the greatest bubble in history'.[3] This is not just modern hyperbole. Charles Mackay, in the third edition of *Memoirs of Extraordinary Popular Delusions and the Madness of Crowds*, wrote that the Railway Mania was greater than anything that had preceded it.[4] Karl Marx, in *Das Kapital*, referred to it as the '*großen Eisenbahnschwindel*', which literally means the 'great Railway Mania'.[5]

Two decades prior to the Great Railway Mania, a new and revolutionary technology was beginning to transform Britain: steam-powered railways. The first such railway in the world had been authorised by Parliament in 1821 and opened in 1825, the year of the previous bubble. Parliamentary authorisation was necessary because of the need to force landowners to sell the land along the railway's proposed route, as well as to acquire the right to incorporate.[6] The next railway to be authorised was the Liverpool and Manchester Railway in 1826. This railway, which was the UK's first passenger railway, opened in 1830. The official opening was a disaster, with William Huskisson, the MP for Liverpool, fatally wounded by George Stephenson's Rocket locomotive in front of the Prime Minister.[7] This tragic beginning, however, did not prevent the Liverpool and Manchester Railway from quickly becoming a success – particularly for its shareholders, as by 1835 its dividend rate was close to 10 per cent. The early success of the Liverpool and Manchester Railway is perhaps unsurprising given that it had a monopoly.

The success of the Liverpool and Manchester Railway encouraged promoters to approach Parliament with railway schemes for other parts of the country. In 1836 and 1837, Parliament authorised 59 new railways and 1,500 miles of track. This mini promotion boom was accompanied by a boom and bust in railway share prices, with share prices rising by 65 per cent and then falling by 45 per cent between May 1835 and May 1837.[8] This episode is sometimes referred to as the 'first railway mania' because it served as a portentous warning of what was to come several years later in the Great Railway Mania.[9]

The collapse of share prices sent the railway industry into a lull, and very few railways were authorised between 1838 and 1843. In 1840 railway development even went into reverse, with more miles of railway abandoned than were authorised.[10] As of 1843, despite the technology being over 20 years old, England and Scotland together had just over 40 railway companies with an average of 36 miles of track. The following year, however, William Gladstone, anticipating that improved economic conditions might re-stimulate railway development, initiated a parliamentary select committee to consider their future regulation. Gladstone was particularly keen to constrain their potential monopoly power, but he was also keen to develop a national rail network, which would avoid unnecessary duplication. A national rail network would also create network externalities: if the railway network covered most of the country, people would use trains much more often, benefiting existing railways by creating lots of extra customers for them.[11]

The resulting Railways Act was passed in July 1844, requiring at least one train per day per company to carry passengers at a rate of one penny per mile. The Act also allowed the government to sanction new competing lines; they could even nationalise lines authorised after 1844 if the lines generated dividends of more than 10 per cent. This latter threat signalled to investors that railways were very profitable enterprises which were expected to generate huge dividends – well beyond what any other industry was paying at the time.

A further product of Gladstone's Railway Act was a new way of processing applications for railways. The parliamentary private bill system, which had worked well for all previous transport developments in the UK, such as the locally based canals and turnpikes, did not operate as effectively for railways because the national interest was neglected at the expense of the local.[12] Thus in August 1844 a 'Railway Board' was established to scrutinise projected railways, with the purpose of rationing schemes and building an integrated national rail network.[13] The main intention of the Railway Board was to prevent duplicate and competing lines from being constructed. *The Economist*, cheerleaders for free trade and competition, declared that whether new railway companies should be established in competition with existing ones should not be left to the likes of Mr Gladstone; rather (and somewhat unfortunately as events would prove), they suggested that those who invest their money are the best judges.[14]

The excitement generated by Gladstone's Railway Act in the first half of 1844 can be seen from Figure 4.1, which charts a railway stock index and, for the purposes of comparison, an index of returns on the 20 largest non-railway companies in this era. Railways were extensively promoted around this time, and 199 applications for new railways were presented for consideration in the 1845 parliamentary session, which at the time typically ran from February to July.[15] Since many believed that the network effects from new railways would make existing railways even more profitable, railway stock prices skyrocketed, and many more

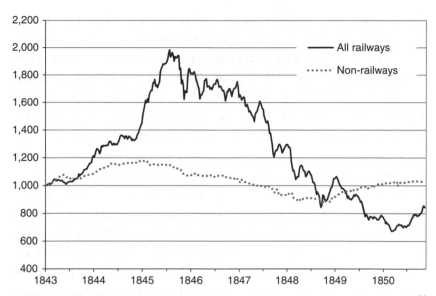

Figure 4.1 Weekly stock indexes of British Railways and non-railway blue-chip companies[16]

promoters devised railway schemes for consideration in the 1846 session of Parliament.

The buoyant atmosphere of the time and the resultant promotion of new railway schemes was best described in *The Glenmutchkin Railway*, a satirical tale published in the aftermath of the bubble.[17] The story tells of two protagonists – Augustus Reginald Dunshunner and Bob M'Corkindale. Both were hard up, averse to exertion and connoisseurs of the finest Oban malt whisky. M'Corkindale was the business brains of the pair, having once leafed through Adam Smith's *Wealth of Nations*. In 1844, observing how the newspapers teemed every week with new railway schemes which were rapidly subscribed for, they joined the speculative rush with their combined funds of £300. But in 6 months they never received an allocation of original shares because of their low social status, and had gained only £20 by buying and selling railway shares on the stock market.

In 1845, frustrated at their lack of success, Dunshunner and M'Corkindale decided to promote their own railway, which was to be 12 miles long and based in the mythical valley of Glenmutchkin in the Scottish Highlands. They drew up a prospectus overnight, which described

Glenmutchkin as a highly populated and prosperous valley. They packed the provisional board of directors of the railway with names resembling those of Celtic chieftains or Scottish lairds, which they believed to be 'sonorous to the ears of the Saxon'. They decided to have a leading Presbyterian businessman on the board to attract the money of other Presbyterians, who could supposedly 'smell a [bargain] from an almost incredible distance'. To further attract Scottish Presbyterians as investors, the prospectus stated that the company was opposed to all Sunday travelling and would distribute 12,000 evangelical tracts to the poor.

To set up a railway company, promoters had to make a detailed application to Parliament in the November preceding the parliamentary session. This application had to include, among other things, the rationale for the railway, estimates of costs, traffic and working expenses. It also had to include the names and details of individuals who had jointly undertaken to provide 75 per cent of the capital that the company required, and already paid 5 per cent of the capital they had promised.

Scrip certificates (or scrip as they were commonly known) were issued to individuals who had been allocated shares and paid up their 5 per cent. The fictional Glenmutchkin Railway issued 12,000 shares of £20 each, which meant that successful subscribers initially paid only £1. Dunshunner and M'Corkindale hoped to make a lot of money trading scrip, which was actively traded even though it was illegal to do so.[18] Scrip were made out to bearer, making them easy to transfer without fear of legal reprisal. However, the original holder of a scrip certificate remained legally liable for all the debts of the railway until it was incorporated, and buyers of scrip would have been in a dubious legal position if they had wanted to sue the promoters for losses.[19]

When an application reached Parliament, it was then sponsored by MPs using Parliament's private bill procedure. The private bill was reviewed by a parliamentary committee, and it could be contested, which would dramatically increase the costs to the promoters of getting the bill through Parliament. It also had to get approval from Gladstone's Railway Board. If successful, a parliamentary private bill was passed that authorised the construction of the railway and the purchase of the necessary lands and incorporated the railway as a limited liability company. At this stage, the investors who had had shares allotted to them were issued with share certificates. They were also expected to meet future calls on capital as and when they arose. The railway company was also free at this point to raise additional capital. The application of the Glenmutchkin Railway failed, much to the relief of Dunshunner and M'Corkindale, whose scam would have been exposed if their application to Parliament had been successful.

During the 1845 parliamentary session, major problems with the railway authorisation process became increasingly clear. The Railway Board was routinely ignored: 35.5 per cent of its recommendations were not implemented. It was subsequently disbanded on 10 July 1845.[20] This made it more likely that a railway bill would be evaluated on its local social costs and benefits, in isolation from national considerations, a process which took no account of network externalities or the potential wasteful competition arising from the duplication of routes.[21] This resulted in a mad rush of railway schemes being developed for parliamentary approval in the 1846 session.

By the autumn of 1845, an astonishing 562 new railway petitions had been submitted to Parliament.[22] Notably, many other projected railway companies never reached the stage of applying for parliamentary authorisation – *The Times* estimated that 1,238 new projects were initiated in 1845 alone.[23] The scale of railway promotion in the autumn of 1845 is illustrated in Figure 4.2, which plots the word count of the advertisements promoting new railways in the *Railway Times*, the leading railway periodical at the time. The first blip in this series occurred in the autumn of 1844, when the railways that were applying to be considered during the 1845 parliamentary session were being promoted and raising capital. However, this was completely overshadowed by the scale of promotion adverts that were placed in the autumn of 1845. Such was the level of promotion that the two leading railway periodicals printed up to three weekly supplements during September and October 1845 to cope with the demand for advertising new railway schemes in order to attract investors.[24] As can be seen from Figure 4.2, this explosion in promotional activity coincided with the tipping point of the railway share index.

The boom in share prices and promotion boom were accompanied by a boom in railway periodicals, with 16 periodicals circulating in 1845. Most of these were short-lived, lasting no longer than a few months, and

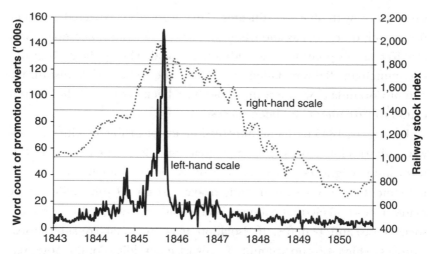

Figure 4.2 Railway stock market index and weekly word count of railway company promotion adverts[25]

their median circulation was 10,750 per week, compared to circa 355,000 for the *Railway Times*.[26] *The Economist* also entered the fray of railway reporting in January 1845, when it introduced a section devoted to the railways. These newspapers tended to reflect the positivity of the railway market, with upward price movements typically followed by positive press coverage. Surprisingly, however, newspapers do not appear to have reinforced market sentiment: positive newspaper coverage was not associated with subsequent price increases.[27]

The increase in promotional activity that followed the demise of the Railway Board began to cause concern that duplicate lines would be authorised.[28] In particular, a series of articles in *The Times* from July 1845 onwards warned about the detrimental effects of the new proposed railways.[29] The financial press, which had been conceived in the aftermath of the 1825 bubble, was acting as a watchdog for investors, barking at signs of trouble. And it was not any old dog which was barking – *The Times* was by some distance the leading daily newspaper in the 1840s in terms of circulation and influence.[30] Its editorials were extremely critical of 'excessive speculation' in railway shares. On 18 October 1845, the weekend before the beginning of the market crash, its editorial was scathing: 'the mania for railway speculation has reached that height at which all follies, however absurd in themselves, cease to be ludicrous, and become, by reason of their universality, fit subjects for the politician to consider as well as the moralist'.[31] In a supplement on 17 November 1845, *The Times* published an exposé of the madness of railway speculation.[32]

Henry Tuck, an author of railway shareholder manuals, laid the blame for the collapse of the market at the feet of *The Times*.[33] The *Railway Times* used scurrilous language, accusing *The Times* and its reporters of bearing the market for their own gain and of being habitual liars for fraudulent purposes. Such was its ire that the leading article in the *Railway Times* each week between 18 October and 13 December 1845 focused on the role of *The Times* in causing the collapse of the market for railway stocks.[34] However, a study on the effect of negative editorials on the market for railway shares suggests that *The Times* had a negligible effect on the market.[35] Although the newspaper may have played a role in the crash by calling attention to the railway promotion boom, it was a confluence of major events at this time which really caused the bubble to burst.

First, the abolition of the Railway Board and the free-for-all promotion craze meant that, rather than benefiting from the positive externalities of a well-organised network, railway firms began to compete wastefully against one another. Second, there was a very poor harvest in England and Scotland, and a disastrous one in Ireland, where the potato crop failed due to blight. By the middle of October, the severity of this situation had become clear.[36] In December 1845, it sparked a political crisis when the Prime Minister, Robert Peel, temporarily resigned his office because his cabinet did not support his desire to repeal the Corn Laws (which placed tariffs and restrictions on grain imports).

Third, the outflow of gold due to problems with the harvest prompted the Bank of England to increase its interest rate from 2.5 to 3 per cent on 16 October and then to 3.5 per cent on 6 November.[37] Some commentators have suggested that the decline in railway share prices was attributable to these rises in the Bank of England rate – the Bank was in essence pricking the bubble.[38] However, *The Economist's* analysis at the time is probably closer to the truth – the rate rise 'only determined the great majority of the holders of shares to do then what they contemplated doing sooner or later, to sell most of the shares they held'.[39]

Fourth, the sharp fall in railway share prices may have been precipitated by the large calls on capital made by the railways which Parliament had just authorised in July and August 1845. These substantial calls were made as railways began the construction of their lines. These calls dwarfed any that had been made in the previous 3 years and signalled the beginning of large and frequent capital calls upon railway shareholders. After the previous heady months, this may have been a reality check for many investors.

As can be seen from Figure 4.2, after the dark days in the last quarter of 1845, the market for railway shares stabilised somewhat in early 1846, with investors neither regaining their former enthusiasm nor succumbing to panic. However, from August 1846 share prices once again declined. When it finally reached its bottom in April 1850, the market for railway shares had fallen 66 per cent from its peak of the summer of 1845.

As with many other bubbles, the bust of the Railway Mania revealed and induced dubious practices. In 1848, a pamphlet was published which alleged that the railways controlled by George Hudson, the 'Railway King', were charging expenses to capital rather than revenue, allowing them to report artificially high profits and pay higher dividends than were warranted.[40] In 1849, several committees of inquiry established by shareholders found that Hudson had over-allocated scrip to himself, made related-party transactions between railways that he controlled and manipulated company accounts to overstate profits and dividends.[41] Hudson was not fraudulently pumping up earnings and dividends during the boom, but trying to sustain his empire after the crash. He resigned from his chairmanships and was sued for various debts. He lost everything and became a bankrupt, going into exile when he lost his seat as an MP, which had afforded him legal protection from imprisonment for unpaid debts. However, Hudson's fraud appears to have been an isolated incident rather than a systemic feature of the railway boom. Neither committees of inquiry into other companies nor a parliamentary report on railway accounting found evidence of fraudulent practices.[42]

The bursting of the Railway Mania also resulted in the Dissolution Act being passed in 1846 to enable shareholders to force company promoters to wind up any railway which had not received parliamentary authorisation. As for those which were authorised, Parliament passed a bill in 1850 to facilitate their abandonment if 60 per cent or more of the shareholders requested it.[43] Of the 8,590 miles authorised by Parliament in the 1845–7 sessions, 1,560 miles were abandoned by promoters under this second Act, and a further 2,000 miles, worth about £40 million of capital, were abandoned before Parliament's formal consent had been granted.[44]

The magnitude of the Great Railway Mania and transformative effect on the industry is illustrated in Figure 4.3, which shows the unprecedented scale of expansion and investment in railways between 1845 and 1847. The vastly greater part of capital formation (i.e. increase in physical capital such as railway lines, bridges and locomotives) and increases in paid-up capital occurred after 1845 because it took time to construct the new railways, and capital was called up from shareholders on a schedule which ran parallel to the construction of the rail network. The greatness

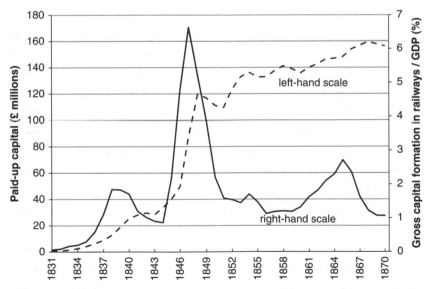

Figure 4.3 Gross capital formation by UK railways as a percentage of GDP and paid-up equity capital of UK railways[45]

of the Railway Mania can also be considered in relation to the rest of the stock market. In 1838, railway shares constituted 14 per cent of all quoted stocks and 23 per cent of total stock market value. By 1848, railways made up 48 per cent of quoted stocks and 71 per cent of total stock market value.[46]

CAUSES

During the Railway Mania, marketability increased in several ways. Parliament became much more liberal in granting corporate charters to railway companies, with hundreds of companies receiving authorisation. Even before authorisation was granted, the process required promoters to form company-like organisations which had marketable shares in the form of scrip certificates. The market in railway shares brought an unprecedented level of activity to the stock market: unlike most other company shares, the shares of railway companies traded daily during the Railway Mania.[47] Indeed, the marketability of railway equity was such that 15 new stock exchanges opened around the country during the Mania to meet the demand from the growing speculator franchise.[48] Seven of these new provincial stock exchanges shut down when the Railway Mania came to an end.[49]

The next side of the bubble triangle is money and credit, without which there is no fuel to feed a bubble. In the case of the Railway Mania, the Bank of England's discount rate was reduced in September 1844 to 2.5 per cent, an historic low in the 150 years since the Bank had been established. In addition, the fall in interest rates meant that the yield on the government's main debt security fell to 3 per cent for the first time in over a century.[50] According to the *Railway Times*, one effect of low interest rates was that it led investors to reach for yield by investing in railway stocks.[51] There is, however, very little evidence of investors borrowing to buy railway stocks. One reason for this is that the part-paid nature of railway stocks meant that leverage was built into them – investors could take highly leveraged positions in railways by simply paying a 10 per cent initial deposit. This in-built leverage contributed to the increase in shareholder returns during the boom.[52] Indeed, in order to stimulate railway investment, Parliament lowered the required deposit to 5 per cent in

February 1844, thus increasing the leveraged nature of railway shares.[53] This decision was reversed in July 1845, just as the next tranche of railway schemes was being prepared for Parliament.

As easy money and credit conditions intensified the boom in railway share prices, so the tightening of money and credit had the opposite effect. The raising of interest rates and the calls upon shareholders for capital accentuated the fall in railway share prices during the bust. Indeed, the bursting of the Mania coincided with the increase in the Bank of England's discount rate, while calls on capital became much larger and more frequent in late 1845, and continued to grow over the subsequent 3 years.

Speculation is the final side of our bubble triangle. The share price rises during the Railway Mania attracted much in the way of speculative money. Investing in the bubbles of 1720 and 1825 was chiefly limited to those of means – those from the upper middle classes and gentry who could, in some sense, afford to lose their investment stakes. However, during the Railway Mania, thanks to low share denominations and partly paid shares, many members of the middle and working classes were enfranchised into the speculating class. In the case of the fictional Glenmutchkin Railway, which was typical of most real railways, investors only needed £1 to buy a share in the railway, with the remaining £19 to be called up if the railway was authorised and as it was built. To put these figures in context, civil servants at the time earned about £180 per annum, teachers about £80 and labourers about £50.[54]

Many speculators of little means would have hoped to flip their shares before the railway was authorised or before any calls were made. Part-paid shares had also played their role in 1720 and 1825 in attracting speculators, but the growth of the middle classes and the fact that very low initial investments were required up front meant that part-paid shares played a major role in democratising speculation during the Railway Mania. The appearance of popular investment guides, such as the *Short and Sure Guide to Railway Speculation*, *The Railway Speculator's Memorandum Book* and *How to Make Money in Railway Shares*, further indicates that speculation was being democratised.

As with other famous bubble episodes, the anecdotal and circumstantial evidence points to naive, amateurish and impecunious individuals investing during the Railway Mania. Contemporaries even went as far as suggesting that these amateurish investors in their clamour for railway shares drove prices up and, in their panic, contributed to the collapse of railway share prices.[55] But many of these representations of investors come from the satirical press and contemporary literary sources.[56] One of the epigraphs to this chapter is from William Makepeace Thackeray's satirical poem *The Speculators*, where he depicts impecunious rogues talking about becoming rich through their investments in railways. But how closely did these caricatures resemble reality?

Historians of the railways have pointed to the participation of inexperienced investors such as women and clergymen and the significant role played by the *nouveau riche* middle classes.[57] For example, literary giants such as Charlotte Brontë and William Makepeace Thackeray and leading scientists such as Charles Darwin invested in railway shares during the Mania.[58] Using the lists of subscribers to the railway schemes that came before Parliament in 1845 and 1846, we are able to look beyond the caricatures and stereotypes.[59] These lists only give an insight into the initial subscribers who invested in the run-up to the Mania rather than into the many speculators who bought shares during the Mania. To that end, the lists will underrepresent the middle classes because railway promoters preferred to have their subscription lists packed with the upper classes and gentry. Nevertheless, women made up 6.5 per cent of subscribers and clergymen 0.9 per cent, which is not insubstantial, and middle-class professionals made up 13.1 per cent of subscribers and manufacturers, merchants and retailers made up another 37.8 per cent. Even the working classes got in on the action, making up 1 per cent of subscribers.

Short selling during the bubbles of 1720 and 1825 had been inhibited by squeezes and rigs, whereby insiders had cornered the market for shares. The same was likely true during the Railway Mania. The presence of cornering is difficult to prove – it can usually only be observed when a short seller or their stockbroker are unwilling to pay on their contracts and are taken to court. However, a corner is the main way that Dunshunner and M'Corkindale, the promoters of the fictional Glenmutchkin Railway, made money on their scheme. One of the members of their provisional board – a prosperous Presbyterian coffin maker called Samuel Sawley – started to bear the shares by short selling. Getting wind of this, and watching as the share price tumbled back towards £1, Dunshunner and M'Corkindale launched a corner by buying up every available share offered for sale. When Sawley's contract fell due, he had to buy shares he had sold short. However, nearly all shares were under the control of Dunshunner and M'Corkindale, and within a matter of days the shares had risen to £17 because of Sawley's need to meet his contractual obligations. After a week of paying such high prices, Sawley had still not managed to fulfil his obligations, and was forced to visit Dunshunner to see if he would sell him some shares. Sawley arrived in full funeral costume and 'a countenance more doleful than if he had been attending the interment of his beloved wife'. He confessed to short selling – 'the devil tempted me, and I oversold' – and ended up paying nearly all he had to buy 2,000 shares from Dunshunner.

The development and passage of Gladstone's Railway Act provided the spark that ignited the bubble. This Act provided a boon to the market by suggesting that the government expected future profitability to be so high that they might later have to consider nationalisation. But more importantly, this Act established the Railway Board. Railways were not a new technology – passenger railways had been around for over 15 years and there were over 1,400 miles of railroad before the Mania – but the rail network was not an integrated national one. The establishment of the Railway Board signalled to investors and potential promoters that the government would only seek to approve new railways which added to the network. This would create network externalities for existing railways, greatly increasing their passenger numbers.

The Railway Board was needed because the structure of Parliament was not suited to building a national rail network. MPs at that time had much more of an electoral incentive to promote the interests of their local constituency than to promote the national interest. Politics was thus dominated by local rather than national interests, and these interests resulted in competition between towns to obtain railway schemes rather than a desire to form a national integrated rail network.[60] Gladstone's failure to give the Railway Board the power to overrule these local interests was a major political blunder, and when its impotency became clear in the summer of 1845, it was abolished.[61]

The abolition of the Railway Board signalled the end of parliamentary co-ordination in the attempted construction of a national rail network. Consequently, in the autumn of 1845, Parliament was flooded with applications, and ultimately authorised many duplicate and uneconomic schemes that destroyed one another through wasteful competition. The devastating effect of this competition was commented upon by one contemporary – 'the obvious effect of the concession of a competing line is to diminish, if not destroy, the profits of the old line; and it is not likely that it can, by entering into competition with the old line, itself be highly profitable'.[62] It is not surprising that this was when railway share prices started to collapse. Indeed, *The Economist* later noted that lines which had emerged in the Mania period had shown little or no profit.[63] An illustration of this is that the return on equity on the York and North Midland's pre-Mania network was 10.1 per cent compared to -0.3 per cent for the part of its network constructed during the Mania.[64] The *Railway Times* summed it up by stating that 'railway rivalry and railway ruin are terms nearly synonymous'.[65]

One change which had taken place since the 1825 bubble was that MPs could no longer sit on committees reviewing proposals in which they had a vested interest, whether as a director for the proposal or as the MP for the constituency in which the railway was based. This should have reduced the local versus national tension in Parliament. However, politicians could circumvent this restriction by 'logrolling', in which two or more politicians agreed to vote for each other's railway schemes.[66] Herbert Spencer, the famous biologist and philosopher, suggested that MPs acted in an opportunistic fashion during the Mania.[67] But broadly speaking this was not the case: they were simply responding to local constituency rather than national interests. Indeed, there is no evidence to suggest that MPs profited from their investments any more than other investors did.[68]

The construction of rail networks in other parts of the world in this era is instructive in this regard. The aim in France and other parts of the Continent was to have no duplicate or competing lines, and this was achieved through state involvement (or ownership) in the construction of rail networks.[69] This explains why continental Europe did not experience its own railway mania. In the case of the US railroads, which were wholly private enterprises, state governments effectively rationed railroad charters so as to reduce the effects of harmful competition.[70] Although there was unrestrained charter granting, sub-national governments in the United States played a key role in the construction of the rail network by providing capital for the routes which it had decided were viable. State and local governments provided half of the capital for early railroads, and every significant American line constructed before 1860 received finance from sub-national governments.[71] This *de facto* control over the construction of railroad routes may partially explain why the United States similarly did not experience a railway bubble.[72]

The local versus national tension was built into the British parliamentary system and simply reflected the unique way in which the UK political system had evolved. In contrast, the political institutions and incentives of other countries were much more heavily weighted towards national rather than local interests, which is possibly why they avoided having railway manias of their own.

An alternative explanation for Parliament's failure is that, since Britain was the first country to attempt to develop a national network via private enterprise, it suffered from a first-mover disadvantage. As the long-established method of parliamentary procedure had worked well for the development of canals and turnpikes, which were all local enterprises, parliamentarians were lulled into thinking that such a procedure would be equally good for railways. However, they did not appreciate the importance of network externalities. On the other hand, during parliamentary debates some MPs noted the danger of using their established procedure for reviewing applications of railway schemes.[79]

Why were existing railways so willing to enter into ruinous competition? In a counterfactual analysis, along with a colleague, one of us has examined the strategies open to railway companies faced with the threat of competition from newcomers.[74] The main finding was that the worst thing that they could have done is nothing and the best strategy was the one they followed, namely to expand their own network to protect themselves from competition. Railways were willing to build branch lines that would only bring loss because that was better than having a rival build them and being driven out of business.[75]

CONSEQUENCES

How much did the newly enfranchised speculating class suffer in the downturn? The novelist Charlotte Brontë, while reflecting on her heavy losses from railway investments during the Mania, thankfully compared her situation to the thousands of middle-class investors who suffered immensely because of the collapse of railway share prices. She wrote 'many – very many are – by the late strange Railway System deprived almost of their daily bread; such then as have only lost provision laid up for the future should take care how they complain'.[76] Previous bubbles had investors who lost fortunes, but the Railway Mania involved many middle-class speculators who had very little to lose. Although many individuals suffered when railway share prices collapsed, the question remains as to what the consequences of the Railway Mania were for the overall economy.

In October 1847, exactly 2 years after railway shares peaked, there was a financial crisis in the UK. Pressures in the money market had been experienced since January 1847, with the Bank of England raising its discount rate four times in the first quarter of 1847. The Bank also rationed its lending and discounting of bills. This culminated in the so-called 'week of terror' from 16 to 23 October, during which several banks suspended payments and even well-run banks had to seek help from the Bank of England. The pressure on the money markets eased only when the Prime Minister and Chancellor of the Exchequer, at the end of the week of terror, sent the Bank of England a letter allowing it to disregard the recently passed Bank Charter Act. As a result, the Bank was able to end the crisis by expanding its note issue, helping banks facing liquidity difficulties.

The proximate cause of the crisis was the failure of many merchants, particularly those involved in the corn business. The price of wheat had doubled in the first half of 1847, following a poor harvest in 1846. However, the high wheat price eventually attracted imports, which then resulted in the wheat price collapsing by about 50 per cent in the summer of 1847. This caught many corn merchants and speculators unawares and ultimately resulted in their failure. These mercantile failures exacerbated the already tight pressures on the money market, resulting in the week of terror in October 1847.

Although the Railway Mania does not appear to have been responsible for the financial crisis of 1847, it seems to have indirectly aggravated the pressures in the money market.[77] The fact that railway shareholders paid up their capital in instalments as railway lines were constructed meant that there were many calls for capital in 1847.[78] As can be seen from Figure 4.1, there was an enormous increase in the paid-up capital that entered the railway sector in 1847, and the scale of gross capital formation in the railways in 1847 was unprecedented. The calls for capital throughout 1847 meant that shareholders had to withdraw money from their banks or raise it elsewhere, which put a great deal of pressure on the money markets.[79]

Lord John Eatwell suggests that the Railway Mania is a *prima facie* example of a useful bubble, in that after the bubble had burst, investments of real social value were left behind.[80] There is no doubt that the national rail network which emerged as a result of the Railway Mania was transformative. The huge reduction in the time and money costs of travelling made journeys possible for the masses, and more frequent (and comfortable) journeys possible for the middle and upper classes. Dionysius Lardner, a contemporary railway commentator, noted that in 1835 there were only 7 daily stagecoaches between London and Edinburgh that took 2 days, but by 1850, there were several trains per day carrying passengers and freight, with a journey time of less than 12 hours.[81] Insofar as it is possible to quantify the social benefits of railways to their full extent, economic cost–benefit analyses suggest that the railway network which emerged from the Mania delivered tremendous welfare gains throughout the nineteenth century and beyond.[82] In order to estimate the welfare gains ushered in by the railways, economic historians have used the concept of social savings, i.e. the cost to society of doing the same as the railways did, without them. One study has estimated that the social savings from railways in terms of time and money were as much as 2 per cent of GDP by 1850 and were close to 10 per cent by 1900.[83] This was a major boon to the productivity of the Victorian economy.

However, one must ask whether the social usefulness was as high as it could have been had the process of authorising the railways and establishing a railway network not been so laissez-faire or ad hoc. One must also ask if a bubble was a prerequisite for creating a national rail network.

The means of authorising the railways and establishing a railway network was inefficient and resulted in a sub-optimal rail network with unnecessary and duplicate lines. One study has estimated that the circa 20,000-mile rail system which had emerged by 1914 contained about 7,000 miles more than was necessary – the same social benefits could have been obtained with substantially less investment.[84] The inefficiencies in the rail system that were locked in during the Railway Mania contributed to the subsequent poor performance of the railway companies and widespread inefficiencies which have plagued British railways down to the present day.[85] Thus, rather than the bubble being useful for society, it created a higgledy-piggledy network and a railway system full of long-term inefficiencies. In addition, too much investment was wasted in building this sub-optimal network. A socially useful rail network and one that was profitable in the long run could have been constructed without the Mania. But this would only have been possible if the political calculus of Parliament had been less wed to regional interests and thus better able to create an efficient national rail network, repressing unnecessary competition and duplicate lines. With such an approach, the Railway Mania would never have happened.

The Railway Mania democratised speculation. The financial press, which was meant to protect investors and warn them of bubbles, called the Railway Mania far too late to be of any use to the new speculating class. According to its author, the moral of the Glenmutchkin Railway satire was caveat investor. Investors needed to look out for themselves because no one else would.

Within a decade of the end of the Railway Mania, any semblance of government regulation of joint-stock companies in the UK was removed when enterprises were granted the freedom to incorporate without needing prior government approval. Marketability was unconstrained and speculation was democratised. However, the only leverage during the Railway Mania was part-paid shares; the bubble was overwhelmingly fuelled by money rather than credit. Investors were still risking their own money. What if they started speculating with other people's money?

CHAPTER 5

Other People's Money: The Australian Land Boom

In Melbourne more particularly the spirit of speculation ran mad, and financiers and adventurers of every kind had a regular carnival of dissipation with other people's money: obtained with too little difficulty from the Melbourne banks, many of which, unfortunately for themselves and the country, were driven to advancing on unimproved land, yielding no income, and dead securities of all kinds by the keen competition that existed between them.

Nathaniel Cork[1]

BY THE END OF THE NINETEENTH CENTURY, FREEDOM OF incorporation and marketability of ownership shares were established principles across many countries, and the ability to speculate had been extended to the middle classes. Apart from the Mississippi Bubble, however, bubbles had typically not had long-lasting negative economic effects. Losses were still mostly borne by those who could afford them, the bankruptcies that occurred did not cascade into widespread defaults, and the affected industries were not so systemically important that they could undermine the entire economy. As the continuing popularity of Mackay showed, bubbles were remembered largely as mildly humorous fables, read by the middle classes as a form of entertainment.

The Australian Land Boom of the 1880s was different. Its bursting plunged Australia into the longest and deepest depression in its history, with widespread poverty, homelessness and hunger. One poignant account given by Rev. J. Dawborn illustrates the predicament of the masses in 1893.[2] One day a haggard mother of six came to the door of his vicarage in Melbourne with a baby in her arms. Her husband was a mason and out of work. She had not eaten in three days and she had fed her children on the stalks of cauliflowers and cabbages, which she had boiled and mashed. Yet a few years before, her husband, their family and all of Melbourne were enjoying a land boom, marking a period of unprecedented prosperity. In contrast with Mackay's flippant accounts of previous bubbles, histories of Melbourne's land boom are pure human tragedies. One historian compares 'Marvellous Melbourne' to the biblical city of Babel: a wealthy and prosperous place which was eventually subjected to judgement and plagues in the form of financial crises, bankruptcies and lost fortunes.[3]

This economic catastrophe originated in 1885 when a marriage boom, a rising population and urbanisation increased the demand for suburban single unit homes in Melbourne and Sydney.[4] Since many Melburnians had emigrated from dank industrial cities, the suburban lifestyle was particularly appealing: one historian describes suburbanism in this period as 'the opiate of the middle classes'.[5] The sudden increase in demand caused land prices to skyrocket: land which had sold for 15 shillings per square foot in 1884 was selling for twenty times as much in 1887. For example, land in Burwood, which was 9 miles from the centre of Melbourne, had risen from £70 to £300 per acre.[6] In the central business district of Melbourne, prices were doubling every few months, and the quantity of house sales exploded. In its review of 1887, the *Australasian Insurance and Banking Record* stated that an extraordinary amount of property had changed hands during the year, involving everyone from labourers to property investment companies.[7]

Much of this boom was fuelled by foreign capital, almost all of which came from the UK. Attracted by the high rate of economic growth, British investment in Australia grew precipitously throughout the 1880s, as can be seen from Table 5.1, and by 1888 it had reached £22.8 million – more than 10 per cent of Australian GDP. Initially this money was mostly invested in securities, but gradually spilled over into the land boom as the decade progressed. This process accelerated after January 1887, when the Associated Banks of Victoria, a coalition of the ten Australian trading banks headquartered in Melbourne, cut its key interest rate from 6 to 5 per cent. This was followed by a second rate cut in August 1887, this time to 4 per cent. Somewhat presciently, but with supportive effect, the *Australasian Insurance and Banking Record* stated that this would stimulate

TABLE 5.1 *Australian GDP, GDP per capita and overseas borrowing*[8]

	Nominal GDP (£m)	GDP per capita (£)	British investment in Australia (£m)
1881	147.8	64	5.7
1886	177.4	62	17.9
1887	195.6	67	15.2
1888	201.5	65	22.8
1889	221.4	68	22.0
1890	214.9	64	15.6
1891	211.6	67	12.6
1892	179.7	57	5.6
1893	160.6	53	-1.0
1899	190.4	55	6.0
1900	198.3	57	5.8

share prices and business activity.[9] But this economic stimulus had an uneven effect, because the reduced interest on safe assets encouraged investors to take more risks. According to H. G. Turner, then the General Manager of the Commercial Bank of Australia, savers responded to these interest rate cuts by searching for a better yield.[10]

The demand for higher-yielding investments was met by the emergence of large land and property companies. Since these companies had much greater access to financial resources than the traditional small contractors and builders, they were able to purchase large tracts of suburban land and subdivide them into single-dwelling building plots. These plots were then either sold to developers for a profit or developed by the companies themselves.[11] With property prices rising rapidly, this business model was extremely lucrative, resulting in a deluge of new property development companies. As Figure 5.1 shows, 40 such companies were incorporated in Victoria alone in 1887. Many of these found additional finance by borrowing from Australia's 28 established trading banks. Although stipulations in bank charters forbade loans on real estate, banks regularly found a way around these regulations. In 1887 the Royal Commission on Banking Laws gave this practice its unofficial blessing, and in 1888 the Victoria government passed legislation removing this regulation for banks incorporated in the state.

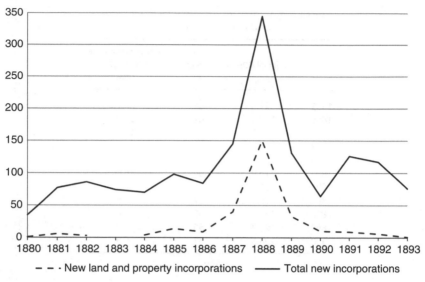

Figure 5.1 New company formations in Victoria[12]

As the land boom developed, property financing and speculation were increasingly dominated by two other types of institution: building societies, and land-boom companies. Building societies were traditionally the major providers of housing finance for individuals who wanted to buy a single-dwelling house. However, during the land boom they began to change their business model, providing finance for the emerging builder-speculators and property developers.[13] The land-boom companies had a hybrid business model that combined property speculation, property investment and mortgage banking. In order to finance their own property operations or those of others, they took advantage of the lax banking regulatory environment to morph into shadow banks, raising funds from the public and from depositors in the UK. They were particularly aggressive when it came to raising deposits, drawing many depositors away from the trading banks by offering hugely tempting interest rates. In New South Wales they were so successful in attracting deposits that they largely supplanted the building societies.[14]

Over the first few months of 1888, the value of central Melbourne land increased by about 50 per cent and the value of suburban property doubled or even trebled in some cases.[15] For example, 6.25 acres of land on the south side of the Yarra River were bought for £100,000, then resold for £300,000 only 6 months later.[16] In the first half of 1888, suburban land was often sold three or four times over, without any enhancements being made to it and with its price trebling.[17] Over the same period, land values in the more desirable parts of the central business district went from £400 to £1,100 per foot.[18] As a result, 12-storey skyscrapers were erected in the central business district to rival those of London. The amount of land speculation in September and October 1888 was such that the *Argus*, one of Melbourne's main newspapers, expanded its land sale advertisements from a page and a half to four pages. Although Sydney did not experience anything like the boom in Melbourne, the price of a block of land in Sydney rose in 1888 from £191 to £304.[19]

A study of 100 Melburnian land investors, which examines how much they bought and sold a piece of suburban land for (allowing for subdivision), finds that, during the 1880s, the average annual return on land was 39.8 per cent. This explains why so many people were keen to participate in the land boom. In terms of land prices, the same study finds that the average price per acre rose from £39 in 1882 and £166 in 1885 to £303 in 1888. By 1890, however, average land prices had fallen to £154.[20]

Figure 5.2 tracks the changes in Melbourne house prices over the last three decades of the nineteenth century. The index of house prices, which had been trending upwards from 1880, accelerated upwards in 1887 and 1888 and peaked in 1889, having nearly doubled since 1870. However, after 1889, house prices fell precipitously until 1895, when they were 56.5 per cent below their peak. By the end of the century, house prices had recovered slightly, but only to their 1870 level.

Sydney in the 1880s did not experience the same increase in house prices as Melbourne – prices over the decade increased by about 32 percent.[21] In addition, unlike house prices in Melbourne, those in Sydney did not start to fall until 1892. However, by 1894 they had fallen by 50 per cent. The housing market in both cities took a long time to recover – it was 1912 in Sydney and 1918 in Melbourne before they got back to their 1889 levels. Land prices also remained low for a long period: the average price of a block of land in Sydney was £123 in 1907, having been £303 in 1888.[22]

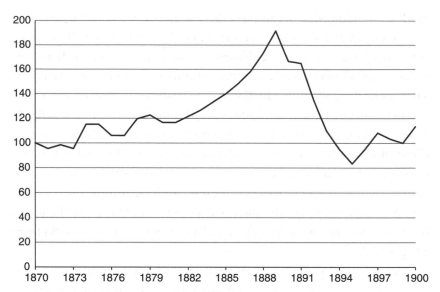

Figure 5.2 Melbourne House Price Index[23]

As well as the boom in the price of land and houses, there was a promotion boom of land companies in 1888 (see Figure 5.1). Many deliberately alluded to their status as quasi-banks, with names like the Australian Land Investment and Banking Company. Shares in land-boom companies were attractive to ordinary individuals who lacked the funds to deal directly in land, but wanted to profit from the boom.[24] Insolvency records reveal that carpenters, drapers, labourers, priests, spinsters, teachers and widows invested in land-boom companies.[25] The democratisation of speculation which we witnessed in the Railway Mania was alive and well 43 years later and over 10,000 miles away.

Such was the demand for shares of land-boom companies when they came to market that they were vastly oversubscribed and immediately sold at a premium. One commentator observed that 'sometimes a newly-formed company is in the position of some of the creations at the time of the South Sea Bubble – it does not know exactly what line of business to take up, its shares going to a premium notwithstanding'.[26]

Figure 5.3 contains a stock index of the land-boom companies which were traded on the Stock Exchange of Melbourne. Between December 1887 and July 1888, this index more than doubled. However, this index

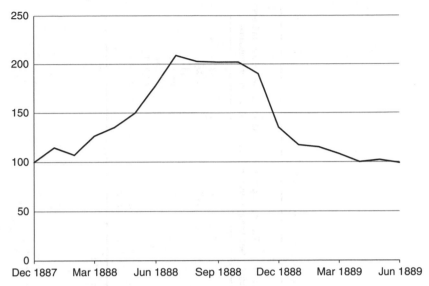

Figure 5.3 Monthly index of land-boom company stocks on the Stock Exchange of Melbourne[27]

may lead us to underestimate the increase in the share prices of land-boom companies because it includes only 25 companies, presumably the larger ones, and thus ignores the smaller and more speculative ventures that may have been traded on Melbourne's other stock exchanges.

The end-of-year values of all the land-boom companies on the Stock Exchange of Melbourne are shown in Table 5.2. This table illustrates the growth of the land-boom companies and the way in which market and paid-up values diverged during the boom years. It also reveals that the number of transactions on the Stock Exchange of Melbourne trebled in 1888. The increase in the volume of business was so great that the clerical staff of the exchange struggled to cope with it, staying in their offices until late in the evening to process trades.[28] This was only one of six stock exchanges operating in the same city, so the total number of trades would have been much greater.[29] Apart from the Stock Exchange of Melbourne, all these 'bubble' exchanges disappeared after the cessation of the land boom.[30] The increase in trading was also reflected in the money earned by brokers and in the price of

TABLE 5.2 *The Stock Exchange of Melbourne and the land-boom companies*[31]

	Number of non-mining companies	Number of land-boom companies	Total market capitalisation (£m)	Total paid-up capital (£m)	Total market capitalisation of land-boom companies (£m)	Total paid-up capital land-boom companies (£m)	Number of transactions on Stock Exchange of Melbourne
1886	85	7	25.0	17.9	1.0	1.3	6,494
1887	95	8	34.1	20.0	2.6	1.5	14,913
1888	153	25	44.1	26.9	8.5	3.5	59,411
1889	152	22	47.7	28.8	4.1	3.9	45,118
1890	152	18	48.6	29.6	4.1	3.6	77,282
1891	154	18	23.9	25.5	2.9	3.9	57,018
1892	121	3	23.9	25.5	0.2	0.6	36,440
1893	112	3	10.7	23.7	0.0	0.3	n/a

a seat at the exchange, which rose from £300 in December 1887 to £1,500 in March of the following year.[32]

Just as a cut in interest rates by the Associated Banks of Victoria coincided with the escalation of the land boom, the increase of 1 per cent in their interest rate on 22 October 1888 marked its end. This increase was accompanied by a new policy of credit rationing by discriminating against the discounting of land bills. The Associated Banks took these steps because they recognised that the cheap money policy which they had introduced in 1887 was contributing to the over-expansion of credit; the speculation in land and the speculation in land-boom companies.[33] This policy change had an almost immediate effect on the prices of land-boom companies: by December the index of land-boom companies (see Figure 5.3) had fallen 35 per cent from its peak. The credit squeeze also brought speculation in real estate to an abrupt end.[34]

In its December issue, the *Australasian Insurance and Banking Record* applauded the Associated Banks for their action, because it had brought to light the unsound condition of the property business.[35] Almost immediately, ten small property companies failed and the shares of land-boom companies became unsaleable. However, the land-boom companies did not collapse for another 3 years.[36]

There are four reasons why the liquidation of the land boom proceeded so slowly. First, there were improvements in the wider economy which slowed the panic selling of land-boom company shares.[37] Following the collapse of the land boom in Victoria, public and private investment in New South Wales increased.[38] After plentiful rainfall, an abundant harvest, the largest wool clip on record and a rise in the European demand for wool, the economic prospects for Victoria looked much brighter.[39] Second, there was a boom in silver-mine shares in 1889, which temporarily stimulated the economy and may have distracted attention from the perilous condition of the land-boom companies.[40] The boom centred around the silver mines of Broken Hill and, in particular, the Broken Hill Proprietary Company. The shares of Broken Hill Proprietary increased in value by 188 per cent in 1889.

Third, the trading banks, which had stayed somewhat aloof from the land boom itself, increased their lending and overdrafts to building societies and land-boom companies, believing that their troubles were temporary. This extension of credit meant that, even at the end of 1890, 2 years after the collapse of the boom, very few building societies or land-boom companies had failed.[41] It was only when the trading banks started calling in their overdrafts in 1891 that large numbers of building societies and land-boom companies started to fail.[42] The extension of credit by many trading banks after the collapse of the boom in 1888 would ultimately contribute to their own demise.[43]

Fourth, and most importantly, the land-boom companies, hoping that the property market would recover, developed survival strategies which stayed their demise. Most offered fixed-term deposits or debentures with a 12- or 24-month duration, so when the boom collapsed suddenly, these institutions were less vulnerable to a run than normal trading banks were. Nevertheless, as the deposits matured they did face a funding issue. In response, they intensified their efforts to attract deposits, particularly from the UK. Many opened offices in London and Scotland; some even changed their name to include the word 'bank' or imply an association with the UK. For example, in September 1889 the Victoria Freehold Bank changed its name to the British Bank of Australia.[44] Scottish newspapers teemed with advertisements from these companies, offering unusually high interest on deposits.[45] But these deposits were being used merely to pay off other maturing debts.[46] This ultimately turned these land-boom companies into Ponzi schemes. Several companies, such as those associated with Sir Matthew Davies, the speaker of the Victorian Parliament, engaged in creative accounting practices, paid dividends out of capital or borrowed funds, and used company funds to keep their share price from falling.[47]

Of course, these zombie banks could only survive for so long. Between 1889 and mid-1891, the only major institution to fail was the Premier Permanent Building Association of Melbourne. Its failure brought to light fraudulent balance sheets and directors exceeding their powers. The *Australasian Insurance and Banking Record* warned that this financial impropriety would scare off British savers from putting their money on deposit in Australia.[48] However, British investors began to probe the situation in Australia more closely only after the collapse of Barings Bank in November 1890. Table 5.1 shows how the flow of British investment started to slow down in 1890. By July 1891, with their deposits maturing and with investors unwilling to renew, the zombie land-boom companies and building societies in Melbourne and Sydney began to topple like dominoes. Over the next 6 months each wave of failures further dented the confidence of British investors.[49] By 1892, the flow of British investment had slowed to a trickle.

By March 1892, 31 major land-boom companies and 9 building societies had failed in Melbourne and Sydney alone. These 40 institutions had total assets of £22.8 million and deposits of £12.7 million. Their depositors did not fare well – about one-eighth of their savings were lost altogether and the rest were locked up for a long time.[50] The institutions had supposedly been backed by uncalled capital of £5.5 million, theoretically available to investors in the event of such a crisis. In practice, however, depositors received less than 30 per cent of this £5.5 million. This was because large shareholders were absolved from their liability through secret 'compositions': special bankruptcy proceedings for the privileged elite that allowed them to evade such responsibilities.[51] For example, F. T. Derham, the Postmaster-General of Victoria from 1886 to 1890, owed his creditors £550,000 over a series of land-boom transactions. The secret composition he made with his creditors kept him solvent because he only had to pay one old penny to the pound. There were 240 pennies in a pound at the time, so this allowed Derham to write off 99.6 per cent of his debt.

By the middle of 1892, the liquidation of the land boom appeared to have run its course. But in its final stages the established trading banks were teetering on the brink of calamity. They too, as we shall see below, would have to pay a price for the excesses of the 1880s.

What role had the media played during the boom and bust? In the boom phase, occasional misgivings had been expressed by the weekly journal *Table Talk* and the *Australasian Insurance and Banking Record*.[52] The daily newspapers did little to question the boom, possibly because they benefited handsomely from the advertising fees from land-boom companies and building societies seeking deposits. Indeed, Nathaniel Cork, when asked about the state of Australian finance by London bankers, would show them a copy of the *Argus* newspaper he had kept from his antipodean visit; one glance at their advertisements told them everything they needed to know.[53] As with the Railway Mania, the substantial advertising money that newspapers received from bubble companies gave them a powerful incentive not to question the boom.

When it came to the bust, the mainstream press avoided investigating it at all whenever possible. One exception was *Table Talk*, a weekly gossip magazine based in Melbourne. Under the editorship of its founder Maurice Brodzky, who has been described as the original muckraker, *Table Talk* ran a series of exposés on unscrupulous behaviour by land-boom company directors.[54] The British press also played an important role in the bust, particularly after the collapse of Barings, by calling the attention of British investors to the major structural weaknesses in the Australian financial system.[55]

CAUSES

Although previous bubbles had followed the removal of restrictions on establishing firms with marketable shares, the Australian bubble was the first in which there was true freedom of incorporation. In other words, entrepreneurs could establish companies with marketable shares without requiring prior authorisation from the government or legal system.

As a result of financial engineering, land also became much more marketable. Land-boom companies raised money from shareholders and depositors, and used the proceeds raised to buy property and land. These shares had relatively low denominations and could be bought with a small deposit, with the remaining balance paid off over 2 to 3 years. During the boom multiple stock exchanges opened, meaning that investors could buy and sell shares at several different locations for the first time. The increase in liquidity was compounded by a threefold increase in trading volume, making it easy to find a buyer or seller.[56] Whereas previously land speculation was restricted to those wealthy enough to buy and sell plots of land, this financialisaton of land by the land-boom companies enabled ordinary investors to speculate in land by simply buying and selling shares in land-boom companies.

Money and credit, the second side of the bubble triangle, were in abundant supply during the land boom. The main sources of credit were the trading banks, the building societies and the land-boom companies,

TABLE 5.3 *The growing vulnerability of the Australian banking system*[57]

	Deposits from overseas (% of total deposits)	Median capital ratio (%)	Median liquidity ratio (%)	Number of branches
1870	12.0	52.6	12.9	381
1875	10.0	36.1	12.5	613
1880	12.8	32.8	16.7	844
1885	18.6	21.2	10.4	1,159
1888	22.8	22.3	12.6	1,404
1889	24.4	21.7	11.8	1,465
1890	25.5	19.4	13.2	1,543
1891	27.1	19.6	11.3	1,553
1892	25.4	18.3	12.3	1,519

many of which were *de facto* banks. During the 1880s, the trading banks aggressively expanded their deposit-gathering and loan portfolio. As can be seen from Table 5.3, in the 1880s the trading banks expanded their branch network to capture domestic deposits and they increasingly sought deposits from the UK. Some banks even went as far as hiring touting agents for this purpose. Between 1880 and 1888, the trading banks doubled their Australian deposits, to £88.5 million, and nearly quadrupled their overseas deposits, to £24.0 million.[58] Table 5.3 reveals that this expansion of deposits was not matched by a concomitant increase in capital, with the result that banks became much more leveraged. In addition, the liquidity ratios in Table 5.3 suggest that, by 1888, a greater proportion of their deposit base was being lent out than in 1880. The deposits raised by many of the trading banks were increasingly either lent to property speculators and developers or lent against the security of land.[59]

The building societies also aggressively expanded in the 1880s, particularly from 1885 onwards. By 1888 they had more than doubled their deposits to £5.3 million. Their loans to the property sector in these years also greatly increased, from £2.5 million of new loans granted in 1887 to a staggering £4.4 million granted in 1888.[60] Much of this credit extended by the building societies was advanced to property speculators rather than their traditional borrower – the owner-occupier. The building societies during the 1880s also made significant changes to their lending policy. They lengthened their repayment periods on average from 8 to 12 years and they reduced the security that they required of borrowers, both of which decisions made it much more attractive to borrow from them. From the perspective of the land boom and property speculators, the greatest change to their lending policy was that loans could be repaid at any time without incurring a penalty.[61] This greatly facilitated the practice of flipping, i.e. buying land with borrowed funds, subdividing the land, quickly selling it at a profit and repaying the loan.

The land-boom companies were highly leveraged institutions, which in some cases had the appearance of banks because they raised substantial deposits from the domestic and UK public. In 1890, it is estimated, the land-boom companies in Victoria held £7.3 million in deposits and debentures.[62] However, these deposits, instead of being advanced to borrowers and invested in safe securities, were invested in property schemes.

The leveraging of land and property purchases during the land boom was twofold. First the property developer or land-boom company borrowed extensively to purchase the land. Then, once they subdivided the land, the usual practice was to offer it on extended credit terms to those they sold it to.[63] This applied also to the purchase of shares in land-boom companies. Initial subscribers had to pay only a small initial instalment and were subject to future capital calls. This practice leveraged the purchasing of shares in highly leveraged companies.

As in previous bubbles, the element that most caught the attention of contemporaries was speculation, which was often perceived as the result of widespread moral weakness. In 1893, a recently repatriated English journalist attributed the bubble to the inherent inferiority of Australians, stating that 'the gambling spirit inherent in the people forms an element of serious weakness in the national character'.[64] As an explanation for the bubble, this is somewhat undermined by the fact that vast quantities of the money invested in the bubble came from the UK. Anecdotal evidence, however, suggests that speculation was widespread. Nathaniel Cork, a UK banking expert, visited Australia in 1888 and observed that:

In Adelaide the street in which the Stock Exchange was situated was crowded with men, women and boys in a state of excitement from 9 o'clock in the morning. All seemed to be having their fling, and some men in responsible positions were not ashamed to pass the first half hour of their day in this scene of excitement. The whole population from statesmen to servant girls, were in the whirlpool.[65]

The same held true in Melbourne, with members of the stock exchange finding it difficult to get into their offices through the vast crowds of speculators who gathered each day on the streets outside the exchange.[66] James Service, the Premier of Victoria until 1886, concurred with this view, adding that 'there was not a man and hardly a woman in the colony who did not go in head-over-heels to make a fortune during the land boom'.[67] Notably, the stories of fortunes being made simply by flipping land several times generated a get-rich-quick mentality among investors and encouraged some to speculate well beyond their means.[68] The official history of a notable Melburnian stockbroker suggests that the speculative fervour of the land-boom years had its roots in the discovery of new gold and silver mines in the 1880s.[69]

The spark which ignited the land boom was the 1887 liberalisation of the restriction on banks from lending on the security of real estate. This was the final act in a 25-year liberalisation process. By the time of the boom, Australia was a *prima facie* example of a free banking system because it had few legal barriers to entry, few regulations, freedom for banks to issue their own notes and no central bank or lender of last resort.[70] In 1862, the British Treasury had devolved responsibility for bank supervision to the individual colonial governments. For a time, the colonies implemented the regulations bequeathed by the British, the most important of which was that banks must not grant mortgages on real estate. However, the colonies gradually diverged from the British Treasury principles towards 'a situation in which banks were subject to a minimum of legal restraint'.[71]

Despite this laissez-faire milieu, the trading banks were forbidden from lending on the security of real estate. However, in 1887, the Victorian government appointed a Royal Commission on the state's banking laws, with a particular focus on this last major vestige of regulation. Reporting in July 1887, it recommended that lending on real estate by banks should no longer be restricted. The Commission argued that, although lending against property might be imprudent for English banks, land in Australia was marketable, and 'that experience shows that there are no better securities than those effected on land'.[72] The Victorian government passed this recommendation into law in December 1888, but puzzlingly, section one of the Act calls the legislation the Banks and Currency Amendment Statute 1887.[73] Quite possibly this back-dating was to provide legal cover for those banks that had acted in advance of the legal change, following the fact that the Royal Commission, before reporting in July 1887, had already directed the drafting of a bill to pass its recommendations into law.[74]

The report of the Royal Commission had two effects. First, it signalled to the public and depositors that land and property were high-quality assets. This, no doubt, was a huge fillip to the land-boom companies that were raising deposits and investing in property. Second, banks started lending in a substantial way on the security of property. Thus, the Commission helped generate the spark that would kindle the land boom.

Why did politicians remove the restriction on lending on real estate? A kind appraisal is that they were asleep, intoxicated with the growth of Melbourne, or too harassed by lobbyists to take the necessary action.[75] Michael Cannon, in his polemic-cum-exposé *The Land Boomers*, is much less kind to the political elite – he argues that the Victorian Parliament became a land speculators' club in which the use of public office for private gain was commonplace.[76] Most of the cabinet of Duncan Gilles, Premier of Victoria from 1886 to 1890, had directorships in land-boom companies, and some were speculators in their own right who were bankrupted in the crash. Outside the cabinet, the lower and upper houses were packed full of land speculators and directors of land-boom companies. No fewer than thirty members of the legislative assembly were directors in land-boom companies.[77] The Imperial Banking Company, the first of the major land-boom companies to fail, had been set up by Sir Benjamin Benjamin, the Lord Mayor of Melbourne between 1887 and 1889. Notably, the special bankruptcy commissions established in the wake of the crash let many prominent land boomers evade repaying their debts.

The influence of the land boomers on politicians and the political machinery is perhaps best exemplified by Sir Matthew Davies, the former speaker of the Victorian Parliament, whose network of companies degenerated into Ponzi schemes. All four of the main companies within his 'Davies group' were chaired by senior politicians. It collapsed in 1892, precipitating Davies' own bankruptcy and that of his companies, after which several unsuccessful attempts were made to prosecute him for conspiracy to defraud by issuing false balance sheets. This same Matthew Davies had chaired the 1887 Royal Commission on Banking.

CONSEQUENCES

The liquidation of the land boom did not end with the collapse of the land-boom companies and building societies. The trading banks – the very heart of Australia's financial system – would also pay a heavy price. In March 1892, two of the twenty-eight Australian trading banks suspended payment – the Mercantile Bank of Australia and the Bank of South Australia. This prompted the Treasurer of Victoria to coerce the Associated Banks of Victoria into a public declaration that they were 'willing to render financial assistance to each other on such terms and to such an extent as may seem justifiable to each of them, if and when the occasion arises'.[78] The sense of panic abated.[79] However, this public declaration of mutual assistance proved worthless when, in January 1893, the Federal Bank, a member of the Associated Banks, closed its doors.

The Associated Banks sought to re-establish public confidence by declaring that their mutual assistance pact was secure and claiming that the Federal Bank had not asked for help before closing.[80] Subsequently, the Treasurer of Victoria pressured the Associated Banks into declaring in March 1893 that 'the associated banks . . . have agreed to act unitedly in tendering financial assistance to each other should such be required, and that the government of Victoria have resolved to afford their cordial co-operation'.[81] However, the Bank of Australasia, which had not been involved in crafting it, required the statement to be reissued with the clarification that 'banks would assist one another to such an extent as to each might seem fit', and the Victorian Premier declined to endorse it.[82] This undermined the credibility of the mutual assistance pact with the public. These doubts were proved correct in April 1893 when the Associated Banks refused to bail out the Commercial Bank of Australia. A panic ensued and by 17 May a further eleven trading banks had suspended payment (i.e. they had closed their doors and depositors could not withdraw their deposits) and the remaining thirteen were experiencing major runs and deposit withdrawals. At this point, fifteen of Australia's twenty-eight trading banks had either failed or suspended. These fifteen banks controlled 56.8 per cent of the total assets of the Australian banking system.

In an attempt to stop the panic, the government of Victoria declared a 5-day bank holiday on 1 May 1893. Instead of calming the situation, depositor excitement 'rose to fever heat and it was hastily assumed that all the banks would have had to suspend had it not been for the Government's intervention'.[83] As a result, several banks, including the 'Big Three', chose to stay open to signal their strength to depositors.[84]

In contrast to the apparent bumbling of the Victorian government, the New South Wales (NSW) government approached the crisis with an assured touch – it passed three measures applicable only to banks with a head office in NSW. The first measure was to declare that the NSW government was willing, if necessary, to act as a lender of last resort. This decree followed the collapse of the Australian Joint Stock Bank, one of the larger trading banks, on 21 April 1893. The second measure was the Bank Issue Act. This made bank notes a first charge on assets, gave the Governor of NSW power to declare bank notes legal tender and granted the government the right to inspect banks. At the start of May 1893, Timothy Coghlan, a government statistician, was dispatched to persuade the five major banks operating in NSW to accept the Act, but without success.[85] However, when the NSW government learned of the imminent closure of the Commercial Banking Company of Sydney, it declared the notes of this bank plus the notes of the 'Big Three' to be legal tender. Notably, none of the 'Big Three' failed, and within a few days deposit runs had ceased and the crisis was ended. The final measure that the NSW government passed in late May 1893 enabled the government to advance 50 per cent of the sums owed to current account depositors of suspended banks in the form of Treasury notes which had the status of legal tender. Put simply, 'this was the traditional policy of choking a panic with cash'.[86]

Most of the banks that suspended during the crisis were allowed to engage in financial reconstruction through converting some deposits into preference shares, converting some short-term deposits into long-term fixed deposits, calling in unpaid capital and raising new capital from bank shareholders. Such reconstruction was criticised at the time by the British press, with some advocating the liquidation of failed banks.[87] However, liquidation might not have been possible because bank assets and collateral were unsaleable and might even have been nearly worthless due to fire-sale losses.[88] It is worth recalling that many depositors at the time believed that the reconstructions were the best outcome for them.[89]

The fundamental reason why the banking crisis occurred is that, in the 1880s, many Australian banks became much more vulnerable and fragile because of the risks they were taking in an unregulated environment. After the liquidation of the property boom in 1891 and 1892, it was only a matter of time before the riskier trading banks themselves collapsed. The banks which failed or suspended during the crisis had riskier profiles than the banks which did not close, in that they: (a) were overdependent on deposits from the UK, which could quickly dry up; (b) had higher leverage and lower liquidity, meaning that they had less skin in the game and less of an ability to meet large deposit outflows; and (c) had a much greater proportion of their loans in Victoria, the epicentre of the land boom.[90]

The land boom helped many Australians fulfil their dream of living in the suburbs and owning a single unit dwelling, thus escaping the squalor, cramped conditions and lack of privacy in the city centre. However, for many, this blissful existence was short-lived because they returned after the crash to their old landlords in the city centre.[91] During the boom too many homes were built and after the crash vacancies soared to over 12,000.[92]

The economic costs of the liquidation of the land boom outweighed any ephemeral benefits while it lasted. As Table 5.1 shows, there was a long depression in the 1890s, with nominal GDP and GDP per capita falling substantially. Although there was a global depression at this time, its depth was minor in comparison to that of Australia. Indeed, it would be the late 1890s before real GDP returned to the levels prevailing on the eve of the land boom, and it would be the early 1900s before GDP per capita returned to the levels witnessed in 1888.[93] Given that the land boom was concentrated on Melbourne, it is unsurprising that Victoria experienced a longer and deeper depression than NSW.[94] It was also substantially longer and deeper than that experienced by Australia during the Great Depression of the 1930s.

The main reason for the severity of the 1890s depression was the 1893 financial crisis. Because deposits were locked up in suspended banks, the money supply fell dramatically and there was a credit crunch, with surviving banks becoming much more cautious.[95] Furthermore, as can be seen from Table 5.1, the funds flowing from the UK dried up; as one history of the crisis put it, 'the British investor would have rather buried his money under the floor boards than entrusted it to an Australian bank'.[96] This obliged Australian banks to contract their balance sheets. In addition, the reconstruction and recapitalisation of the banking system during the 1890s resulted in a continuous contraction of credit until the early 1900s. This crippled businesses for most of the 1890s and very little investment occurred.[97]

As in any deep economic depression, the raw numbers conceal a significant human cost. The contemporary press and subsequent historians recount stories of destitution among the working classes and the formerly well-to-do – malnourished families, families broken up and women forced to turn to prostitution.[98] Thanks to the bursting of the property boom and subsequent financial crisis, Australia endured many years of economic hardship and human misery. Melbourne was no longer so marvellous.

The Australian Land Boom showed that bubbles can have substantial economic and human costs when they are financed with other people's money. It also revealed that the financial system can take assets such as land and turn them into objects of financial market speculation. This would not be the last time that a property bubble would be financed with other people's money, and it would not be the last time that clever financial engineering would turn land or houses into objects of financial market speculation. One hundred and twenty years after the peak of the Australian Land Boom, the world would once again experience a bubble which not only was devastating for the economy, but which would also undermine the political stability of major democracies.

CHAPTER 6

Wheeler-Dealers: The British Bicycle Mania

Money poured into the coffers of men who had done nothing to build these businesses; they had only been astute enough to see that the market was ripe for flotation, and as the public cried for cycle shares they got them. The result of all the flotations and the buying and selling of the various concerns was that a limited few made money and a large number of people, many of them workers in the various businesses, lost their savings of many years.

W. F. Grew[1]

A cynical writer has said that, while panics run in cycles, the present mania began with a run on cycles.

Money[2]

THE ABUNDANT MARKETABILITY, MONEY AND CREDIT IN BRITain at the end of the nineteenth century meant that, for the first time, bubbles could form without any specific government involvement. Any sufficiently interesting innovation, especially if it were accompanied by high-profile early success stories, could attract enough speculation to start a bubble. The circumstances that made bubbles more frequent – abundant money and a preference for risky investments – also provided fertile ground for fraudulent schemes. Both innovation and fraud were present during the British Bicycle Mania, which, while sparked by a series of major improvements to bicycle technology, was abetted by financial entrepreneurs who were inventive, creative and ethically questionable.

Although bicycles were used from the early nineteenth century, early models were highly impractical. The penny-farthing design had an enormous front wheel which, by giving the pedals additional leverage, allowed cyclists to achieve high speeds. However, this also made the bicycles unstable. When cyclists fell off, as they often did, they had a long way to fall to reach the ground. Of particular danger was 'taking a header': flipping over the handlebars, often after hitting one of the many potholes on mid-nineteenth-century roads. The bicycles were usually made entirely from wood and wrought iron, and as a result had comically poor suspension. One of the most popular models was nicknamed 'the boneshaker' on account of the uncomfortable riding experience it provided.

Bicycles did not become a serious transport option until the 1880s, when a series of innovations significantly increased their utility. In 1885 the penny-farthing design was replaced with the 'safety' model, which used a chain to give the pedals leverage without the need for a large front wheel. The safety model was soon itself superseded by the diamond-shaped frame, which provided additional stability. Improvements in the manufacture of weldless steel tubes allowed bicycles to be both stronger and lighter, and the addition of J. B. Dunlop's pneumatic tyre in 1888 allowed for a much smoother ride.[3] The transformation was remarkable: in the space of a few years, archaic and impractical devices turned into something closely resembling the bicycles we still use today.

The British bicycle industry grew steadily in the late 1880s and early 1890s, and was largely based in the West Midlands. In Birmingham the number of bicycle manufacturers rose from 72 in 1889 to 177 in 1895, and the number of manufacturers in Coventry more than doubled.[4] By the summer of 1895, there had been a notable increase in the number of cyclists in British towns and cities; many contemporary writers commented on how widespread cycling had become, particularly among women, for whom cycling was said to have become fashionable.[5] The breakthroughs of the 1880s opened the door to further innovations in the field, and the number of cycle-related patents issued rose from 595 in 1890 to 4,269 in 1896, when it accounted for 15 per cent of all new patents issued.[6] Inventions ranged from incremental improvements in tubes or chains to a raft that allowed bicycles to cross water and a velocipede fire engine.[7]

Initially most bicycle, tube and tyre firms were privately owned, but in the early 1890s a few of the larger firms incorporated, with most share trading activity occurring on the Birmingham Stock Exchange. One such firm was the Pneumatic Tyre Company, established in 1892 with a nominal capital of £300,000, which held the patent to produce Dunlop-branded pneumatic tyres. Because Dunlop tyres had an exceptional reputation, this company was uniquely well placed to profit from the increasing popularity of cycles. Its potential was spotted by a local tycoon called Ernest Terah Hooley, who came up with a plan to profit by buying the company out, then re-floating it on the stock market at a higher valuation.

The Pneumatic Tyre Company shareholders asked Hooley for £3 million, ten times its original value and well above the market rate. Hooley had to borrow almost all of the £3 million; the purchase could be thought of as an early example of a leveraged buyout. Attempting to re-float the company for a higher valuation also required an expensive marketing campaign: gentlemen with 'good reputations' were paid to put their names to the prospectus, and various newspapers were paid to provide positive coverage. But these efforts were ultimately successful, and in May 1896 the newly renamed Dunlop Company was launched, with £5 million of shares successfully issued.[8] Hooley later told a bankruptcy court that the marketing campaign had cost so much that his profits only amounted to somewhere between £100,000 and £200,000, a relatively low rate of return considering the riskiness of the venture.[9]

News of Hooley's acquisition offer had first reached the market in March 1896, and the Pneumatic Tyre share price rose accordingly, peaking at £12.38 on 25 April 1896 – a 1,138 per cent profit for those who had subscribed to the shares.[10] Investors soon learned that another publicly traded tyre firm, Beeston, was set to pay a 100 per cent dividend in anticipation of a Hooley-led recapitalisation. Unlike Dunlop Beeston's fundamentals were poor, and the company was unsuccessful in the long term. Although it was not proven, there is reason to believe that the money for the 100 per cent dividend came from Hooley's own funds for the purposes of market manipulation.[11] If so, this ploy was spectacularly successful: Beeston shares rose from £1.05 to £7.75 between 7 April and 9 May.[12]

The enormous capital gains of these two companies brought the cycle share market to national attention. The *Financial Times* published its first

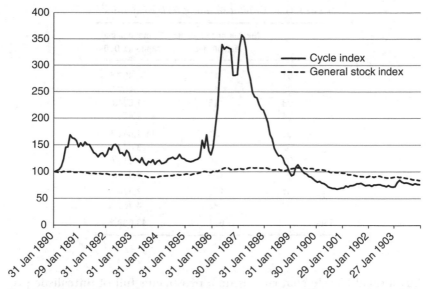

Figure 6.1 Monthly general and cycle share indexes, 1890–1903[16]

article on cycle shares on 22 April 1896, claiming the Birmingham Stock Exchange had 'gone mad' in response to rapid rises in cycle share prices.[13] This sentiment was repeated a week later in an editorial that suggested that the shares would soon become 'as inflated as the tyres'.[14] These price rises were dismissed as a result of pure gambling, and the newspaper compared profits in cycle shares to 'a run of luck at Monte Carlo'.[15] But despite its sceptical editorial line, developments in the cycle share market were usually reported without comment. As the trade in cycle shares grew more popular, the *Financial Times* steadily increased its coverage, devoting a daily section to the cycle share market from April 1896 onwards. The resulting publicity probably had a more significant effect on the market than the newspaper's sporadic criticism, and prices continued to rise. An index of cycle shares, shown in Figure 6.1, rose by a total of 258 per cent between 31 December 1895 and 20 May 1896.

The success of the Dunlop Company in attracting investment encouraged large numbers of existing cycle firms to go public. As Table 6.1 shows, 70 cycle, tube or tyre firms had been floated in 1895; in 1896 the number was 363, with a further 238 floated in the first 6 months of 1897. Hooley's promotion of the Dunlop Company established the template:

TABLE 6.1 *Capitalisation of cycle companies*[17]

		Number of companies established	Total nominal capital (£'000s)
1895	Q1	17	357.5
	Q2	12	182.5
	Q3	15	1,624.0
	Q4	26	1,476.1
1896	Q1	34	1,641.1
	Q2	94	13,847.2
	Q3	96	5,316.6
	Q4	139	6,454.6
1897	Q1	156	7,370.0
	Q2	82	4,763.6
Total		**671**	**43,033.2**

buy a small bicycle company, issue a prospectus full of unrealistic promises, pay influential figures to support the flotation and offer it to the
public for a much higher price than you paid. On balance sheets, the
discrepancy between the price paid by the promoter and the price
offered to the public was resolved by placing unjustifiably large valuations
on patents, or by referring to the intangible asset of 'goodwill'.[18] This
practice could be incredibly lucrative: one firm was reportedly issued to
the public for a price ten times as large as the promoter had paid for all its
constituent private firms combined.[19]

The methods used in promotion could be remarkably creative. For
several years before the boom, J. G. Accles had run an unprofitable
Birmingham bicycle factory which he could not sell privately. In 1896 he
sought to take advantage of the boom by incorporating as Accles Ltd. and
recruiting the services of John Sugden, a former manufacturer of ostrich
feather products with a history of financial chicanery.[20] In order to attract
investors, Sugden and Accles formed another company, Lum-in-um Cycles,
and placed an order on its behalf for 20,000 Accles bicycles. This order was
then displayed prominently on the Accles Ltd. prospectus, with no mention
of the fact that the company was effectively buying products from itself (in
fact none of these bicycles was ever produced).[21]

This strategy initially managed to attract only £85,000 of the
£300,000 required, so the promoters formed another firm, Accles

Arms Manufacturing Ltd., which purchased a further £100,000 shares in Accles Ltd. These shares were then quietly and gradually sold on the secondary market, with almost half successfully offloaded by December 1898.[22] It is doubtful whether Accles Ltd. ever had any intention of manufacturing a bicycle: its total revenue for the first 17 months of its existence was just under £71, consisting solely of transfer fees and interest on overdue share calls, and soon after this it filed for bankruptcy.[23] Although Sugden was declared bankrupt in 1899, neither he nor J. G. Accles seems to have faced criminal charges for fraudulent behaviour.[24]

It was also common for cycle company promoters to make payments to newspapers, either to publish 'puffs' that recommended their company or simply to keep quiet about its shortcomings. These payments sometimes took the form of call options, which gave the newspaper an incentive to generate as high a first-day share price as possible. During Hooley's bankruptcy proceedings, he named the *Financial Post, Financial News* and *Pall Mall Gazette* as three of the papers that he paid off during the promotion of the Dunlop Company, as well as the financial journal *Corporation of British Investors*.[25] The two managing directors of the *Financial Post* were jailed for libel in January 1898, having published a defamatory article about a company that refused to pay an extortion fee.[26] However, these conflicts of interest were not made public until much later; in the short term, a positive press could generate capital gains that appeared to vindicate the stance of the newspaper.

Other parts of the news media, however, did an excellent job of informing investors. *The Economist* frequently criticised cycle share promoters, warning as early as May 1896 that false rumours of consolidation and strategically placed news articles were being used to manipulate share prices.[27] One cycle company prospectus was so weak that *The Economist* accused it of demonstrating 'a very robust faith in the gullibility of the average investor'.[28] But *The Economist* could also be somewhat coy, almost never referring to fraudulent promoters by name.

The most comprehensive analysis of the market was provided by *Money: A Journal of Business and Finance*, a twice-weekly publication consisting of financial news and investment advice. *Money* identified three features of the cycle share market that suggested overpricing.

First, vendors generally took very few shares in the companies they promoted, which, it was ironically suggested, 'showed the faith these gentlemen have in their own concerns'.[29] Second, the profits of many cycle companies would clearly be unsustainable in the face of future competition. *Money* gave the example of a cycle hire company renting a £3 bicycle for £0.75 per week in early 1896, resulting in large profits, on the basis of which the company was quickly recapitalised. But such pricing was only possible because the sudden increase in demand had caused a temporary shortage of bicycles, whereas the company's valuation assumed that it could be sustained indefinitely. Third, *Money* highlighted the vast difference between public and private valuations. Public firms were much more marketable, but liquidity advantages could not explain this discrepancy – it could only be the result of large-scale speculation.[30] Furthermore, *Money* was not afraid to name promoters it felt were taking advantage of naive investors. When Harry J. Lawson, a close associate of Hooley's, attempted to float the New Beeston Company in May 1896, *Money* described it as 'absolutely certain to fail', destined for 'the large grave which is allotted to Mr. Lawson's promotions in the financial cemetery'.[31]

On the other hand, there were plenty of true believers who did not need to be paid to publish propaganda about cycle promotions. As during the Railway Mania, periodicals for enthusiasts were a persistent cheerleader for the bubble. *Cycling* ran a weekly financial section in which it discussed developments in the market, generally with a very positive slant. Though the main focus was on reporting specific financial news, the column also frequently criticised the mainstream financial press for its negativity towards the industry. At first, *Cycling* argued that the financial press failed to appreciate the revolutionary nature of the new technology, stating, 'the prospects of the trade are so vast and the possibilities so unlimited, that it is an impossibility to form any idea of what this enormous growth may bring forth'.[32] As the crash intensified, the magazine often suggested that negative articles were the work of short sellers trying to engineer a market crash.[33] This preoccupation with motives allowed the magazine to avoid addressing the content of critical articles, and it is unlikely that *Cycling* itself was an impartial observer. Its financial columnist almost certainly held bicycle shares, which may have influenced his decision to repeatedly urge investors to hold shares in the expectation of a 'reaction' or 'turn of the tide' in the spring and summer of 1897.[34]

Promoters understood that even the most well-informed investor could be attracted by the prospect of making quick profits by re-selling them to a 'greater fool'. Promotional materials made liberal use of stories in which small investors grew rich overnight as a result of their investments in cycle shares. The Beeston Tyre Rim Company, one of several doomed companies to emerge from the reconstruction of the original Beeston firm, opened its prospectus by selectively quoting a *Financial Times* article in which 'a plunger who invested the lordly sum of 15s (£0.75) ... has lately realised a profit of £345'.[35] Such dramatic profits were extremely rare, but investors who managed to time their transactions well could make substantial gains.

The deluge of promotions, many of which had very large capitalisations, might have been expected to put competitive pressure on existing firms. But in fact, cycle share prices remained at a relatively high level throughout 1896, and actually rose during the first 3 months of 1897. Large positive returns after a firm was listed were common: in the middle of March 1897, the eighty-one cycle companies listed in the *Financial Times* were, on average, trading at 44 per cent above their subscription price.[36] This made it possible to profit by subscribing for shares and immediately re-selling them on secondary markets. As a result, the company's initial owners, the promoters, the aristocrats paid to act as directors, the newspaper proprietors paid to provide flattering coverage and some initial subscribers all stood to benefit from the boom. The full extent of the losses, meanwhile, would fall on whoever was left holding the shares after the crash.

The bicycle bubble did not so much burst as suffer a slow puncture, with prices falling gradually over the course of several years. The cycle share index fell by 21 per cent between its peak in March 1897 and July of the same year. The decline accelerated in July after the *Financial Times* published a pessimistic front-page editorial on the market, noting that, despite appearing to record impressive sales figures, cycle companies were still paying fairly modest dividends. The *Financial Times* also highlighted the potential for American competition, and that those working in the industry had expressed concerns about slackening demand.[37] The editorial concluded that 'the majority of companies are over-capitalised' and predicted that 'the end of the present year will see disaster'.[38] This proved accurate, and by December 1897 the index had lost 40 per cent of its value in the space of 9 months. In several cases, profits fell so far short of the promises made in prospectuses that shareholders instigated legal proceedings.[39]

The market for cycle shares fared just as badly in 1898, ending the year 71 per cent below its 1897 peak. The cycle share market did not reach its nadir until the end of 1900, by which time 69 of the 141 cycle firms listed at the peak of the boom had failed. The industry continued to struggle in the early years of the twentieth century; by 1910 only 21 of the 141 firms were still extant. Winding-up orders show that these firms rarely folded without damage to their shareholders. Forty-three firms declared bankruptcy, which almost certainly resulted in shareholders losing the full extent of their investment, while 52 were wound up voluntarily or for unknown reasons, with final share prices suggesting that subscribers would have lost two-thirds of their initial investment. Twenty-seven others were reconstructed, which generally meant that shareholders accepted a reduction of more than 50 per cent of the par value of the shares.[40]

Of those firms that survived, a small number went on to become household names. Dunlop struggled in the immediate aftermath of the crash, but later became a global success by moving into the manufacture of car tyres. Rudge-Whitworth thrived as a result of a series of astute managerial decisions: it was one of the very few firms not to recapitalise at a higher valuation during the boom, it paid relatively low dividends in order to retain enough capital to prevent bankruptcy during the crash, and it quickly cut prices in response to keener competition.[41] The firm continued its success after 1912 with the production of a series of iconic motorcycles. Shifting production into related technology was a recurring practice for the long-term successes: Riley and Rover moved into motor car production, and Hughes Johnson Stamping moved into aeroplanes. Only Raleigh thrived by exclusively producing bicycles, and it did so only after a series of reconstructions that imposed heavy losses on its initial investors.[42]

Contemporaries tended to have little sympathy for cycle share inves-tors. George Gissing's *The Whirlpool,* a fictional drama published in 1897, features a downwardly mobile aristocrat called Hugh Carnaby, who frit-ters away his inherited fortune to end the book bankrupt and embroiled in various scandals. In order to illustrate his fiscally irresponsible char-acter, the author shows him investing heavily in the cycle industry and persistently holding his shares in the expectation of a recovery.[43] Carnaby neatly illustrated the type of person Victorian society would have expected to buy cycle shares: wealthy, frivolous and naive.

However, shareholder registers of cycle companies, which are sum-marised in Table 6.2, suggest not only that the base of investors was much broader than the stereotype suggests, but that it changed considerably over time. Rentiers like Carnaby, who listed their occupation as 'gentleman' or 'esquire' because they were either retired or wealthy enough not to work, held only 16 per cent of cycle shares before the crash. In comparison, a sample of shareholder registers from the broader stock market shows that rentiers accounted for 45 per cent of shares.[44] Unlike other companies, bicycle firms attracted professionals and those close to the industry, parti-cularly manufacturers, as share buyers. We can also see that, as in previous bubbles, the Bicycle Mania attracted investors from a wider range of socio-economic background than was typical for the period.

TABLE 6.2 *Proportion of capital contributed by occupational groups*[45]

	Cycle companies pre-crash	Cycle companies post-crash	Wider stock market
Manufacturers (of bicycles)	21.3 (10.3)	20.0 (7.0)	5.9
Merchants and retailers	9.5	8.2	11.3
Institutional investors	10.0	7.7	1.2
Financiers	5.7	6.7	2.1
Professional classes	26.1	17.2	12.1
Rentiers	16.0	27.7	43.4
Women	4.3	5.9	13.2
Working classes	5.9	5.1	0.5
Agricultural workers	0.3	0.4	1.5
Military	0.9	1.2	2.1
Executors/trusts	-	-	4.7
Company directors	25.7	18.7	26.4*

The cycle shareholder base after the crash looks quite different, suggesting that some groups successfully rode the bubble and exited before the crash. Company directors reduced their holdings by 27 per cent, exploiting the absence of insider trading laws, while cycle manufacturers reduced their holdings by 32 per cent. The professional classes and manufacturers also reduced their holdings substantially. Most of these shares were sold to rentiers, suggesting that there was some truth in the stereotype of worthless cycle shares being sold to gentlemen with more money than sense. The sell-off of insider shares at the peak of the boom continued a notable theme of the Bicycle Mania: the exploitation of outside investors by those with privileged information.

CAUSES

Although technological innovation provided the immediate spark for the bubble in cycle shares, it was only possible because all three sides of the bubble triangle were present. By 1896 shares in Britain were already sufficiently marketable for a bubble to occur, and marketability increased in two important ways. First, large numbers of cycle firms went public, making it much easier to buy and sell parts of their ownership. Before the cycle boom, firms with a profile like theirs had seldom incorporated, and were thus very illiquid.[46] Second, cycle firms were almost all floated with small-denomination shares, usually £1 each and sometimes even less.[47] In comparison, the average share denomination prevailing at the time was about £32, equivalent to around £3,800 today.[48] By issuing shares in small denominations, cycle companies signalled their intention to attract as wide a range of investors as possible.[49] This gave many of the firms a relatively dispersed ownership, which further increased liquidity.

By some measures, monetary conditions were looser than they had ever been. The Bank of England's minimum discount rate was reduced to 2 per cent, the lowest on record, in February 1894, and not raised until August 1896. This was the longest period of a 2 per cent bank rate ever in the Bank's then-200-year history. Traditional assets were producing very low returns for investors: in May of 1896, the month in which the Bicycle Mania initially peaked, the yield on British consols (consolidated annuities) fell to 2.25 per cent, the lowest it had ever been since consols were first issued in 1753.[50]

As with other bubbles, contemporary reports of the Bicycle Mania often commented on speculation in disapproving tones: 'rampant speculation', 'gambling' and 'harum-scarum' were all used by the financial press to describe the market for cycle shares.[51] Although there was undoubtedly an element of moralising in this coverage, share transfer records suggest that speculation was common: many shares were sold very soon after being allocated.[52] One trading strategy, known to contemporaries as 'stag' investing, was to subscribe for shares with the intention of selling them at a profit on the first day of trading.[53] Often, these sales would already have been agreed before the shares had even been allotted. This practice was encouraged by promoters, because agreed sales at a premium to the subscription price would be reported in the financial press, advertising to potential investors that they would be getting a good deal. Inducing speculators to 'come on the feed' was said to be one of the keys to a successful promotion.[54]

It was also possible to speculate in the opposite direction, selling shares short in the expectation of future falls in price. Because short selling was not strictly regulated, this was theoretically simple: a trader could agree to sell shares in the future at today's price, then wait until just before the settlement date to purchase them. If the price had fallen by then, the bears, as short sellers were known, would profit from the difference in price.

During the Bicycle Mania, however, directors, promoters and market manipulators found that they could exploit this bear strategy by buying a controlling stake in a company that was sold short – a strategy known as a market corner or short-squeeze. Since bears had entered into a contract to sell the shares, the market manipulator could then name their price. The use of this strategy was rare, occurring only three times during the bubble, but the losses they imposed on short sellers were substantial. During the Bagot Tyre corner, one investor was forced to pay twenty-one times the face value of Bagot shares and subsequently faced a loss of £2,318; executing the strategy successfully would have earned a profit of only £26. Having initially refused to reimburse his brokers, he was taken to London's High Court, where the consensus of the judge and jury was that short sellers who lost money in a corner were getting what they deserved.[55]

The presence of corners during the Bicycle Mania contributed to the bubble in two ways. First, the risk of cornering created an asymmetry in speculation: it was much easier, especially for non-specialists, to bet on prices rising than to bet on prices falling. Financial advice columns at the time typically cautioned against speculation in general, but were particularly wary of 'speculating for the fall' (i.e. short selling), while noting how rare it was among the general public.[56] Second, although corners were usually engineered by insiders, their beneficiaries were often individual investors. Only 5.5 per cent of the Bagot Tyre corner profits went to company directors, industry insiders or those working in the finance industry. The remainder went to ordinary investors, including several members of the armed forces, a hotel keeper and a student of theology.[57] Since these profits represented quick and spectacular returns, they undoubtedly played a role in attracting further speculative investors during the boom of 1897.

The presence of easy money, marketability and speculation poses the question of why the bubble did not spread to the overall stock market. There were some features of existing shares, such as their high denomination, which made speculation less practical. But the most important reason was that the stock market, like the market for government debt, was already at a very high level. Railways, banks and industrials, the three major issuers of shares, were all paying dividends that by historical standards were small: the 100 largest companies in 1898 had an average dividend yield of only 3.79 per cent.[58] There was therefore little room to generate the capital gains necessary to attract speculative investors. Indeed, the limited potential for high returns elsewhere almost certainly played a role in driving the investment in bicycle shares.

That is not to say that bicycle shares were the only outlet for speculative investment. The period saw a series of booms in exploratory mining companies, the volatile nature of which encouraged speculation.[59] The greatest of these was in 1895 when, in response to excitement about the potential levels of gold in the Witwatersrand escarpment, shares in the Rand Mines Company rose by 360 per cent in the space of a few months. Almost all of these gains were lost by the end of the year. This was accompanied by a promotion boom that largely focused on Western Australia, in which 401 mines floated in 1895 alone, with a total nominal capital of £40.8 million. Trading in these shares spread to Paris and Berlin, as issuers attempted to further expand their base of potential investors.[60]

Breweries provided another outlet for funds, with a wave of new promotions brought to market in 1896 and 1897. Government restrictions on the number of available pub licences, combined with new refrigeration and bottling technology, left small breweries at a severe competitive disadvantage. As a result, many tried to grow by incorporating at large capitalisations: between 1890 and 1900 the total equity of public brewery companies trebled.[61] These companies initially paid high dividends, providing investors with good returns. Many, however, had grown over-capitalised due to the abundant money and credit in the mid-1890s, and struggled in the medium term. Shareholders eventually suffered comparable losses to investors in bicycle firms; between 1897 and 1908 brewery shares lost 84 per cent of their value.[62]

CONSEQUENCES

The effect of the crash in the cycle share market on the Birmingham area is difficult to determine. Studies of the area have highlighted the loss of trade after the closure of so many factories, but they also note how effectively their machinery could be adapted to manufacture different products.[63] Perhaps the most high-profile example of this flexibility is Birmingham Small Arms, which initially produced weaponry, moved into bicycle production during the boom years, and later manufactured a series of iconic motorcycles. But there was a period of recession before industry could adapt, and regional estimates show that GDP per capita in the West Midlands was 7.5 per cent lower in 1901 than it had been in 1891, making it the worst-performing region in England in this period.[64]

On a national level, the crash does not appear to have had any adverse macroeconomic effects. On the contrary, the years 1895 to 1900 are associated with strong economic growth. GDP estimates show the UK economy consistently growing in real terms in the aftermath of the cycle boom; the growth rate reached 5 per cent in 1898 and 4 per cent in

1899.[65] Unemployment fell from 7.3 per cent in 1895 to 4.3 per cent in 1899.[66] Outside the West Midlands, the effect of the bubble's bursting was minimal.

Several factors alleviated its adverse effects. First, the bicycle industry constituted a relatively small section of the economy, and bicycle shares constituted a relatively small section of the stock market. As a result, the fall in consumption associated with investor losses and recession in the industry had little macroeconomic impact. Second, the bicycle industry was not important to the wider economic system. Recession in a small industry might spread to the wider economy if it was an important part of several production chains. But for the bicycle industry this was not the case: the associated technology was not adapted into the existing economy in the way that, for example, internet technology later would be.[67] Third, relatively few of the shares were leveraged; 145 of the 182 shares listed by the *Financial Times* in April 1897 had no uncalled capital at all, and those that did were typically smaller enterprises.[68] As a result, third parties were not generally exposed to bankruptcies or defaults resulting from losses on cycle shares.

Finally, and most importantly, financial institutions on the whole did not invest in bicycle shares, and thus there was no risk of a financial crisis resulting from the bubble. Notably, none of the shares accounted for in Table 6.2 was held by a bank. Banks were keen to publicise this fact: in July 1897, in response to rumours that they were exposed to a crash, several Birmingham banks issued a statement reassuring the public that they did not hold cycle shares, and stressing their reluctance to accept cycle shares as collateral.[69] This mirrored their position on mining shares during the previous year's boom, when the refusal of major banks to accept the shares as collateral had precipitated the crash.[70]

Why were banks so reluctant to involve themselves in speculative industries? The first thing to note is that institutions in this period rarely held significant numbers of any shares at all: in the 1890s, institutional investors accounted for just above 1 per cent of capital in the British equity market, and very much the greater part of this was held by investment trusts rather than banks.[71] It was therefore rare for a bank to be directly exposed to a stock market crash. They might have suffered losses indirectly, however, if they had accepted shares as collateral or issued loans to over-capitalised public companies. But in the case of the cycle boom, banks publicly distanced themselves altogether from the industry.

Given its minor economic impact, the Bicycle Mania would appear to offer a particularly clear illustration of the usefulness of bubbles. The most obvious benefit was technological. A feature of the boom years was the excessive valuations placed on patents, which, though potentially irrational from the perspective of an individual investor, encouraged innovation. These innovations had a general applicability that was not obvious at the time. The bicycle boom, for example, led to further improvements in tyre quality, which later helped the development of the motor car and motorcycle industries. In some instances, the potential applications were even wider: bicycle production led to improvements in automated machine tools and the use of ball bearings in construction.[72]

The forced contraction of the bicycle industry also produced some positive outcomes for consumers. During the boom years, it was conventional for British bicycles to be relatively expensive, competing mainly on quality. When Rudge-Whitworth first cut prices in July 1897, rival companies felt entitled to object.[73] However, they were soon compelled to follow suit, and the firms which attempted to maintain high prices often went bankrupt.[74] Firms that branched into alternative industries, such as motor cars, were more likely to survive the recession. In contrast with the unnecessary and wasteful competition of the Railway Mania, the Bicycle Mania is perhaps an illustration of Schumpeter's principle of creative destruction, in which the failure of inefficient companies paves the way for more innovative ones.[75]

Finally, the overabundance of affordable bicycles resulting from the bubble had some clear positive social and political effects. Unlike horses and motor cars, the use of bicycles provided health benefits, did not produce harmful waste products, and posed significantly less of a threat to the safety of pedestrians. Numerous commentators have also noted the positive effects for women's rights, since cycling gave women an unprecedented level of personal mobility.[76] As well as allowing for ease of congregation, it eroded the social norm that expected upper-class women to be chaperoned, and the difficulty of riding in the restrictive corsets of the time resulted in a 'rational clothing' movement and the development of more practical dresses.[77] Even before the bubble, cycling was already becoming popular, but the bubble gave companies additional capital to innovate and advertise, improving the technology while helping to bring it to national attention. The combination of minor economic damage and positive externalities makes it possible that, unlike many more famous bubbles, the Bicycle Mania brought benefits that outweighed its costs.

CHAPTER 7

The Roaring Twenties and the Wall Street Crash

I decided to go East and learn the bond business. Everybody I knew was in the bond business, so I supposed it could support one more single man. (Nick Carraway, in *The Great Gatsby*)

F. Scott Fitzgerald[1]

Over-investment and over-speculation are often important; but they would have far less serious results were they not conducted with borrowed money.

Irving Fisher[2]

W HILE HISTORY OFTEN CONSISTS OF LONG-TERM TRENDS, occasionally a proverbial meteorite arrives: an unforeseen shock that stimulates enormous change in a very short period of time. One of the clearest examples is World War I, which precipitated the breakup of several empires, the emergence of the first great communist power, and the disintegration of class and gender hierarchies all over the world. Whereas in Britain the democratisation of financial markets took two centuries, World War I brought it to the United States in the space of only a few years. In the United States, the decade following the conclusion of the war was then characterised by abundant money, as the newly unlocked savings of the middle classes continually looked for new investment outlets. When a technological spark eventually brought this money into the highly leveraged market for equities, the result was a bubble that encompassed the entire stock market and culminated in one of history's most spectacular crashes.

Like many financial developments throughout history, the demo-cratisation of US financial markets came about as part of an effort to raise money to pay for war. The United States entered World War I in April 1917, believing that its outcome hinged on its ability to mobilise its forces as quickly as possible, creating urgent funding requirements for the government. Expenditure rose from $1.9 billion in 1916 to $12.7 billion in 1917, and was to rise further to $18.5 billion in 1918, far greater sums than could be funded through taxes alone.[3] Woodrow Wilson's administration concluded that the best way to fund the war effort was to sell vast amounts of bonds to the American public.

In order to ensure that these bonds were sold, the government launched a spectacular marketing campaign. The bonds were rebranded as 'Liberty bonds' in a direct appeal to the patriotism of US citizens. In advance of the initial $2 billion issue in May 1917, a series of posters were issued, some stressing their potential returns, some appealing to the fear of a German victory and others appealing to a more general sense of national pride. Rallies were arranged featuring movie stars such as Charlie Chaplin and Mary Pickford, and the Boy Scouts of America were enlisted to solicit subscriptions on doorsteps.[4] The marketing drive might not have been so successful, however, had the government not skilfully used the existing financial system to make buying the bonds as easy as possible. The recently established Federal Reserve began accepting Liberty bonds as collateral, giving financial institutions a strong incentive to hold them. These institu-tions then acted as a distribution network, with investors able to purchase the bonds at their local branch. Many institutions also allowed investors to buy the bonds on credit.[5]

The first Liberty bond drive was followed by four more, all of which were heavily oversubscribed. As a result, large numbers of Americans invested their savings in securities for the first time. The fourth subscrip-tion alone attracted almost 23 million subscribers, at a time when the total US population was just over 100 million.[6] This included unprece-dented numbers of working- and middle-class investors. Of those earning under $1,020 per annum, 36.7 per cent purchased a Liberty bond in 1918–19; to put this into context, the proportion of Americans of equiva-lent real income holding *any* security in 2013 was only 11.4 per cent.[7]

The Liberty bond issues introduced the American public to the principles of investing and created a distribution network that made doing so much easier. As the 1920s progressed, record rates of economic growth created even more money for savers to invest. The decade was thus characterised by large and increasing sums of capital searching for profitable investment opportunities.

Initially, much of this went into corporate bonds, with $1.4 billion in bonds issued in 1920 compared to $540 million in stocks.[8] When the yield on government bonds fell from 1921 onwards, corporate bonds became increasingly attractive to investors. At first, large companies were happy to meet this demand because it was difficult for them to meet their capital requirements through the banking system: branch banking was restricted and there were strict limits on the proportion of loans that could be given to one company.[9] But bond issues were outpaced by the quantity of capital entering the market, causing the price of corporate bonds to rise to the point where they were no longer such an appealing investment: the yield on Aaa-rated bonds fell from 6.38 per cent in 1920 to 4.93 per cent in 1922.[10] The market was becoming saturated, and savers began to look for alternatives.

One such alternative was housing. Few houses had been built during the war because industry had been reoriented towards munitions, resulting in a temporary shortage of new homes. After the war, construction increased to plug this gap: as Figure 7.1 shows, in 1925 work started on 937,000 new houses, up from 247,000 in 1920. This was accompanied by a nationwide increase in house prices of around 40 per cent.[11] The primary source of finance for these new homes was mortgage debt, which was rapidly expanded by commercial banks, insurance companies and savings associations. In contrast to later housing booms, however, the easing of credit was relatively minor, and by today's standards the mortgage terms were very restrictive. The boom was instead driven by a combination of easier access to existing credit and increased demand.[12]

Mortgages allowed investors to speculate on housing using credit, but many mortgages were also packaged into securities, thereby increasing their marketability. The level of outstanding real-estate bonds grew from $500 million in 1919 to $3.8 billion in 1925, at which point real estate accounted for 22.9 per cent of all new

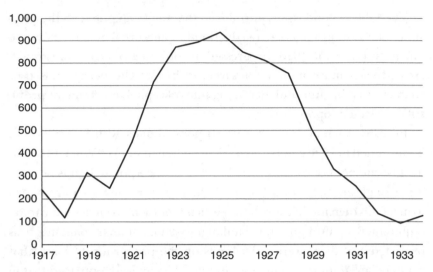

Figure 7.1 Number of new non-farm houses on which construction started in the United States, 1917–34 (thousands)[13]

corporate bond issues. These bonds were conceptually similar to the mortgage-backed securities that were to wreak havoc in the 2000s, but unlike in the 2000s, institutions were very reluctant to hold them, preferring to limit their exposure to mortgages they could monitor themselves. This stance was ultimately justified, as the real-estate bonds performed very poorly, losing 75 per cent of their value between 1928 and 1933.[14] When the construction boom ended after 1925, house prices initially remained relatively steady, falling by only 8.1 per cent nationwide between 1925 and 1929. However, as economic conditions worsened, the housing market collapsed, and by 1933 prices had fallen 30.5 per cent from their peak value.[15]

The speculative element of the housing boom can be seen most clearly on a local level, especially in Florida, where bankers were most successful in recruiting politicians to their cause in order to bypass regulations.[16] Driven by the innovative marketing techniques of the entrepreneur Carl G. Fisher, the image of Florida was transformed into that of a Mediterranean-style tourist paradise, driving demand for its land.[17] In Miami, the price of building permits rose by 700 per cent between 1923 and 1925.[18] The Floridian land market was structured to make speculation as easy as possible, partly through the extension of short-term credit. Investors could buy land for a deposit of 10 per cent, with a further 25 per cent not due for another 30 days, at which point it would often have already been resold for a quick profit.[19] The scale of speculation can be seen from the remarkable increase in the volume of trades: the number of Miami real-estate transactions rose from 5,000 in July 1924 to 25,000 in September 1925.[20]

Florida also saw the growth of new and innovative forms of fraud. The most famous scheme was that of Charles Ponzi, who provided a template for fleecing investors that is still followed today. Ponzi issued 'unit certificates of indebtedness' for $310 each, promising a dividend of 200 per cent in 60 days, supposedly the profits of his land development work near Jacksonville. In practice, most investors agreed to reinvest their profits with Ponzi, relieving him of the need to pay these dividends. The small minority of investors who insisted on cash were paid with the money of subsequent investors. When the scheme eventually collapsed, Ponzi was convicted of securities fraud and served 7 years in prison after a failed attempt to escape to Italy.[21] However, the willingness of so many investors to believe in the prospect of such extravagant returns suggests a fertile atmosphere for legal but misleading promotion schemes.

Another alternative investment was foreign bonds. In August 1924, convinced that the recovery of the German economy was a geopolitical necessity, the US government, along with several major European powers, negotiated the Dawes Plan. The essence of the Plan was that J. P. Morgan would sell high-interest bonds to American investors in order to fund Germany's economic reconstruction and war reparations. Since most politicians and bankers agreed that American interest in the bonds was unlikely to be sufficient to raise the agreed $110 million, the Federal Reserve encouraged uptake by cutting the discount rate from 4.5 per cent to 3 per cent, the lowest in the world. This rate cut was accompanied by another extensive government marketing campaign encouraging investors to buy foreign bonds, and came on the back of a 1922 ruling that deregulated the process for issuing them in the United States.[22]

This turned out to be overkill: the full quota of bonds was sold within 15 minutes, and the issue was oversubscribed several times over. German local governments spotted an opportunity and placed their own bonds in the US market, and German businesses soon followed.[23] Demand for German bonds quickly spilled over into demand for those of other foreign countries. The quantity of newly issued dollar loans from the United States, almost all of which were in the form of bonds, rose from $600 million per annum in 1921–3 to $1.3 billion in 1924–5. Following another discount rate cut in the second half of 1927, this figure increased to $1.7 billion, dwarfing the sums raised in London. Thirty-two countries issued bonds in the United States during the 1920s, with around half of the total volume issued coming from Europe and another quarter issued coming from Latin America.[24]

In early 1928, several factors combined to steer American capital into domestic stocks. House prices and house production had both peaked, and real-estate bonds were already performing poorly.[25] Germany went into recession when its central bank raised interest rates, and its foreign bond issues had begun to fall in 1927.[26] In the same year, National City, the country's largest investment bank, began to handle stock issues, having previously restricted itself to bonds in an effort to maintain an image of conservatism.[27] All of the institutional framework and market-ing nous that had been developed to sell bonds was therefore suddenly directed towards the stock market. Furthermore, recent history sug-gested that stocks were a much more promising investment than bonds or housing. Between August 1921 and January 1928, the Dow Jones Industrial Average (DJIA), shown in Figure 7.2, had risen by 218 per cent.[28]

Although these price increases seemed dramatic, they reflected a genuine increase in profitability: an index of dividend payments by Dow Jones companies closely tracked the DJIA until January 1928.[29] The economy was in the midst of a remarkable boom: GDP grew at an annual average of 4.7 per cent between 1922 and 1929. Both the high profit-ability and economic growth owed much to technological innovation, particularly in electricity and mass production, both of which contribu-ted to significant increases in productivity.[30] But innovation was by no means limited to these areas; major breakthroughs also occurred in the chemicals, food processing and telegraph industries. Investors were especially keen to invest in firms that spent heavily on research and development, with innovative firms trading at a premium.[31]

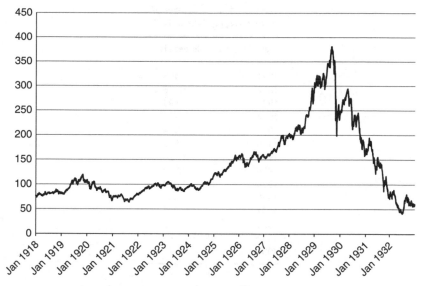

Figure 7.2 Dow Jones Industrial Average, 1918–32[32]

In February 1928 the Federal Reserve, concerned that large price increases would attract speculative investors, moved to dampen the stock market. The New York Fed's discount rate was raised by ½ per cent, and further increases that summer brought this rate to the relatively high level of 5 per cent.[33] The Federal Reserve also pressured banks to curtail the issuing of broker loans, whereby money was lent for the purpose of buying stocks.[34] But neither of these measures was effective. The discount rate increases inadvertently encouraged capital to return to the United States, because higher interest rates than were available at home had been one of the most attractive features of foreign bonds. Much of this capital then found its way into domestic stocks, either directly or via the banking system.[35] When domestic banks were pressured by the Federal Reserve to reduce broker loans, the gap was plugged by private investors, corporations and foreign banks. The quantity of these loans continued to grow despite the sharp rise of the interest rates on them, indicating substantial demand for buying on margin (i.e. investing with borrowed money).[36] During 1928, the DJIA rose by a further 50.9 per cent.

With stock prices at such a high level, equity became a historically cheap source of finance, and corporations moved en masse to issue more

TABLE 7.1 *US corporate stock issues, 1921–34*[37]

Year	Issues ($m)
1921	455
1922	1,146
1923	1,399
1924	740
1925	1,034
1926	829
1927	1,396
1928	3,850
1929	4,808
1930	1,493
1931	223
1932	12
1933	61
1934	36

shares. As Table 7.1 shows, $3.85 billion of shares were issued in 1928, followed by a further $4.81 billion in 1929, where the previous high had been $1.4 billion in 1923. Investment trusts issued more capital than any other sector in 1929, and since these trusts primarily purchased stocks, equity prices were driven even higher. The numbers of stocks and their prices were both increasing, and they were changing hands much more frequently. The daily average trading volume on the New York Stock Exchange rose from 1.7 million shares in 1925 to 3.5 million in 1928 and 4.1 million for the first 9½ months of 1929.[38] Although the DJIA did not change much during the first 5 months of 1929, it rose a further 27.8 per cent between the end of May and the end of September.

Newspapers were split over whether stock prices were excessive or representative of a new financial era. Alexander Dana Noyes, the financial editor of the *New York Times*, was a notable sceptic, his perspective informed by having written a financial history of the United States dating back to 1865.[39] His columns were often too diplomatic to attack the bull market explicitly, however, and his cautious advice was often undermined by editors who were reluctant to contradict the more optimistic views of well-known bankers.[40] The *Wall Street Journal* essentially acted as a cheerleader for the stock market. One article, in July 1929, argued that although the market 'has had big reactions ... it always comes back ...

because general business refuses to slump with it'.[41] This enthusiasm was usually genuine, but not always: two of its journalists accepted payments for stock recommendations in the mid-1920s, which the *Journal* was forced to cover up by offering them minor jobs at the paper. *New York Daily News*, which at the time was the most-read newspaper in the country, had a more systemic bribery problem: its financial columnist was later shown to have taken money from traders in exchange for a share of their profits.[42]

The summer months were normally quiet on the exchanges, but in 1929, both brokers and investors forwent holidays to continue trading stocks. The peak was on 3 September, when the DJIA reached a value of 381.2; since the beginning of 1927 it had risen by 231 per cent.[43] Prices then began gradually to fall, which some contemporaries interpreted as an inevitable levelling-off. The Yale economist Irving Fisher stated on 16 October that stocks had reached 'what looks like a permanently high plateau'.[44] Prices were extremely volatile, however. A 4.2 per cent drop in the DJIA on 3 October was followed by a 6.3 per cent gain on 7 October, which was then the largest movement in the post-war era. These volatile conditions continued until Tuesday 22 October, when the DJIA sat at 326.5, 14.3 per cent below its peak.

On Wednesday 23 October, a sharp sell-off in automobile shares precipitated a general fall in stock prices on the New York Stock Exchange. The volume of shares traded reached 6.4 million, with the final hour of trading being particularly frantic. The ticker tape, which telegraphed stock prices around the country, ran for 104 minutes after trading ended, so traders had an agonising wait to discover how much money they had lost. When the dust settled, the DJIA had ended the day down 6.3 per cent, at that time the greatest daily fall since before 1914. And worse was expected to come because these losses triggered margin calls – recalls of broker loans that forced leveraged traders to immediately sell their stocks to avoid default. The sell-off was expected to be so fierce that the New York Police Department closed off one entrance to Wall Street, with wagons and men stationed throughout the financial district.[45]

The Thursday morning trading was as frenzied as expected, with 1.6 million shares changing hands in the first half hour, mostly from ruined margin accounts. The downward momentum led many holders to 'sell at the market' – in other words, to accept any price for their stocks. As news of the crash spread, crowds began to gather outside the New York Stock Exchange to watch the panic unfold, and the police presence was doubled. But, remarkably, the market recovered. At 1:30pm, following a meeting with several major bankers, the vice-president of the Exchange began conspicuously buying large quantities of blue-chip stocks at above the market price. This deliberately evoked the panic of 1907 which, it was widely believed, had ended due to the intervention of a cartel of bankers led by J. P. Morgan. This gambit initially appeared to have worked because stocks quickly recovered most of their losses. The DJIA, having at one point been down 10.8 per cent, ended the day down just 2.1 per cent.[46] Although this day later became known as Black Thursday, the damage was confined almost entirely to small stocks.

The remainder of the week was relatively calm, and many assumed that the following week would see a return to normality. The *New York Times* praised 'Wall Street's banking leaders' for 'arresting the decline', reporting that 'the feeling was general that the worst had been seen'. *New York Daily Investment News* was much more direct, printing a four-word front-page headline: 'Stock Market Crisis Over'.[47] The Chairman of the Irving Trust, one of the country's largest investment banks, issued a statement warning that 'whenever fundamental values are lost sight of by the unthinking majority it is time for courage on the part of those investors who have a real sense of basic worth'.[48] Remarkably, this was intended as an argument for buying.

When trading reopened on Monday morning, however, it was immediately clear that there were many more sellers than buyers. Whereas Black Thursday had been characterised by pockets of illiquidity where shares could not be sold, on Monday their prices simply dropped substantially, often by \$1–\$2 at a time. These sales came primarily from two sources: shareholders who had been issued with margin calls over the weekend; and foreign investors, particularly British investors, many of whom had recently had funds frozen due to the bankruptcy of a major British financier.[49] Prices fell further in the afternoon as it became clear that neither the Federal Reserve nor the private banks were prepared to intervene. The DJIA finished the day down 12.8 per cent, which was by far the largest fall in its history.

Once again, the *New York Times* led the following morning with the story that 'the storm had blown itself out', a conclusion reached on the basis of 'statements by leading bankers'.[50] This line was repeated by *New York Daily News*, giving it the unwanted record of having advised investors to buy shares on every single day of the crash.[51] But when trading reopened, prices continued to fall. The size of sell orders rose considerably on the previous day, suggesting that institutional investors and large shareholders were now leaving the market. This was later compounded by the withdrawal of local banks, corporations and individuals from the call loan market, meaning that many would-be buyers could not borrow money to purchase stocks. The New York Fed decided to act, purchasing $100 million in government securities to provide the market with liquidity in order to prevent an immediate credit crisis.[52] Nevertheless, the DJIA ended the day down a further 11.7 per cent. The aggregate loss was barely believable: it had fallen by 23.6 per cent in 2 days for no obvious reason. To put this fall into perspective, the Japanese attack on Pearl Harbor resulted in the DJIA falling only 6.3 per cent over 2 days.

The remainder of the week saw a considerable recovery, but this was immediately reversed when trading resumed the following week, as stocks continued to display unprecedented levels of volatility. The DJIA finally bottomed out on 13 November at a value of 198, having lost 48 per cent of its value in 2 months. The new year saw a recovery, and the DJIA touched 292 in the April of 1930, making it seem as if the crisis was finally over. However, the stock market fell further during the rest of 1930 as the economy entered a deep depression. The DJIA did not reach its minimum until July 1932, when it fell to 41, an incredible 89.2 per cent loss from its 1929 peak.

What role had the news media played during the bubble? Generally speaking, newspapers were uninterested in valuing the market independently, instead uncritically reporting the self-serving words of bankers, traders and politicians. John Brooks's financial history of the era mockingly describes the emergence of the 'transatlantic shipboard interview', in which an 'enigmatic' major banker or business leader 'reluctantly' offered comments to journalists on financial matters while travelling to Europe on a luxury cruise-ship.[53] By 1929 the comments of powerful men had become so uniformly positive that they were nicknamed 'the prosperity chorus'.[54] Newspapers continued to use the chorus's over-optimistic opinions in lieu of facts throughout the crash: the *New York Times* headline on the morning after Black Thursday was 'Worst Stock Crash Stemmed by Banks; Leaders Confer, find Conditions Sound'.[55]

While previous bubbles also saw the emergence of famous 'characters', the extent to which the press focused on the role of high-profile individuals in the 1920s bubble is unusual. It could be argued that this made financial stories more relatable for a general audience, reinforced the idea that market movements happened for good reasons, and made it appear as if someone was in charge. Needless to say, most of these articles aged very badly. Journalists frequently based stories on comments by the National City Bank directors, but the terms of a proposed merger with the Corn Exchange Bank gave these directors an enormous vested interest in keeping stock prices high.[56] Other high-profile figures eventually ended up in prison for financial crime, most notably Richard Whitney, who had been vice-president of the New York Stock Exchange during the crash.

In addition to making for more compelling stories, the sycophantic editorial style served three purposes. First, it allowed newspapers to develop close relationships with the country's most powerful men, and thereby access a reliable source of future stories. Second, it ensured that the newspapers could not be blamed for sparking a panic. If a major newspaper had correctly predicted the crash, it would have been heavily criticised for causing it. Third, reporting only what other people were saying ensured that they could evade responsibility when events did not transpire as expected. In the aftermath of the crash, newspapers often mocked the exact theories that they had been citing for several years as expert opinion. This strategy thus helped the news media to walk the tightrope of maintaining some credibility without contradicting the special interests and access on which they depended.

While the 1920s bubble was primarily an American phenomenon, it also had an international element. Global stock markets were highly connected during the 1920s, meaning that several countries experienced a stock market boom at the same time as the United States.[57] French stocks rose by 231 per cent between 1922 and 1929, then fell by 56 per cent between 1929 and 1932.[58] Swedish stocks rose by over 150 per cent between 1924 and 1929, but had lost all of these gains by 1932.[59] The German stock market more than doubled during 1926, but the central bank intervened to burst the developing bubble.[60] Although the UK had a stock market crash in 1929, stock prices recovered relatively quickly, reaching their pre-crash level by 1935.[61] None of these countries came close to experiencing the 89 per cent price drop witnessed in the United States.

CAUSES

The decade before the crash saw a continuous increase in marketability, as a series of reforms and innovations made it much easier to buy and sell securities. The first of these was the financial network set up to distribute the Liberty bonds, which allowed them to be bought in local bank branches, department stores and through payroll deductions.[62] After the war, private banks moved to replicate this network in an attempt to tap into the market for small investors. The total number of brokerage offices rose from 706 in 1925 to 1,658 in 1929, allowing investors to buy securities without going near Wall Street. The National City Company effectively became a financial chain store, selling corporate bonds, foreign bonds and common stocks all over the country. This was accompanied by marketing campaigns that aimed to educate the public in the basics of investment. This benefited investors directly by making it harder for fraudsters to take advantage of them in financial markets, but it also benefited genuine companies, because it was easier to sell stocks and bonds to more confident investors.[63]

On secondary markets, transaction costs were remarkably low in the second half of the 1920s: the average one-way total transaction cost in 1929 was around 0.5 per cent, lower than any level on record before the 1980s.[64] Traders also benefited from the expansion of communications technology: telephone use expanded by 70 per cent over the decade. By 1929 the New York Stock Exchange had installed 323 telephone lines connecting it to brokerage firms.[65] As in previous bubbles, increasing marketability was, to an extent, self-perpetuating: higher marketability increased the volume of trades, which in turn made stocks even more liquid.

For the purpose of explaining the stock market bubble, the most significant form of credit growth was in broker loans. Investment trusts had barely existed in the United States before 1920, but when they did arrive, they were much riskier entities than they had been in the UK. Many were enormously leveraged: trust managers were allowed to purchase stocks on margin for a deposit of only 10 per cent, meaning that up to 90 per cent of their investments could be purchased with borrowed money. The number of these trusts grew from 40 in 1921 to over 750 in 1929, when they issued more new capital than any other sector. Trading on margin was just as common among individual traders, who borrowed from brokers, who in turn borrowed from banks.[66] Margin trading transformed stock trading from a staid and technocratic profession into an activity that could appeal to compulsive gamblers, who had few other outlets, because almost all forms of gambling were illegal throughout the United States. The extent to which this exacerbated the stock market boom is evidenced by the fact that the quantity of broker loans almost exactly tracks the DJIA for the period 1926–31.[67]

The Federal Reserve has often been blamed for allowing the boom to develop through excessively loose monetary policy during the 1920s. This argument, however, does not fit the evidence. Given the prevalent economic conditions, discount rates in the period 1922–9 were not particularly low.[68] In the latter part of the decade, the Federal Reserve became acutely worried about stock market speculation, raising interest rates three times in 1928. It successfully pressured banks to curtail broker loans from the end of 1927 onwards, and the subsequent increase in these loans came from individuals, corporations and foreign banks, which the Federal Reserve had little control over. The minutes of its meetings suggest that the Federal Reserve was, if anything, excessively concerned with curtailing margin lending when other areas of finance were more systemically important.[69]

While the roles of marketability and credit are widely acknowledged, the popular memory of the bubble is based largely around speculation. In J. K. Galbraith's famous history of the crash, he argues that its key feature was that 'all aspects of [stock] ownership became irrelevant except the prospect for an early rise in price'.[70] This was widely observed at the time: the *New York Times* noted in August 1929 that 'the present modus operandi in the market appears to be the buying of leading issues for the purpose of passing them on to someone else at a higher price'.[71] Several pools of investors were set up explicitly for this purpose, many of which involved leading businessmen and financiers. These pools were soon joined by individual margin traders, many of whom had given up their jobs to become day traders.[72]

The spark for the bubble came from technological change. American society, as well as its economy, was transformed by electrification in the years preceding the crash: per capita electricity production grew by 9.2 per cent between 1902 and 1929.[73] As well as providing considerable benefits to consumers, cheaper electricity was useful in many other industries, and complemented another major economic shift: the rise of mass production. Famously pioneered by Henry Ford in the automobile industry, the 1920s saw mass production extended into almost every area of manufacturing, dramatically increasing the quantity of goods produced and lowering the costs for consumers.[74] In combination with electricity, it made all kinds of consumer goods cheaper to produce, from telephones to washing machines to refrigerators – many of which could now be purchased on credit.

New technology sparked the bubble in two ways. First, it provided companies with extraordinary profits in the mid-1920s, much of which was paid out to shareholders. The dividends accruing to the DJIA grew by 120 per cent between 1922 and 1927.[75] This caused the DJIA to grow by a similar amount, providing shareholders with large capital gains. It was these capital gains that initially attracted speculative investors. Second, new technology provided investors with a powerful rationalisation for the fact that stock prices far exceeded the level implied by traditional metrics. The 1920s saw the growth of modernism, a philosophy which contended that new technology had rendered most previous models for explaining the world obsolete.[76] By the end of the decade this worldview was often applied to investment. In March 1928 the *New York Times* reported that the 'widely-held opinion of market participants' was that 'all former yardsticks must be disregarded and that new measures, if the market is to be judged aright, must be adopted'.[77]

In previous studies of 1929, it has been more common to ask 'what caused the crash?' than to ask 'what caused the bubble?' Several possible triggers of the crash have been proposed, including the bankruptcy of Clarence Hatry in London, the passage of the Smoot-Hawley tariff and the New York Fed raising the discount rate on 9 August 1929. However, none of these can plausibly explain the timing or scale of the crash.[78] This has led some to conclude that the crash was caused either by a sudden unexplained change in investor sentiment, or was simply a 'mystery'.[79] In fact the crash was neither a response to a specific incident nor a mystery: it was simply a consequence of the market's underlying structure. The quantity of outstanding broker loans in the autumn of 1929 meant that any sufficient fall in prices would lead to a significant number of margin calls. This in turn would force traders to liquidate, depressing prices further. Essentially, the fuel for the bubble could be removed at any moment. This vulnerability was widely understood, since the quantity of broker loans was publicly available, and as a result the market became much more volatile. In such circumstances, any particularly large noise trade could have triggered a crash, and this is likely what happened on 22 October 1929.

CONSEQUENCES

The Wall Street Crash was followed by a collapse in consumer spending. One cannot be certain that these two events were linked: the stock market's relative economic importance suggests that it ought not to have caused Americans to reduce their spending as much as they did. But US consumer spending overreacting to a stock crash would not be unusual – consumer spending is historically very responsive to share price movements – and, while subsequent spending reductions can be attributed to deflation, there is no other obvious explanation for the reduction of 1929.[80] Although it is difficult to know for sure why consumers would have reacted to the crash in this way, it could be that the apocalyptic tone of media coverage during the crash led households to anticipate a disproportionate economic impact, and households cut spending in response.

This reduction in spending was accompanied by the end of the credit boom. After the crash, the sudden contraction in broker loans was followed by a similar contraction in mortgages and consumer durable loans.[81] These concurrent falls in spending and lending led to a deficiency in aggregate demand, ushering in deflation and pushing the American economy into recession. In the first half of 1930, industrial production increased because corporations expected the recession to be relatively mild. However, consumer spending remained persistently low, and it quickly became clear that the recession would be significant: by the end of 1930, GDP had fallen by 11.9 per cent for the year. The end of 1930 also saw the period's first financial crisis when banks holding $552 million in deposits failed in November and December. This aggravated the economy's deflation problem: the consumer price index fell by 2.5 per cent in 1930, 8.9 per cent in 1931 and 10.3 per cent in 1932.[82] This, in turn, discouraged economic activity while increasing the real value of bank liabilities, resulting in waves of further bank failures.

The key to escaping this economic spiral would have been to stop deflation and protect credit channels. The easiest way to do so would have been to flood markets with liquidity and have the Federal Reserve act as a lender of last resort to failing banks. But the government feared that doing either would undermine its commitment to keeping the value of the dollar fixed to gold.[83] As a result, banks continued to fail, and the economy continued to self-destruct. When the United States finally left the gold standard in 1933, nominal GDP had fallen by 45 per cent, unemployment had reached 23 per cent, and the number of banks in operation had almost halved since 1929.[84]

The Great Depression was a truly global catastrophe, exacerbated by the importance of the United States to the inter-war economy. Its severity varied, however, and was closely linked to how quickly a country left the gold standard.[85] The Japanese economy shrunk by 24 per cent between 1929 and 1931, the UK economy shrunk by 10 per cent between 1929 and 1932, and the French economy shrunk by 33 per cent between 1929 and 1934. The German economy, which had grown dependent on American credit, was affected especially badly: its GDP fell by 37 per cent in 3 years, while industrial unemployment reached 44 per cent.[86] In human terms, this meant increased homelessness, increased infant mortality and increased rates of suicide.[87] The secondary political effects were even worse, with the Depression a major factor in the collapse of several European democracies and, consequently, World War II.[88]

The 1920s bubble is often thought of as one of the most destructive. The extent of margin trading made financial networks much more vulnerable to a crash than they had been in previous bubbles, and these networks could have collapsed had the New York Fed not provided emergency liquidity in October 1929. In practice, however, the number of important institutions that collapsed due to stock market losses or broker loan defaults was negligible. If the crash caused the subsequent recession, it could only have done so through its effect on consumer spending, a mechanism which not all economists find convincing.[89] Assuming that the crash did cause the recession, it still cannot explain its extraordinary severity. The Great Depression was instead the result of the vulnerability of banking networks, the rigidity of the inter-war gold standard, and the failure of governments and monetary authorities to adequately address the resulting deflation.[90]

If the aftermath of the bubble had been successfully managed, it might not be remembered as such a disaster. The boom made it remarkably easy for highly innovative firms to raise capital.[91] One of the companies to experience the most substantial bubble was the Radio Corporation of America, which was central not only to radio technology but to the later development of both black-and-white and colour television.[92] Another company caught up in the boom was Burroughs Adding Machine, which went on to become one of the world's largest producers of mainframe computers. The Columbia Graphophone Company, which had a market value over 50 times its book value in 1929, survived the crash by merging with the Gramophone Company and becoming a record label.[93] It was later responsible for launching the careers of Chuck Berry, Pink Floyd and Cliff Richard. Without the overinvestment of the 1920s, these long-term achievements might have been impossible.

However, it could also be argued that any positive effects on investment in new technology were offset by underinvestment in subsequent years. In the aftermath of the crash it was almost impossible to raise funds through stock issues. As Table 7.1 shows, in the whole of 1932 only

$12 million of stock was issued, a 99.8 per cent fall from the quantity issued in 1929. This was despite the fact that the gains from new technology had not even come close to being realised and innovations were ongoing. In any recession there is an unobserved cost of companies with great potential folding early due to a lack of investment, and, given the severity of the Great Depression, this unmeasurable cost may well have been substantial.

The experience of the Roaring Twenties offers two key lessons on bubbles. First, the optics of the crash matter. The economic significance of a bubble does not straightforwardly derive from its direct effects on the incentives of shareholders and businesses: how it is viewed by society is also important. When stock markets become culturally significant, a spectacular crash can affect consumer behaviour, and thereby have unexpected economic effects.[94] Second, managing the bubble is much less important than managing its aftermath. In 1928 and 1929, the Federal Reserve grew obsessed with curtailing stock market speculation, but none of the measures introduced to do so were effective. As it turned out, stock market speculation was little more than a sideshow: what really mattered for the economy was the stability of financial institutions, which the authorities comprehensively failed to uphold. This failure explains why the 1920s bubble has remained one of financial history's most infamous episodes.

CHAPTER 8

Blowing Bubbles for Political Purposes: Japan in the 1980s

Han ne hachi gake ni wari biki
(When the market has halved, take 80 per cent of that figure and add a 20 per cent discount; only then should you buy.)

Japanese rice traders' proverb[1]

THE 1920s BUBBLE, IN THE VIEW OF THE F. D. ROOSEVELT administration, fatally undermined the case for leaving US stock markets largely unregulated. The Securities Act of 1933, introduced almost immediately after Roosevelt assumed the presidency, required all companies issuing securities to disclose more information to potential investors, including independently certified financial statements. This was followed by the Securities Exchange Act of 1934, which established the Securities and Exchange Commission to oversee securities markets. Generally speaking, this Act attempted to prevent future bubbles by targeting speculation and credit, with relatively few new restrictions on marketability. Insider trading and various forms of market manipulation were banned, with the Act arguing that manipulation was responsible for 'sudden and unreasonable fluctuations of security prices and ... excessive speculation on such exchanges and markets'. In response to the extensive margin trading of 1929, strict limits were placed on how much money could be lent for the purposes of buying shares.[2]

After World War II the US government was faced with a new challenge: rebuilding a Japanese economy which it had spent most of the war destroying. In normal circumstances such a task would be considered, at best, low priority. But Japan had emerged from the war in a surprisingly advantageous position: under the control of the world's leading capitalist power, but situated beside the world's great communist powers. Since post-war American foreign policy was to do whatever it took to illustrate the superiority of capitalism, Japanese prosperity became a key strategic interest. The United States thus made a serious effort to encourage its economic development.

The occupying forces, lacking in cultural knowledge and language skills, generally attempted to replicate economic policies that had been implemented in the United States. Harry Truman's administration enacted a series of New Deal-inspired reforms, which encouraged labour union growth and attempted to dismantle the oligarchical conglomerates (or *zaibatsu*) that had dominated Japanese industry. It also invested heavily in education, overhauling the curriculum to better reflect American interests.[3] Japanese financial market regulation was based heavily on the Acts that had been passed in response to the Wall Street Crash. The (Japanese) Securities and Exchange Law of 1948 made stocks much less marketable than they had been before the war. All stock trading was required to take place exclusively at stock exchanges, and futures trading was banned. Although these restrictions were gradually loosened in subsequent years, stock trading remained relatively tightly controlled.[4]

Economic policy subsequently evolved to reflect changing American priorities and renewed Japanese authority. Moves were made to curtail union power, and efforts to dismantle the *zaibatsu* grew increasingly half-hearted. Economic planners instead directed their energy towards encouraging mechanisation, first in the agricultural and coal sectors, then in manufacturing. The latter was given a major boost by the Korean War, which created a boom in demand for Japanese goods, and the economic recovery quickly gathered pace. By 1955, output had reached its pre-war level, and the 1960s saw miraculous levels of growth, with GDP rising by 144 per cent over the course of the decade.[5] By 1980 Japan was a fully developed economy, with comparable income levels to the UK.[6]

The spectacular growth of the 1960s was achieved through the economic strategy of developing specialist manufacturing skills, and exporting the resulting consumer goods. The success of this strategy was partly due to the efficiency of Japanese companies, who pioneered the just-in-time method of production to take advantage of the world-leading engineering abilities of the Japanese workforce. But it was also important that these goods could be sold abroad at a competitive price. This was ensured by fixing the yen to an exchange rate which was, by the mid-1960s, artificially low, making Japanese goods cheap for foreign consumers. This required the co-operation of the countries to which these goods were sold, who often risked undermining their own manufacturing industries. But this co-operation was typically forthcoming, for three reasons. First, consumers benefited from cheap, high-quality goods. Second, Japanese imports initially constituted only a small part of the market, as the world economy did not rapidly integrate in the immediate aftermath of the war. Domestic manufacturers, perhaps with a hint of complacency, rarely felt threatened by Japanese goods. Third, for geopolitical reasons, the economic success of Japan was considered to be in the interests of the Western bloc.

From the early 1970s onwards, however, the United States began to push back against this arrangement. President Nixon, concerned by high unemployment and inflation, suspended the convertibility of the dollar into gold in 1971, hoping to allow the dollar to devalue. This heralded the end of the Bretton Woods System, and by 1973 most major currencies had moved to a managed float. No longer fixed to a low valuation, the yen began to appreciate. At the pegged rate, which was sustained throughout the 1950s and 1960s, $1 had cost ¥360, but in 1973, $1 cost only ¥272.[7] From 1980 onwards, however, the appreciation of the yen slowed, largely because of Japan's conservative fiscal policies. A large current account surplus developed, suggesting that the low value of the yen was once again providing a distinct advantage to Japanese exports.[8]

Frustrated by exchange rates rendering their products uncompetitive, American businesses stepped up the pressure on the US government to find a solution. President Reagan was initially reluctant to devalue, fearing that it would adversely affect the financial sector. However, he was eventually convinced that devaluation was a necessary alternative to protectionist measures. The unwanted prospect of protectionism was, in turn, used to achieve the international co-operation required for a dollar-devaluation policy to work. The result was the Plaza Accord: an international agreement, signed in 1985, in which Japan agreed measures to increase the value of the yen with respect to the dollar.

The Plaza Accord committed Japan to implementing three major economic reforms. First, they agreed to pursue 'vigorous deregulation measures' to encourage private sector growth. Second, they agreed to loosen monetary policy and liberalise financial markets, both with a view to ensuring that the yen 'fully reflects the strength of the Japanese economy'. Third, they were compelled to reduce the government deficit, thereby reducing the economic size of the state. Since this could cause an economic contraction, the reduction in demand was to be offset by 'measures to enlarge consumer and mortgage credit markets'.[9] Japan's export-led growth model, in which the state had played a significant economic role, was to be dismantled. The new economic strategy was to encourage banks to lend enormous amounts of money, particularly for the purchase of housing, so that the economy continued to grow despite an appreciation of the yen and a reduction in government spending.

In some ways, the agreement simply gave Japan an excuse to accelerate reforms that had already begun, or to pursue reforms that the government wanted to implement anyway. Financial liberalisation was a continuation of policies that had been pursued since the early 1970s. The oil shock of 1973 had forced the Japanese government to run large deficits, leading the Bank of Japan to worry that it could no longer underwrite the full quantity of outstanding government bonds. The government's response was to establish secondary government bond markets, thereby relinquishing control over interest rates for the first time in the post-war era. The Foreign Exchange Law of 1980 removed most capital controls, allowing Japanese residents to invest internationally without government authorisation. The potential for investors to benefit from foreign interest rates created arbitrage opportunities, which further shifted control of interest rates from the government to the market. Restrictions on the size and term of deposits that could earn market-determined interest rates were gradually removed.[10]

The difference after the Plaza Accord, however, was that financial deregulation was now accompanied by extremely loose monetary policy. The Bank of Japan's discount rate was reduced from 5 per cent when the Plaza Accord was signed to 3.5 per cent in May 1986 and 2.5 per cent in

February 1987, despite GDP growth having been above 3 per cent in every year since 1981. This, combined with the unprecedented freedom of banks to decide how much to lend, dramatically increased the amount of leverage in the financial system. Japanese household debt rose from 52 per cent of GDP in 1985 to 70 per cent of GDP in 1990, as government policy eroded cultural norms against borrowing money.[11] This in turn caused a substantial monetary expansion, which was compounded by the fact that the Plaza Accord implicitly encouraged the movement of funds into Japan to take advantage of the expected appreciation of the yen. M3, a broad measure of the money supply, grew by a total of 141 per cent between 1980 and 1990; for comparison, between 1990 and 2010, M3 grew by only 40 per cent.[12]

What was all of this money invested in? As a result of low interest rates, safe assets were unappealing: in 1987, Japanese treasury bills were yielding only 2.4 per cent, at that time the lowest in their post-war history.[13] Instead, investors piled into land and stocks.

For many Japanese, land ownership was still closely linked to social status, perhaps as a result of the country's relatively recent feudal past. This was especially true for the older generation, who generally had the most money to invest.[14] Since Japan was one of the world's most densely populated countries, land also had scarcity value. Landholders were often very reluctant to sell at a loss, so the nominal price of land rarely fell, perpetuating the belief that it was an extremely safe asset. But this apparent safety did not preclude the possibility of abnormal returns: there were substantial land price booms in 1961, 1974 and 1980, each of which was associated with a loosening of monetary policy. But only the 1974 boom was followed by a fall in nominal prices, and even this correction was relatively modest.[15] Land price booms were familiar to the Japanese public, and previous booms had never ended particularly badly.

The catalyst for the latest boom, which began after 1985, was the shifting of the Japanese economy towards the service sector. With jobs moving from factories to offices, the demand for urban office space suddenly increased, especially in Tokyo.[16] This was quickly compounded by government efforts to stimulate urban development as a way of increasing demand. In keeping with its commitment to reducing the

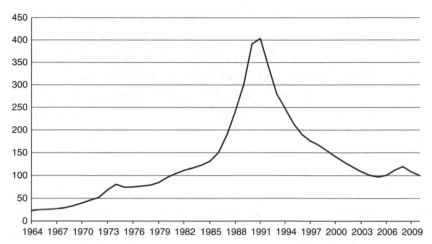

Figure 8.1 Japanese land price index for six major cities, 1964–2010[17]

economic role of the state, the government decided not to direct urban development itself. Instead, a series of tax breaks, subsidies and financing initiatives were granted to private real-estate companies, while the Ministry of Construction heavily deregulated the process of urban planning.[18] This, combined with the liberalisation of mortgage lending and ultra-low interest rates, massively increased real-estate investment.

The subsequent effect on urban land prices can be seen in Figure 8.1. Between 1985 and 1987, the price of land in the six major Japanese cities rose by 44 per cent. This attracted the attention of Japanese corporations, who found that capital gains on land were dwarfing the profits from their main operations. These corporations responded by shifting funds from core operations to land, creating an additional influx of money into the sector. Much of this money was borrowed to take advantage of the prevailing low interest rates.[19] As a result, prices continued to rise, and the price of land was soon completely out of proportion with the income it could generate. By 1991, land in Tokyo cost 40 times as much as comparable land in London, whereas rents were only twice as high. At this stage, urban land prices had risen by 207 per cent in 6 years, and the total land value in Japan was around $20 trillion – five times the value of all the land in the United States, and twice as much as the entire world's equity markets.[20]

Stock markets, meanwhile, had been radically transformed since the American occupation. Efforts to prevent corporations from controlling the stock market, as they had done in the pre-war era, were gradually reversed after the revision of anti-trust laws in 1949 and 1953. Formerly *zaibatsu*-owned shares that had been sold to the public were bought up by *zaibatsu*-affiliated banks, and conglomerates of corporations began to hold substantial amounts of each other's shares. Financial difficulties at securities companies in the mid-1960s led to the establishment of the Japan Joint Securities Corporation and the Japan Securities Holding Association, conglomerates of businesses intended to support stock prices. In practice, these associations tended to buy from individual investors and sell to either conglomerates of corporations or financial institutions, who were themselves closely connected to Japanese business. As a result, although corporations held only 39 per cent of shares in 1950, by 1980 this had risen to 67 per cent. Financial institutions alone accounted for 37 per cent.[21]

Corporations dominated the stock market because, while shares held only investment value for individuals, for corporations they also helped sustain networks of co-operation and collusion. By holding each other's equity, corporations created a mutual interest in the continuation of a beneficial relationship, since any breakdown would lead to a large number of stocks of both companies being dumped on the market. This arrangement had the added benefit of guarding against hostile takeovers. Furthermore, because cross-held shares were rarely traded, share prices became easier to control. In particular, the Big Four securities companies – Nomura, Daiwa, Nikko and Yamaichi – were often able to manipulate prices in order to serve the interests of their business relationships. As of 1986, the Big Four controlled more than half of all stock trading and close to 100 per cent of the underwriting market.[22]

From 1980 onwards, a series of deregulatory measures created an incentive for companies to treat stocks as a more speculative investment. A 1983 change in tax law allowed companies to separate long-term stock holdings from short-term investments, with the latter placed into a separate investment fund called a *tokkin*. After 1983, the returns on the *tokkin* fund were taxed at a lower rate, creating the unusual situation in which speculation could be a less expensive investment strategy than buy-and-hold. As a result, the number of stocks in *tokkin* funds exploded from under ¥2 trillion in 1983 to ¥30 trillion in 1987. At the same time,

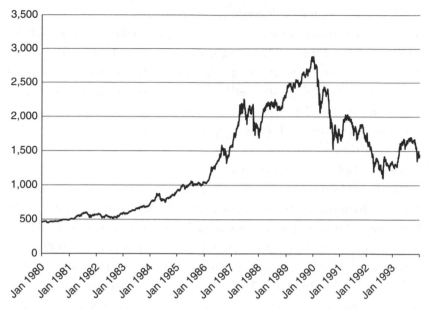

Figure 8.2 TOPIX daily index of Japanese stocks, 1980–93[23]

the Bank of International Settlements announced that it would allow Japanese banks to count 45 per cent of their unrealised capital gains on stocks towards fulfilling capital requirements.[24] This was spectacularly misguided, encouraging banks not only to replace safe assets with risky equities, but to use their considerable market power and lending capacity to stimulate a stock market boom. The incentive to create a boom was compounded by the fact that a substantial part of the stock market consisted of shares in the banks themselves.[25]

Stock prices soared. The Tokyo Stock Exchange's TOPIX index, shown in Figure 8.2, rose by 23 per cent during 1983, 24 per cent during 1984 and a further 15 per cent during 1985. The boom was then supercharged by the flow of money into Japan after the Plaza Accord, and 1986 saw the TOPIX rise by 49 per cent. When it finally peaked in December 1989, it had risen by a total of 386 per cent in just under 7 years. At this stage, Japanese stocks were worth a total of $4 trillion, accounting for almost half of the entire world's equity market capitalisation.[26]

The deregulations of 1983 also relaxed listing requirements, making it much easier for firms to raise money by issuing stocks. As stock prices soared, equity became an incredibly cheap source of finance, resulting in a wave of new promotions: the number of initial public offerings (IPOs) rose from 34 in 1984 to 127 in 1989, and 141 in 1990. These IPOs were typically accompanied by large first-day returns, which averaged 32 per cent over the period 1981–91, making them an excellent speculative investment. This was even more pronounced towards the peak of the boom: new issues in 1988 rose by an average of 74 per cent in the first week of trading.[27]

During 1989, the Bank of Japan grew increasingly concerned that the stock market boom had gone too far. Its response was to incrementally raise the discount rate from 2.5 per cent in April 1989 to 4.25 per cent in December of the same year. This signalled the end of the party, and as soon as the Tokyo Stock Exchange opened at the start of 1990, stock prices began to fall. The fall was slow at first, more of a deflation than a bursting of the bubble. The TOPIX fell by 5 per cent in January, 6 per cent in February and 13 per cent in March. Prices remained stable until mid-summer, but August and September were disastrous, seeing a cumulative fall of 30 per cent. By the beginning of October 1990, the discount rate had reached 6 per cent, and the TOPIX had lost 46 per cent of its peak value.[28] The market recovered somewhat in subsequent months, but from April 1991 prices again began to fall precipitously. The end of the bubble could be dated to August 1992, by which time the TOPIX, having lost 62 per cent of its peak value, finally began to recover. But this recovery was temporary, and in subsequent years the market fell even further as the fallout from the property and stock market bubbles began to bite.

The fall in stock prices forced banks to contract their lending, as it both reduced the value of the collateral they had lent on and wiped out the profits they had been using to fulfil capital requirements. This contraction was compounded by the rise in the discount rate and by the Ministry of Finance finally introducing regulation on loans to property companies in April 1990. This withdrew the fuel from the land bubble, causing the number of new home sales to collapse during 1991. Stripped of the potential for capital gains, investors were left with only rental income, which turned out to be much smaller than anticipated. Although landholders were initially reluctant to sell at a loss, a series of bankruptcies at property companies forced their hand, and land prices began to fall.[29] By 1995 urban land had lost almost half of its peak value, with no sign of the decline slowing down. When prices finally plateaued in 2005, they had fallen by 76 per cent. At this point, land values in real terms were almost exactly what they had been in 1980.

CAUSES

The Japanese land and stock bubbles were purely political creations. Not only did the Japanese government provide the spark, but it systematically cultivated all three sides of the bubble triangle with the explicit goal of generating a boom. This process was clearest in the realm of money and credit, where an expansion was both a central part of Japan's economic policy and, after the Plaza Accord, an international commitment. By lowering interest rates, encouraging the extension of credit and creating the expectation of an appreciation of the yen, the government generated enormous amounts of fuel for speculative investment. Most previous research has identified this monetary expansion as the immediate catalyst for the bubbles.[30]

An additional consequence of deregulation in Japan was an increase in asset marketability. In the post-war period, the buying and selling of stocks had been tightly controlled. Purchases of foreign assets, and the purchase of domestic assets by foreigners, was restricted until 1980, and the Securities and Exchange Law of 1968 placed strict limits on the level of risk that could be taken by securities companies. During the 1980s, these regulations were gradually removed. Perhaps the most significant deregulation occurred in 1983, when investment funds were allowed to buy and sell securities without direct orders from their clients, precipitating the massive growth of *tokkin* funds.[31]

Focusing purely on changes in the law understates the extent of deregulation, however, because the government simply stopped enforcing many laws. Trillions of yen were kept in illegal *eigyo tokkin* funds which the authorities pretended not to notice; one commentator reports that Nomura even managed an *eigyo tokkin* fund for the Ministry of Finance.[32] In a reversal of the post-war situation, corporations could now assume that assets could be bought, sold and repackaged in any particular way unless the sitting government explicitly forbade it, regardless of the letter of the law.

A further increase in marketability resulted from the rise of stock index futures trading. Futures, which are essentially standardised, marketable agreements to buy or sell an asset at a set date in the future, were originally created to allow buyers to reduce their exposure to price fluctuations. In the absence of other risks to offset, however, stock index futures trading is equivalent to betting on the short- to medium-term value of the stock market, so it also appeals to speculators. Futures trading was first introduced by the Osaka Stock Exchange in 1987, where it was an immediate hit with traders: between November 1987 and August 1988, the volume of Nikkei futures trading on Osaka was five times the combined volume of the spot and margin Nikkei trade. Tokyo implemented futures trading shortly afterwards, and it soon accounted for 20 per cent of trades in the TOPIX index. This occurred in the context of a massive expansion of trading volume generally, with the total number of shares traded daily rising from an average of 91 million in 1982 to 328 million in 1988. By 1989 the Japanese stock market had one of the highest turnover rates in the world.[33]

The presence of stock index futures made speculation much easier, and contemporary survey data shows that investors often bought shares with expected short-term rises in mind.[34] In 1989, 39 per cent of institutional investors were advising investors to buy shares despite expecting prices to fall in the long term, because they expected to benefit from short-term price rises. After the crash of 1990, just 9 per cent of institutional investors were recommending this strategy, and the effect of speculation on the market had reversed: 55 per cent were advising *against* buying stocks despite expecting a long-term rise in prices.[35]

Speculation in land, labelled 'land-rolling' by the media, was equally common. A new profession arose, called *Ji-age-ya*, which consisted of buying multiple plots of land, repackaging them into one plot and selling at a large profit.[36] Mostly this occurred in major Japanese cities, and often necessitated the forcible eviction of tenants. Interestingly, this was the opposite activity to the Australian Land Boom companies, which we covered in Chapter 5, who had broken large plots of land up so that tenants and homeowners could move in. As the bubble went on, institutions also began to invest heavily in land overseas: Japanese investment in US property rose from $1.9 billion in 1985 to $16.5 billion in 1988. This was in addition to extensive Japanese lending on American real-estate projects, especially in California, which, not coincidentally, experienced its own land boom at this time.[37]

Land speculation was primarily driven by institutions rather than individuals. Between 1984 and 1990, 38 per cent of land purchases were by specialised real-estate companies, most of which were relatively small operations. Unlike most corporations or households, they did not primarily use the land for living, offices or rental income. Their business model instead involved selling it for a profit soon after its purchase. Although they may have engaged in some level of development work, the vast majority of urban property value consisted of the land rather than the buildings, so the potential value added by this work was relatively small. In practice, profits were derived almost entirely from the continuously increasing value of land. These companies were also highly leveraged, having been funded by loans of approximately ¥44 trillion. Three-quarters of this was invested in property; the remainder was invested in securities.[38] Many of these loans were granted by shadow banks known as 'nonbanks' or *jûsen*, which were almost entirely unregulated before 1990.[39]

The spark then came from Japanese politicians. Japan had explicitly sought to encourage homeownership since World War II, but were reluctant to decrease the wealth of existing homeowners. New builds were therefore accompanied by extensions of mortgage credit, bringing new buyers into the market and thereby ensuring that demand continued to outstrip supply.[40] As a result, house prices almost never fell. When it became clear that the export-led growth model could not continue, in the 1980s the government attempted to use urban regeneration to stimulate the Japanese economy, which increased the price of land for business use. The National Land Agency's *Reform Plan for the Tokyo Area* of 1985 aimed to turn the city into an 'advanced space for international financial business'.[41] One of the proposed means for doing this was to sell public land to private developers. But the ongoing privatisation of land gave the government an interest in rising land prices, since it allowed them to receive more money for their sales. An early indication of the land bubble, and of its potential for generating revenue, was the sale of a 0.7-hectacre government site for ¥57.5 billion in August 1985, around three times its perceived market value at that time.[42]

These policies contributed to the stock market boom, as increasing land values allowed banks to create money to invest in the stock market. But the stock price boom was also a separate element of the government's economic strategy: they wanted to ensure that corporations had low borrowing costs while they navigated the shift away from export-led growth. A senior Bank of Japan official admitted in the 1990s that both the land and stock booms had been deliberately engineered in order to provide a 'safety net' for Japanese business.[43] As the boom went on, efforts to support the market became more explicit. In October 1987 and again in October 1990, the Ministry of Finance ordered the Big Four securities companies to buy stocks in order to support the market.[44]

A unique feature of these bubbles was the way in which the Japanese financial structure created a self-perpetuating relationship between money and speculation. Banks used land as collateral for lending, so the higher the value of land, the more they could lend. Since unrealised stock profits could be used to fulfil capital requirements, stock price rises also resulted in further extensions of credit. The majority of this borrowed money was then invested in either land or stocks, driving prices even higher and freeing banks to lend even more money, which was in turn invested in land and stocks.[45] This circular relationship goes some way to explaining the incredible scale of the real-estate bubble: urban land rose by 320 per cent in 10 years, before losing all of these gains.

Another unusual feature was the degree to which the bubbles were driven by businesses and banks, rather than by the general public. Between 1985 and 1989, the proportion of private land owned by corporations rose from 24.9 per cent to 28.7 per cent, while the proportion owned by individuals fell from 75.1 per cent to 71.3 per cent. Similarly, the proportion of stocks held by corporations rose from an already high 67.0 per cent in 1982 to 72.8 per cent in 1987, most of which was driven by financial institutions and securities companies. The volume of trades accounted for by corporations rose from 19 per cent to 39 per cent, underscoring the extent to which business was responsible for higher levels of speculation.[46] Previously, businesses had almost exclusively pursued buy-and-hold strategies in the stock market.

Commentators at the time often suggested that Japan's culture of consensus thinking created social reasons not to express pessimistic sentiments about land or stocks.[47] This was compounded by the extent of cross-holding, which made it difficult for a corporation to exit the bubble without offending important business partners. Those who did not have an interest in the bubble may have had other reasons not to criticise it. Japanese banks had lent substantial sums of money to Japan's organised crime syndicates, usually with almost no oversight. In one instance, the Industrial Bank of Japan lent $2 billion to the owner of a restaurant chain popular with gangsters. This money was then used to invest in stocks based on the advice of ghosts spoken to during séances.[48] Whatever the money was used for, bursting the bubble would have made it much more difficult for gangsters to raise funds, and they presumably would have been displeased with those deemed responsible. This may partly explain why Japanese investors, politicians and pundits were so reluctant to publicly predict a crash. Whatever their private thoughts, 73 per cent of Japanese institutional investors surveyed in December 1989 stated that they did not believe that stock prices were too high.[49] The small number of sceptics often went to seemingly absurd lengths to keep a low profile. In September 1990, when Japanese television finally decided to broadcast a panel of bearish financial pundits, the pundits insisted on having their faces blurred out.[50]

CONSEQUENCES

Although the end of the two bubbles was signalled by the stock market crash during the first half of 1990, the economy did not immediately enter a recession.[51] GDP growth was 4.9 per cent in 1990, 3.4 per cent in 1991 and 0.8 per cent in 1992. When growth turned negative in 1993, the Japanese government loosened monetary policy and increased government spending. By 1995, the discount rate was 0.5 per cent, while the deficit was 4.4 per cent of GDP. When GDP grew by 2.7 per cent in 1995 and a further 3.1 per cent in 1996, it appeared that the crisis was over.[52] The government, believing that the storm had passed, implemented austerity measures in an effort to prevent a persistent large deficit.

The financial system, however, was crumbling. Its problems first became apparent in the shadow banking system, where 38 per cent of the ¥12.1 trillion loans were non-performing in 1991. A series of government-led debt restructures, having assumed that real-estate prices would not continue to fall, made the situation worse, and in 1995 the proportion of non-performing loans had reached 75 per cent.[53] Acknowledging the level of insolvency in the sector, the Japanese Parliament agreed a bailout funded by a combination of financial institutions and taxpayers, provoking public outrage. In November 1997, the crisis spread to Sanyo Securities, a mid-sized securities firm, which was adjudged to be systemically unimportant and allowed to fail. As part of its bankruptcy arrangements, however, it defaulted on its interbank loans. Although the amount was relatively small, this was the first such default in the post-war history of the interbank market, leading to a severe contraction in it. The Bank of Japan was forced to step in to provide the market with liquidity.[54]

This was followed by the failure of the Hokkaido Takushoku Bank on 14 November 1997, after an attempt to resolve its bad debts via a merger fell through. On 24 November, Yamaichi Securities, one of the four largest securities firms with client assets of ¥22 trillion, announced that it would dissolve. Two days later the Tokyo City Bank declared bankruptcy. Fearing a total financial collapse, the Bank of Japan reiterated its intention to secure all deposits and provide enough liquidity for depositors to withdraw their funds. In February 1998, the government approved a ¥30 trillion taxpayer-funded bailout of the banking sector, massively reversing its earlier efforts to cut the deficit. But the crisis continued to deepen, and the largest bank failure of the crisis came in October 1998, when the government was forced to nationalise the Long-Term Credit Bank of Japan. Six more major banks were placed under government control by the end of 1999.[55]

The government response succeeded in averting a major depression, but at a significant cost: ¥60 trillion of public money was spent on emergency financial measures, around 11 per cent of Japan's GDP.[56] The dire state of the finances at nationalised banks meant that the majority of this money went on covering bad debts. Furthermore, the continued support for failing banks and, by extension, unprofitable businesses had a sclerotic effect on the economy, making it impossible for more efficient firms to compete. The result was a prolonged period of underwhelming economic performance, as the 'lost decade' of the 1990s became the 'lost 20 years'. Japanese GDP in 2017 was only 2.6 per cent higher than it had been in 1997, an annualised growth rate of 0.13 per cent.[57] The contrast with the miraculous growth of the post-war period was stark.

The poor performance of the Japanese economy during the 1990s was especially weak in the context of other developed economies: US GDP grew by 3.4 per cent per year during the decade.[58] This may, however, have resulted in a tendency to overstate the extent of Japan's problems. Although the economy was stagnant, the worst annual growth rate was -1.1 per cent in 1998. Consequently, unemployment never rose above 6 per cent.[59] Furthermore, most contemporary commentary was based on economic data that failed to account for Japan's extremely low population growth. During the 1993–2003 period, the worst 10 years of the crisis, real GDP per capita grew by a total of 9 per cent. For comparison, in the 10 years following the global 2007 crash, the equivalent figure for the UK was 3.6 per cent, and many European countries have performed much worse.[60] Japan's 'lost decade' was a serious downturn, but not on the same scale as the economic collapse that followed the global financial crisis of 2008.

Another consequence of the bubble's bursting was the exposure of a large number of scandals and frauds. In October 1990 the Chairman of the Sumitomo Bank, one of Japan's largest financial institutions, resigned after it emerged that Sumitomo had persuaded its clients to lend ¥23 billion for the purposes of market manipulation.[61] This was followed in the summer of 1991 by Nomura, at that time the largest stockbroking firm in the world, admitting to having used its research division to pump shares it had recently placed with favoured clients (some of whom were prominent gangsters).[62] At the same time it was revealed that almost all Japanese securities companies had been compensating their best-connected clients for their losses on stocks. Such compensation appeared to be in direct contravention of securities law, but the Ministry of Finance had chosen to interpret the law in a way that allowed it to overlook the practice.[63]

A recurring theme in these scandals was the excessively close relationship between the government and the private sector, underlining the bubble's political roots. The scandal with the most far-reaching consequences was the Recruit scandal of 1988, whereby shares in a human resources firm were offered to politicians prior to their issue in return for favours, implicating the entire cabinet and forcing the prime minister to resign.[64] Real-estate companies were regularly involved, too: in 1992, a former cabinet minister was arrested for having accepted ¥480 million in bribes from a Hokkaido property developer.[65] In 1993, Shin Kanemaru, a former deputy prime minister and influential elder statesman, was indicted for tax evasion, having accepted billions of yen in bribes.[66] Combined with economic stagnation, this corruption undermined the authority of the Japanese ruling classes. In July 1993, Kanemaru's Liberal Democratic Party lost its majority in the Lower House for the first time since 1955.[67]

Again, however, the venality of Japanese institutions may have been overstated. It was common in the late 1990s for commentators to encourage Japan to move towards an Anglo-American economic model, in which there was supposedly a healthy distance between business and government.[68] But as the Japanese crisis unfolded, politicians and banks were often held accountable, and at times there was an immediate legislative response. Politicians were arrested, securities companies implemented internal reforms, and the executives of scandal-ridden firms voluntarily took substantial pay cuts.[69] This is not to say that the response was satisfactory. But one could argue that it compared favourably to the degree of accountability in the global financial crisis of 2008.

The Japanese bubbles had few positive effects. Whereas some of the highly innovative companies that formed during the bubbles of the 1920s eventually went on to be successful, companies that listed during the Japanese Bubble performed poorly in the long run.[70] Of the 52 Japanese companies listed in the 2017 Fortune 500, none were originally incorporated during the 1980–92 period – a remarkable failure considering the number of companies that went public during the bubble.[71] The lack of any silver lining underlines a key difference between technological and political bubbles. Technology bubbles often involve large sums of money flowing into extremely innovative sectors of the economy, which might otherwise have trouble attracting enough capital to get off the ground. As a result, they can be beneficial for society.[72] During a political bubble these benefits are absent, as money typically flows into sectors of the economy with much fewer positive externalities. The episode that came after the Japanese Bubble made this contrast abundantly clear.

CHAPTER 9

The Dot-Com Bubble

Clearly, sustained low inflation implies less uncertainty about the future, and lower risk premiums imply higher prices of stocks and other earning assets ... But how do we know when irrational exuberance has unduly escalated asset values, which then become subject to unexpected and prolonged contractions as they have in Japan over the past decade?

Alan Greenspan, 1996[1]

THE DISMANTLING OF POST-WAR FINANCIAL REGULATION that led to the Japanese Bubble ushered in an era of abundant marketability, money and credit. Securities became much more marketable as a result of the removal of restrictions on foreign ownership of firms and an accompanying boom in the use of derivatives, especially in the United States.[2] The 1970s and 1980s saw a global decline in the use of capital controls and fixed exchange rates, making it easier than ever for money to cross borders. Restrictions on banking were gradually removed, giving banks, many of which were now operating internationally, unprecedented control over the level of credit. The global economy effectively became a giant tinderbox waiting for a spark and, as a result, the post-1980 period has seen major financial bubbles become remarkably common.

The first spark after the Japanese Bubble came from computer technology – a literal spark, in one sense, since computing is the use of electrical currents to perform logical functions. In the post-war period this proved useful for a range of industrial and military applications, and by the end of the 1980s it had already had considerable economic impact. Its true potential, however, has turned out to be even greater, and it may even be the most consequential technology ever invented. The key to unlocking this potential, and the catalyst for the bubble, was the creation of a global network of information exchange: the now-ubiquitous Internet.

Although governments and universities had been developing networks of computers since the 1960s, the Internet as we now know it originated in 1989. Tim Berners-Lee, a scientist at the European Council for Nuclear Research, suggested that the organisation would find it easier to keep track of its projects if it had a system which structured information in an easily accessible way. Berners-Lee conceived of a decentralised system of documents, to which any member could upload data. These documents were then connected to one another by hyperlinks. This 'world wide web', as Berners-Lee named it, was simply a way of connecting users and structuring information in order to increase productivity. But it created a feedback loop that exponentially increased the rate of technological change: computing technology was used to create better networks, and these networks allowed programmers to innovate more rapidly, thereby producing even larger and more efficient network systems. The more people used it, the more useful the technology became.

The world wide web was opened to the public in January 1991, but at first grew relatively slowly.[3] To those without a background in computing, it was quite inaccessible. This divide was bridged by browser technology, which provided a means of navigating the web. Mosaic, launched in January 1993 by a 21-year-old computer science major called Marc Andreesen, represented a significant step forward. It was easy to use and install, could be run on all major operating systems, and introduced features such as a 'back' and 'forward' button that made it much easier to use the Internet.[4] As a result, the network rapidly expanded: the number of people online globally rose from 14 million in 1993 to 281 million in 1999 and 663 million in 2002.[5]

Hoping to keep control over the next iteration of his invention, Andreesen then moved to Silicon Valley to found Mosaic Communications Corporation (later, for legal reasons, renamed Netscape). Start-up funding of $3 million was provided by Jim Clark, a veteran computer scientist, and a team of programmers was recruited, largely from those who had worked on the original Mosaic browser.[6] The company's communications officer quickly spotted the news potential of a team of young entrepreneurs working on world-changing technology, which could be leveraged into free publicity. Netscape received positive press coverage from, among others, *Fortune Magazine* and the *New York Times*.[7] The Netscape Navigator was released in October 1994 and quickly became the world's most popular browser.

In June 1995, Andreesen and Clark made the unusual decision to have an initial public offering (IPO) before having turned a profit. In addition to his desire to cash partially out, Clark recognised that an IPO could be used as a 'marketing event': the process itself would generate significant publicity for the company. There were also concerns that Microsoft would soon launch its own browser, which would make it more difficult to sell shares in the future. However, some board members worried that markets would be discouraged by the company's poor performance according to traditional metrics: firms without a reasonably long track record of profits to guide investors had struggled in the past to attract finance from public markets.[8]

Despite these concerns, Netscape's IPO was a resounding success. When its shares went public on 19 August 1995, demand outstripped supply by so wide a margin that trading could not open for two hours.[9] Having been offered at $28 per share, the stock reached a first-day peak at $75 and closed at $58, a first-day return of 107 per cent.[10] Its price continued to rise following the successful launch of its beta version later that year – by December it had reached $170 per share, for a total market capitalisation of $6.5 billion.[11]

The Netscape IPO has been described as the 'big bang' of the dot-com era, providing a template for subsequent internet IPOs. The strategy of going public early and using the IPO for marketing purposes was widely copied: the median age of a publicly offered company in the 1999–2000 period was 5 years, compared to 9 years for the period 1990–4, 8 years for 1995–8 and 11 years for 2001–16. Since younger companies could not use a track record of profits to obtain the trust of investors, they developed a range of new commitment devices and ways to communicate their potential and trustworthiness. For example, many were backed by venture capitalist firms with

a strong reputation: 60 per cent of IPOs issued in 1999–2000, compared to 38 per cent in 1990–8, were backed by venture capital.[12] The
vast majority also committed to lock-up agreements, in which insiders
agreed not to sell shares for some time, usually 180 days, after the
IPO.[13]

The most notable method of attracting investors, however, was under-
pricing: offering shares to the public for a price much lower than the
expected market valuation. Although under-pricing was already common, it was taken to a new level in the dot-com era. IPOs issued in the
United States between 1990 and 1994 had an average first-day return of
11 per cent, whereas the average first-day return in 1999 was 71 per cent,
and in 2000 was 56 per cent. Issuers were, on average, selling their
company for less than two-thirds of its market price. This practice was
known as 'leaving money on the table', and $130 billion was left on the
table in 1999 and 2000 alone.[14] The cost of under-pricing to the company's owners was generally much lower than this figure suggests, however, since they typically retained large majority stakes in the company
after the offering. It was therefore tempting to use under-pricing to
generate positive media coverage on the first day of trading, creating
a momentum that allowed them to sell at a profit later.[15] This practice
was further encouraged by the use of directed share programmes, which
allowed shares to be issued to family and friends at the IPO price.[16]
Whatever the reason for under-pricing, one of its effects was to attract
speculative investors, who could subscribe for shares with the intention of
quickly selling them on the market for a profit.

These financial innovations allowed technology firms to go public in
much greater numbers than had previously been possible. As Figure 9.1
shows, the 1984–91 period saw the issuing of relatively few technology
IPOs, with no single year seeing more than a hundred. They then
increased year on year in the early 1990s, reaching 274 issues in 1996.
After a brief lull, the issue of technology IPOs accelerated, peaking in
1999, when 371 were issued. Their aggregate market value, based on
their first traded price, was even more striking. From a previous high of
$98 billion in 1996, the tech IPOs issued in 1999 and 2000 were valued at
totals of $450 billion and $517 billion respectively. However, this market
immediately collapsed – new technology IPOs issued in 2001 were valued

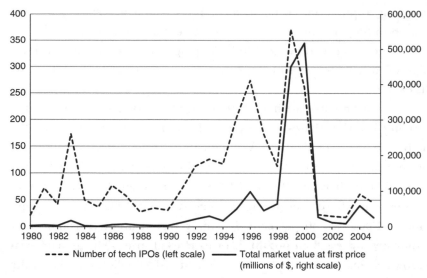

Figure 9.1 US technology IPOs, 1980–2005[17]

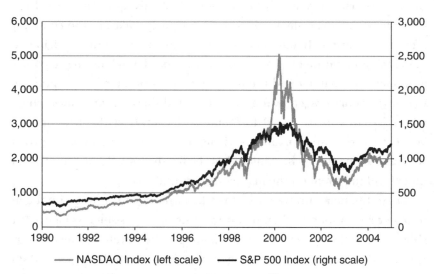

Figure 9.2 S&P 500 and NASDAQ indexes, 1990–2004[18]

at a total of $27 billion, and those issued in 2003 were valued at just
$9 billion.

The IPO boom was accompanied by a boom in the price of existing
equities, shown in Figure 9.2. The S&P 500 index, covering the largest
US-based companies, rose by 115 per cent between January 1990 and

December 1996, prompting concern that the equity market was over-heating. These gains appeared to be somewhat out of proportion with the money being made by its constituent firms. Robert Shiller's cyclically adjusted price-to-earnings ratio (CAPE) stood at 28, meaning that S&P 500 companies were, after adjusting for the business cycle, valued at an average of 28 times their annual earnings. This was well above the long-term average of 15, leading Shiller to advise the Federal Reserve that a correction was due.[19] Alan Greenspan, the Federal Reserve's Chairman, gave what would become an iconic speech 3 days later, in which he questioned the point at which rising asset prices could be said to result from 'irrational exuberance' rather than changes in their intrinsic value. This was accompanied by a warning that inflated asset prices could eventually result in similar problems to those seen in Japan.

In fact, the stock market was not even close to its peak, and fears of a correction were soon forgotten. The S&P 500 rose by another 30 per cent in 1997, 26 per cent in 1998 and 20 per cent in 1999. When it reached its peak in March 2000, its value was 110 per cent higher than when Greenspan made his speech, and its total capital appreciation since 1990 had been 353 per cent. Shiller's CAPE ratio at this stage reached 45, the highest value ever recorded. Before the dot-com era, its highest-ever value had been 33, on the eve of the 1929 Crash.[20]

The boom in technology shares was even more dramatic. The NASDAQ Composite Index, which was heavily weighted towards infor-mation technology firms, rose by 1,055 per cent between March 1990 and March 2000. At its peak in March 2000, the index had more than trebled in value in the space of 18 months. Microsoft and Cisco briefly became the two most valuable public companies in the world. The largest internet firm was America Online (AOL), which had acquired Netscape in March 1999. Having been valued at $61.8 million when it was launched in 1992, AOL achieved a market capitalisation of $190 billion in March 2000, making it the tenth most valuable public company in the world.[21] In February 2000, a $164 billion merger was agreed with Time Warner, at the time the second-largest merger in corporate history.

Much of the money driving these developments came from a massive increase in stock market participation rates. Excluding stocks held through defined pension plans, the number of stock-owning individuals rose from 42.1 million in 1989 to 75.8 million in 1998. This rise was accompanied by substantial growth in the investment management industry: of the 33.7 million additional investors, 6.8 million exclusively held shares directly and the remaining 26.9 million held at least some of their shares through a retirement account or mutual fund.[22] The value of assets held by equity mutual funds rose from $870 per capita in 1989 to over $14,000 per capita in 1999. Concurrently, a shift from defined-benefit to defined-contribution pension plans gave households greater control over the choice to invest in bonds or in equities. Since individuals showed a greater preference for equities over bonds than pension-fund managers had, this had the effect of channelling funds into the stock market.[23]

Many investors were also attracted to the stock market by the emergence of specialist financial television. Three dedicated financial news channels emerged during the 1990s: CNBC, CNNfn, and Bloomberg Television, all of which offered 24-hour coverage of stock markets interspersed with commercials for investment products. This had the effect of marketing stocks to an ever-wider audience.[24] Whereas previous financial news was usually a very sober affair, these emerging channels recognised that more viewers could be attracted by making it as exciting as possible. As a result, they began to overplay the significance of any development, with even minor news reported in increasingly breathless tones. If there was not even any minor news to report, they instead reported analyst recommendations, treating them as though they constituted news in and of themselves.[25] In practice, this almost always meant puffing stocks, because by the end of the decade these recommendations were almost uniformly positive. In 1989, 9 per cent of analyst recommendations were to 'sell' a particular stock; in 1999, only 1 per cent were.[26]

Many of the articles and books published at this time carried a striking tone of delusional optimism. Jim Cramer of *The Street* published an article in February 2000 criticising 'troglodyte value managers' for insisting that the price-to-earnings ratio was still useful in the new economy, accusing them of 'making something psychological into something scientific, and that is WRONG!'[27] Kevin Hassett and James Glassman published a book entitled *Dow 36,000*, arguing that the Dow Jones Index, then at around 10,000, would quickly rise to 36,000 (it peaked at around 12,000 before falling below 8,000 in 2002). It is striking how little effect the failure of these predictions had on their careers: Cramer got his own successful TV show on CNBC, and Hassett later became the head of President Trump's Council of Economic Advisers.

Other elements of the news media were critical of the bubble, advising investors to avoid technology stocks. Some of this advice came too early: *Fortune*, for example, ran an article reporting the willingness of policemen and baristas to offer stock recommendations as early as April 1996.[28] But other advice was well timed, and used arguments that have since aged well. Martin Wolf of the *Financial Times* argued in December 1998 that US equity prices were 'unsustainable', and stressed the need to anchor valuations to a realistic estimate of the equity risk premium.[29] Near the peak of the boom, *The Economist* published an article disputing the validity of several common arguments that tried to justify the level of share prices, concluding that share prices assumed 'an implausible rate of growth in profits'.[30]

Most narratives of the dot-com era date the end of the bubble to the spring of 2000; Rory Cellan-Jones, for example, calls 14 March 'the day the bubble burst'.[31] The next month saw a series of dramatic falls in price: between 10 and 14 April the NASDAQ fell by 25 per cent, a record for a single trading week, while the S&P 500 fell by 10 per cent.[32] Even those sceptical of technology stocks were caught out by the speed of the drop. Stanley Druckenmiller of the Soros Fund quit in April after his portfolio experienced a 4-month loss of 22 per cent, saying 'we thought it was the eighth inning, and it was the ninth'.[33] But although the bubble had peaked, it had not completely burst, and stocks made a considerable recovery during the summer months of 2000. From a low of 3,321 on 14 April, the NASDAQ rose 27 per cent to 4,234 on 1 September, only 15 per cent lower than its March peak. Between a May trough and a second peak in July, internet stocks rose by 42 per cent.[34]

Thereafter, however, the bubble gradually deflated. The NASDAQ fell continuously from September 2000 through to the end of the year, suffering particularly heavy losses in November, when it fell by 23 per cent. By the end of 2000 it had lost more than half its value in the space of 8 months. The S&P 500 initially held up relatively well, ending 2000 only 15 per cent below its peak. But both indexes continued to fall throughout 2001 and for most of 2002, the economic outlook deteriorating due to a series of accounting scandals and adverse geopolitical developments stemming from the 11 September attacks. When the market finally bottomed out in October 2002, the NASDAQ had lost 77 per cent of its value in 2½ years, while the S&P 500 had fallen by a total of 48 per cent.

For internet stocks, the picture is even more remarkable: the sector experienced returns of 1,000 per cent in the 2 years preceding February 2000, and had lost all of these gains by the end of 2000.[35] Some of the failures were spectacular. Webvan, an online grocery delivery service, saw its market capitalisation fall from $3.1 billion to zero in 18 months. VerticalNet, which provided business-to-business portals, lost $7.8 billion in value during March and April 2000.[36] The merger between AOL and Time Warner fared so badly that the Time Warner CEO, having overseen a $99 billion loss, called it 'the biggest mistake in corporate history'.[37] There were, however, some long-term successes. The most notable of these was Amazon, which fell from $106 at the peak of the bubble to $6 by September 2001, but later recovered, eventually reaching over $2,000 per share in September 2018. As of March 2019 it has a market capitalisation of $796.1 billion, making it the fourth-largest company in the United States.[38]

Although the Dot-Com Bubble is often thought to have occurred in Silicon Valley, it was in fact an international phenomenon. The main technology stock indexes for Europe, Japan, and the rest of Asia, standardised to January 1995, are shown in Figure 9.3. All three indexes experienced substantial booms and busts concurrently with the NASDAQ bubble. Between October 1998 and March 2000, the European index rose by 370 per cent, the Japanese index by 299 per cent and the Asian index by 330 per cent. By October 2002, the European index had lost 88 per cent of its peak value, while the Japanese and Asian indexes had fallen by 75 per cent and 67 per cent respectively. The bust was particularly severe in Germany, where the NEMAX 50, the 'new market' stock index, was discontinued in 2004, having fallen by 96 per cent.[39]

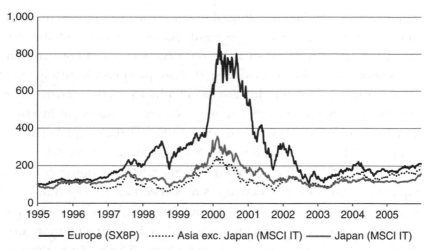

Figure 9.3 Global technology stock price indexes, 1995–2006[40]

CAUSES

During the 1990s, the incendiary conditions left in place by global financial deregulation were aggravated by further increases on all three sides of the bubble triangle. Marketability increased for four reasons. First, as a straightforward consequence of the increase in IPOs, firms which previously would have been privately owned could now be bought and sold on the stock market. Second, transaction costs fell substantially throughout the 1990s, partly as a result of new technology making it less costly to execute trades. The average commission charged by New York Stock Exchange brokers fell from 0.9 per cent in the mid-1970s to 0.1 per cent in 2000, while the bid-ask spread – the difference between the price at which brokers will buy a stock and the price at which they will sell it – fell from 0.6 per cent in 1990 to 0.2 per cent in 2000. Taking both of these trends into account, the average New York Stock Exchange transaction cost between 1990 and 2000 fell from around 0.5 per cent to around 0.2 per cent.[41]

Third, internet technology made stock trading much easier. Three per cent of stock trades in 1993 were facilitated by electronic communications networks (ECNs); by 2000, 30 per cent of trades used ECNs. Securities Exchange Commission estimates suggest that by 1999 there were 9.7 million active online trading accounts in the United States alone. Finally, after-hours trading, although it had been allowed for some time, became much more widespread, partly as a result of the new technology. During 1999, most broker-dealers extended after-hours trading services to small retail investors, who had previously been excluded on the grounds that the thinness of after-hours markets made them vulnerable to market manipulation.[42] As a result, individual investors could now buy and sell shares in the comfort of their own homes, at any time of day, and at a significantly lower cost than before.

Money was relatively abundant during the 1990s, providing sufficient liquidity for the bubble to develop. Alan Greenspan's decision to intervene after the 1987 stock market crash led many to believe that the Federal Reserve would respond to a price drop by cutting interest rates, thereby limiting the potential losses of investors. This became known as the 'Greenspan put' and acted as an incentive to take greater risks. In 1998, just as the bubble was developing, the Federal Reserve cut interest rates in anticipation of an economic downturn, further encouraging investors to reach for yield. The 1990s was also an era of increasing credit, with US household debt as a proportion of GDP rising from 60 per cent in 1990 to 70 per cent in 2000.[43] As in the 1920s, the number of investors borrowing to buy shares rose particularly sharply. Between January 1997 and March 2000, margin lending rose by 144 per cent.[44]

These increases in margin lending and marketability abetted the rise of speculative investment. As more day traders entered the market, turnover increased substantially: the ratio of total shares sold to total shares listed on the NASDAQ market rose from 86 per cent in 1990 to 221 per cent in 1999.[45] This, in turn, made shares even more marketable. Institutional investors did not conceal the fact that many of their trades were for speculative purposes, confident in their ability to exit the market before any crash. One survey of investors in the dot-com era found that 54 per cent claimed to have previously held a stock they thought was overvalued in anticipation of further price increases.[46]

This was by no means confined to institutions, with many of the millions of individuals who invested for the first time in the 1990s also pursuing speculative trading strategies. Trading data suggest that the price increases of 1998 to March 2000 were driven by increased demand from both individuals and institutions. Institutional investors, however, were broadly correct in their belief that they would be more likely than individuals to time their exit from the bubble: demand from institutions dipped sharply between March and June 2000, even as demand from individuals continued to rise. Not every type of institution timed their exit well, however, with independent investment advisers performing exceptionally badly.[47] Mutual funds with younger managers performed worse than average, as they were generally much more heavily invested in technology stocks and more likely to exhibit trend-chasing behaviour.[48] Unsurprisingly, insiders also tended to time their exits well in comparison to the average investor. By one estimate, in the month before the NASDAQ peaked, insiders sold 23 times as many shares as they bought.[49] As is often the case, speculative investment strategies were much more profitable for experienced investors and those with privileged information.

The spark for the bubble was provided by the realisation that network effects would vastly increase the usefulness of computer technology. The 1990s saw spectacular growth at existing firms such as Hewlett-Packard and Microsoft, providing early investors with enormous capital gains. The initial success of newcomers such as Netscape and AOL further demonstrated the potential profits that could be made from investing in dot-com firms. Partly due to the successful integration of information technology systems, there was a wider economic boom during the 1990s, and earnings were high even at non-technology firms. The resulting capital gains attracted speculative investors, whose demand drove prices ever higher.

Prices might not have reached such a high level had these earnings not been accompanied by compelling 'new era' narratives about the transformative power of the Internet. For the purposes of justifying dot-com price levels, these narratives consisted of two arguments: first, that the Internet was an incredibly significant and world-changing technology; second, that this made traditional metrics for valuing stocks irrelevant. The second argument was clearly much weaker, but the first argument was a much more interesting topic of conversation, and therefore formed the basis of most non-specialist discussion. As a result, one's opinion on dot-com valuations was likely to be closely linked to one's opinion on the potential of the Internet. Since people used the Internet increasingly often, its revolutionary potential was widely apparent, and the Internet itself was a powerful means of spreading the new era narrative.[50] In some cases, these theories encompassed broader sociological and political changes as well as technological ones. In a nod to Francis Fukuyama's *The End of History*, perhaps the most influential new era narrative of the time, a 1997 article in *Foreign Affairs* argued that 'changes in technology, ideology, employment, and finance' had precipitated 'the end of the business cycle'.[51]

While new era ideas look foolish with hindsight, as of 2000, pessimistic forecasters had been crying wolf for so long that their warnings were easy to ignore. While much has been written about the naive optimism of the late 1990s, curiously little has been written about the equally misplaced scepticism towards technology firms of a few years earlier. Netscape, for example, was an exceptional investment: those who bought it for $58 on its first day of trading received an average 35 per cent annual return until its acquisition in 1999.[52] But the *New York Times* smugly described the enthusiasm for Netscape as 'juvenile', attributing its first-day returns to 'the belief that these stocks only go up'.[53] The *Financial Times*, often praised for its sophistication at the peak of the market, was completely dismissive of Netscape, accusing its investors of having 'abandoned reality'.[54] There were also plenty of writers who predicted a mid-90s crash that never arrived. James Grant, a public investment strategist, was widely praised for his 'prescient' pessimism at the turn of the century.[55] But Grant had warned of a coming crash as early as 1996, with much of his argument based upon a dismissal of growth prospects in the computer and semiconductor industries.[56] Stock price levels at this stage were fully justified by future developments and, from the standpoint of 2019, 1996 seems to have been an excellent time to buy technology stocks.[57]

While the spark for the bubble was technological, political factors almost certainly contributed to its scale. In Roger Lowenstein's narrative of the bubble, corporate influence over Washington in the 1980s and 1990s led to the removal of regulations that protected investors and the cutting of funds for prosecuting white-collar fraud. Simultaneously, an emerging culture of tying executive pay to a company's share price created an incentive for companies to overstate earnings, often through the use of creative accounting.[58] Before 1998, there had never been more than 60 earnings restatements in a single year in the United States; in

1998 there were 96, in 1999, 204, and in 2000, 163. As a result, investors were led to believe in the 1998–2000 period that profits were rising, but when future revisions were taken into account, they had in fact been steady or falling.[59] This practice culminated in the collapse of Enron in 2001, when it emerged that the $60 billion energy firm had used creative accounting to fraudulently hide substantial losses.

However, the explanatory power of Lowenstein's argument is limited by its exclusive focus on the United States. The stock market crash was much more severe in Germany, where the major trends identified by Lowenstein did not occur. Executive pay rises had been several orders of magnitude smaller than in the United States, and there was no wave of earnings restatements at German firms.[60] Furthermore, although German governments were generally following deregulatory policies, dispersed firm ownership and managerial stock options were extremely rare. As a result, German managers had few, if any, incentives to artificially increase their company's share price.[61] The fact that the bubble occurred simultaneously in several countries with different political environments, and was in each case particularly pronounced in information technology stocks, strongly suggests that its spark was technological.

CONSEQUENCES

The Dot-Com Bubble in the United States was notable for its limited macroeconomic impact. The 2001 recession lasted only 8 months, and was very mild compared to previous recessions, with GDP figures showing positive growth for the year as a whole.[62] There were two reasons for this. First, consumer spending did not fall. The bursting of a bubble often results in deficient demand because those who have lost money cut spending in response. In 2001, this wealth effect was very weak. This may have been because stockholders tend to be wealthy, particularly when compared to house owners. Since the rich are generally less likely to cut spending in response to losses on investments, this will result in a smaller reduction in demand. Alternatively, the wealth effect could have been offset by the effect of lower interest rates: while some consumers cut back spending, others borrowed and spent more.[63]

Second, the banking sector was relatively well insulated from the stock market bust. Banks held very few technology shares: in one sample of investors, the portfolio of banks never consisted of more than 4 per cent of technology stocks, a lower weighting than any other category of institutional investor.[64] Furthermore, the pre-crash profit margins in the banking sector were particularly high, while default rates were low, providing a buffer against the economic downturn.[65] Banks were thus able to continue to supply credit after the crash, and the economy avoided the bank failures, credit crunch and deflation that characterised the 1930s.

The economic effects were also fairly limited elsewhere. The UK experienced continued growth until the global financial crisis of 2007–8. The French economy stagnated in 2002–3, but did not experience a recession, while the Japanese economy experienced a contraction that was mild in the context of its ongoing economic problems. The only moderate recession was in Germany, where GDP growth was negative in both 2002 and 2003.[66] The main reason for this appears to have been the relatively high exposure of German banks to stock market losses. Although there were no high-profile banking failures, both profits and capital-to-loans ratios declined. In response, banks reduced lending, which had a chilling effect on economic activity.[67]

Given the modest levels of economic damage associated with the bursting of the Dot-Com Bubble, it may provide an example of a bubble where the benefits outweighed the costs. There were areas where it had a positive economic impact. Enormous sums of capital were channelled to the most innovative sector of the economy, which might not have occurred if markets had operated efficiently. Some of this capital was used very effectively: household names such as Amazon and eBay started as dot-com companies, and established firms like Apple and Microsoft benefited from increased investment. Firms that did go bankrupt often left behind technology that proved useful in the future, and failures indicated where pitfalls lay in wait for the next generation of internet firms. The infrastructure constructed by telecoms firms, while not particularly efficient or optimal, still constituted an investment with considerable public benefits.[68] The bubble was also closely associated with the emergence of the venture capital industry, which has since provided funds to firms with the kind of high-risk profile that makes it difficult to source finance elsewhere.

On the other hand, it is not necessarily clear that the long-term consequences of internet technology will be positive. At the time of writing, it has become fashionable for the media to express concerns over its secondary social and political effects, such as misinformation, oligopolistic market structures and automation. In the long run, these concerns may even appear trivial. Marc Andreesen, now a leading venture capitalist, argues that the contemporary discourse severely underestimates the impact of computer technology. Software is pervading every aspect of everyday life; it is, in Andreesen's words, 'eating the world'.[69] Others have gone so far as to argue that the only comparable innovations are language and money.[70] We may be no better able to understand its impact than societies could understand how language or money would change the world in the decades after their creation.

Another consequence of the Dot-Com Bubble was the emergence of financial bubbles as a serious academic area of investigation. Academic finance prior to 2000 was dominated by the belief that markets were generally efficient, and many considered the idea that asset prices could diverge substantially from underlying profitability to be faintly ridiculous. On the rare occasion that a prestigious economics or finance journal published an article about a bubble, it was often to argue that the supposed bubble was illusory and that prices during it were mostly 'rational'.[71]

After the dot-com crash, the academic tradition of attributing bubbles to market fundamentals continued. The *Journal of Financial Economics*, one of the leading finance journals, published an article arguing that there was no Dot-Com Bubble, and that the dramatic price changes actually resulted from changes in the expected return associated with technology shares.[72] The basis of this article was that internet shares justified their peak values because their best-case scenarios were so spectacularly profitable: in the words of the authors, 'a firm with some probability of failing and some probability of becoming the next Microsoft is very valuable'.[73] However, even if this were true, it would not account for internet share prices being 90 per cent lower a few months later, when many companies still had considerable potential. Another article, published in the leading economics journal the *American Economic Review*, presented a model arguing that the boom and bust resulted from changes in the risk associated with technology shares during a technological revolution. But even if one were to accept this model uncritically, it only predicted that new technology shares would fall by 50 per cent; in reality, internet shares fell by almost 90 per cent.[74]

Unsatisfied with efficient-markets explanations, academics proposed a range of alternative explanations. Some focused on the difficulty of short selling technology shares: borrowing shares to short sell was often expensive, making it difficult to bet against the bubble.[75] However, while borrowing costs were high for some individual shares, they were relatively low for the overall NASDAQ market, so this is unlikely to explain the overall bubble.[76] Another possibility was that insiders were temporarily barred from selling their shares due to lock-up agreements, and that the crash occurred when these agreements expired. But subsequent research showed that, somewhat surprisingly, the expiration of lock-up agreements at a technology firm was not strongly associated with a fall in its share price.[77]

A more compelling branch of explanations blamed the crash on the rise of investment institutions, which often created conflicts of interest and flawed incentive structures. Mutual funds, for example, typically aim to attract as many new investors as possible. The easiest way to do so is by demonstrating excess short-term returns, which can most easily be achieved by taking on more risk. During the Dot-Com Bubble, this meant investing a higher proportion of funds in the volatile technology sector. Conversely, institutions which went against the herd by avoiding technology stocks risked mass withdrawals if the bubble continued to grow. The Tiger Group of hedge funds began to bet against technology firms in 1998, underperforming its rivals for the next 2 years as a result. In the first quarter of 2000, its investors lost patience and withdrew their funds, forcing its closure only weeks before its strategy would have paid off.[78]

Perhaps the most influential explanation to emerge from the Dot-Com Bubble was that of Robert Shiller, whose bestseller *Irrational Exuberance* was published just as the bubble began to burst. While this book is most famous for emphasising the role of psychological factors in driving share prices, this was only one part of a hypothesis that also referenced the aforementioned incentive problems, steady inflation, tax cuts and cultural factors.[79] The long list of precipitating factors made it difficult to ascertain the relative importance of each one, but in part this reflected the difficulty of explaining a bubble which could not be neatly attributed to a single cause. The impact of the book undoubtedly played a role in Shiller later being awarded the Nobel Prize for economics.

The dot-com crash was expected to be a wake-up call, but if anything its modest economic impact engendered an atmosphere of complacency about the next crash. Central bank and think-tank papers in the years after 2000 praised the role of financial derivatives and securitisation in allowing banks to better manage risk, arguing that these innovations made them less vulnerable to future crashes. The New York Federal Reserve concluded that banks performed well during the dot-com crash because they 'used credit derivatives effectively to prune credit risk', while RWI, a German economics think-tank, recommended that banks could increase lending without increasing risk by 'hiving off loans into securitisation'.[80] Meanwhile, the bursting of the bubble made investors distrustful of stocks, and many poured capital into the real-estate market instead.[81]

After 2000, proponents of cyclical models of bubbles became sceptical that another bubble would develop soon, because the models of Kindleberger and Minsky suggested that the memory of a recent bubble would prevent an immediate repeat. John Cassidy, at that time the *New Yorker*'s financial correspondent, concluded his 2003 study of the Dot-Com Bubble by stating that the next speculative bubble 'probably won't be for quite a while' because America had 'gotten serious' in the aftermath of the crash.[82] But money remained abundant, credit was becoming more and more loose, and the growth of the derivatives market was substantially increasing the marketability of financial assets. Speculation had temporarily declined, but with plenty of money sloshing around the global economy and historically low returns on traditional assets, it would not take much for the fervour of the late 1990s to return. All that was needed was a spark.

CHAPTER 10

'No More Boom and Bust': The Subprime Bubble

Unlike so many other bubbles . . . this one involved not just another commodity but a building block of community and social life and a cornerstone of the economy: the family home.

The Financial Crisis Inquiry Commission[1]

If mortgages did indeed become Dutch tulips, Washington provided a superbly fertile flower bed.

Nolan McCarthy, Keith Poole and Howard Rosenthal[2]

THE TITLE OF THIS CHAPTER ALLUDES TO GORDON BROWN'S continual refrain as the UK's Chancellor of the Exchequer from 1997 to 2007 – 'no return to boom and bust' was a phrase he repeated many times.[3] The Dot-Com Bubble led Brown, among many others, to conclude that bubbles do not have major negative economic or social consequences and that central banks can save us from the excesses of irrational exuberance. Devastating housing bubbles and banking collapses only happened in faraway lands or in the distant past. But Brown's bubble was well and truly burst with the 2008 global financial crisis.

There were Cassandras warning that disaster was impending. A handful of economists such as Yale's Robert Shiller and Raghuram Rajan, during his tenure as Chief Economist at the International Monetary Fund, warned about the housing bubble in the United States. Morgan Kelly, an economics professor at University College Dublin, provoked by the inane utterings of professional economists, simply looked at the data and made the prognosis that not only was Ireland going to have a substantial fall in property prices, but that its banking system would implode in the process.[4] But these were all voices crying in the wilderness. Bertie Ahern, at that time the Irish Prime Minister, dismissed criticism from the likes of Kelly with the line 'I don't know how people who engage in [talking down the economy] don't commit suicide.'[5]

The housing bubble that these Cassandras warned about was unlike all the property booms that had come before it, which may explain why there were so few Cassandras and why they were ignored. Previous property booms had not witnessed the level of financial engineering which turned homes into objects of financial market speculation to be bought and sold by investors around the globe. Company shares had long been marketable, but financial alchemy now meant that people's homes were, in some ways, just as marketable. Furthermore, previous property booms and the effects of their busts had mostly been confined to one country or a region within a country. The property boom of the 2000s, however, was global in nature. At least four countries had a simultaneous major property bubble – Ireland, Spain, the United Kingdom and the United States – and the financing of the bubbles in these economies extended well beyond their own borders. Their bursting then caused substantial problems for several major European banking systems.

Houses in the United States had typically been viewed as a relatively solid investment, their 'bricks and mortar' simplicity contrasting with the ephemeral and abstract nature of stocks and bonds. From 1890 to 1999, as can be seen from Figure 10.1, average house prices in the United States had appreciated by only about 25 per cent in real terms. Then, from January 2000 to summer 2006, the national house-price figures, Composite-10 and Composite-20 figures respectively show an 84.6, 126.3 and 106.5 per cent increase. The fall from this peak to the trough in early 2012 was between 27.4 and 35.3 per cent. However, as Table 10.1 shows, the composite and national indexes masked huge regional variation within the country.[6] Four metropolitan areas experienced increases of more than 150 per cent and four areas experienced falls greater than 50 per cent. Miami, Las Vegas, Phoenix and Washington, DC stand out because of the substantial reversal in their house prices.

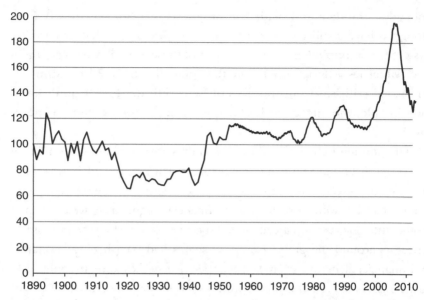

Figure 10.1 Index of real house prices for the United States, 1890–2012[7]

Table 10.1 also reveals the extent of the bubble in the bottom tier of the housing market for each metropolitan area. Bottom-tier house prices in five areas appreciated by approximately 200 per cent or more. While only four areas experienced a fall of 50 per cent or greater in the overall housing market, ten areas experienced bottom-tier falls greater than 50 per cent. In most areas, the overall housing bubble peaked in the summer of 2006, a full year before the problems were manifested in the interbank markets and a full 2 years before the collapse of the banking system. In those areas that experienced the most substantial booms, bottom-tier markets usually peaked much later than the overall market did.

The US housing boom was replicated elsewhere (Figure 10.2). From 1998 to 2007, real house prices in Ireland, Spain and the United Kingdom increased by 133, 103 and 134 per cent. However, by 2012, prices had fallen by 51, 39 and 20 per cent respectively. The housing booms in these three economies peaked one year later than in the United States.

In each country, the boom in house prices was accompanied by a boom in house building, the extent of which is shown in Table 10.2. In the United States, nearly 15 million new homes were completed

TABLE 10.1 *Real house price changes in major US metropolitan areas*[8]

Metropolitan area	Appreciation of overall market from Jan 2000 to peak (%)	Depreciation of overall market from peak to bottom (%)	Appreciation of low-tier houses from Jan 2000 to peak (%)	Depreciation of low-tier houses from peak to bottom (%)
Miami	178.8	50.8	241.1	66.3
Los Angeles	173.9	41.8	239.8	56.5
San Diego	150.3	42.3	196.8	52.6
Washington, DC	150.2	50.8	196.6	46.4
Tampa	138.1	46.9	197.7	65.4
Las Vegas	134.8	61.7	143.9	70.2
Phoenix	127.4	55.9	139.3	70.7
San Francisco	118.4	46.1	176.1	60.7
New York	115.8	27.1	159.7	37.9
Seattle	92.3	32.9	102.4	44.2
Boston	82.5	20.0	119.2	32.4
Portland	81.7	29.0	99.9	36.2
Minneapolis	70.9	38.1	87.7	56.4
Chicago	68.6	39.1	83.6	56.5
Denver	40.3	14.1	37.5	21.0
Atlanta	35.3	39.0	38.1	65.9
Charlotte	29.0	16.0	n/a	n/a
Detroit	27.1	49.3	n/a	n/a
Dallas	25.7	10.7	n/a	n/a
Cleveland	23.2	23.5	n/a	n/a
Composite-10	126.3	35.3	n/a	n/a
Composite-20	106.5	35.1	n/a	n/a
National	84.6	27.4	n/a	n/a

between 2000 and 2008, adding up to 1.47 new homes for each new inhabitant. Given the average household size of 2.57 at the time, this was many more new houses than was necessary. Some estimates suggest that close to 3.5 million houses were constructed where they were not needed during the boom.[9] Indeed, unlike previous building booms, this one increased the number of houses just when the number of new households was falling steeply.[10] The drop in completions after 2008 is remarkable, falling to about one-third of the level during the boom years. Housing starts in the United States fell 79 per cent to a 50-year-low.[11]

In Spain, just over 5 million new houses were completed between 2001 and 2008.[12] To put this into perspective, between 2002 and 2006, Spain built more houses each year than Germany and France combined, despite having less than one-third of their combined population.[13]

TABLE 10.2 *New housing completions (thousands), 1990–2012*[15]

	Ireland	Northern Ireland	Spain	Great Britain	United States
1990s	22	8	268	181	1,330
2000	40	11	416	165	1,574
2001	42	14	505	160	1,570
2002	58	14	520	168	1,648
2003	69	15	506	176	1,679
2004	77	16	565	188	1,842
2005	81	13	591	193	1,931
2006	105	14	658	195	1,979
2007	74	12	647	212	1,503
2008	48	10	632	178	1,120
2009	22	8	425	149	794
2010	10	7	277	129	652
2011	7	6	179	135	585
2012	4	6	133	136	649

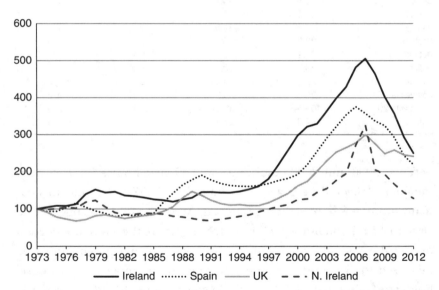

Figure 10.2 Indexes of real house prices for Ireland, Northern Ireland, Spain and the United Kingdom, 1973–2012[14]

When the construction boom peaked in 2006, the number of housing starts in Spain was greater than the combined total number for Germany, France and the United Kingdom. However, after the bubble burst, the number of houses under construction dropped dramatically.

In Ireland, the go-go years of 2005 and 2006 saw almost as many houses completed as in the entire 1990s. From 2000 to 2008, Ireland built over 0.6 million new homes. However, as can be seen from Table 10.2, in the aftermath of the bubble, new home completions almost collapsed altogether. Between 2000 and 2008 in both Ireland and Spain, just over one new home for every new inhabitant in the country was built, a staggering record for two countries with an average household size of 2.7 and 2.6 respectively. In both countries it appears to have been a case of 'build it and they will come'.

In the United Kingdom just over 1.6 million new homes were completed between 2000 and 2008. This was one new home for every 1.78 new inhabitants, a high ratio given the UK's average household size of 2.4 persons. Although aggregate UK figures suggest a relatively small housing bubble, one part of the United Kingdom – Northern Ireland – had a more significant housing bubble than Spain, Ireland or the United States.[16] House prices in Northern Ireland increased by 206 per cent between 1998 and 2007 (see Figure 10.1), and Northern Ireland added just over 119,000 new homes between 2000 and 2008, amounting to one house for every 0.81 new inhabitants!

A significant driver of the housing bubble was a dramatic expansion of credit. During the 2000s, US banks and mortgage companies relaxed their lending standards to borrowers with poor credit-rating histories – so-called subprime borrowers. As a result, there was an unprecedented growth in mortgage credit to high-risk borrowers from the poorer segments of society.[17] Loan-to-value ratios approaching 100 per cent became common, enabling those on low incomes to buy houses. Many were given interest-only mortgages or adjustable rate mortgages with very low 'teaser' rates for the first few years, which initially made the mortgage payments appear much more manageable than they really were.

High loan-to-value ratios, high earnings-to-loan ratios, interest-only mortgages and mortgages with low initial teaser rates also became common in the United Kingdom, Ireland and Spain. In the United Kingdom, for example, institutions such as Northern Rock lent to subprime parts of the market on loan-to-value ratios close to or over 100 per cent. Northern Rock's infamous Together mortgages, which allowed individuals to borrow up to 125 per cent of the value of their homes, were aimed at those on low incomes who needed to borrow to furnish their home, never mind buy it. Lenders in Ireland introduced 100 per cent mortgages in 2004, and by 2008 they constituted 12 per cent of all new mortgages granted.[18]

The expansion of mortgage credit in the United States, Spain and the United Kingdom was supercharged by growth in the securitisation of mortgages.[19] This involved a bank 'distributing' the mortgages which it had originated by selling their associated cash flows. These cash flows were then sliced, diced and packaged into mortgage-backed securities (MBS): financial assets which entitled the holder to the repayments from a set of underlying mortgages. Despite the fact that these underlying mortgages were often very low quality, many MBSs received a coveted AAA credit rating from credit-rating agencies during the boom years, indicating to potential investors that they were essentially risk-free. Riskier tranches which could not be repackaged as MBSs were instead repackaged as Collateralised Debt Obligations (CDOs); these, too, magically received AAA credit ratings. When securitisation firms ran out of actual mortgages to securitise, they created synthetic CDOs, which were essentially a series of bets on other mortgage products.

The securitisation of mortgages during the housing bubble had at least three effects. First, the originate-to-distribute model meant that the originators were less likely to screen borrowers carefully because they did not have to live with the consequences of their lending decision. If the mortgage defaulted, it was not their problem – the losses would land on whoever was left holding the MBS or CDO. This resulted in many poor quality and subprime mortgages.[20] Second, securitisation, by allowing banks to lower their lending standards and thus issue more mortgages, amplified and pyramided leverage in the economy. In addition, MBSs and CDOs were themselves debt financed and were often used as collateral for creating other CDOs financed with debt. Third, securitisation allowed investors to participate in the housing boom without having to buy and sell houses or lend to homeowners.

A consequence of the easily available mortgage credit was that many of the poorest members of society were swept up in the Subprime Bubble. Michael Lewis in his account of the property boom and bust describes a Mexican strawberry picker in California with an income of $14,000 and no English, who was lent all of the $724,000 he needed to buy a house. He also tells of a nanny who had bought six houses in New York City, having borrowed every penny to do so, and a stripper in Las Vegas who had mortgages on five properties.[21] This phenomenon was not confined to the United States: Claire Dempsey, a single Northern Irish woman in her mid-20s, was lent money by her bank in 2006 to buy a £185,000 semi-detached house, with an interest-only mortgage eight times her salary.[22] After the crash she was unable to maintain the mortgage and sold the property for £65,000.

The middle classes also got caught up in the bubble. Many of them bought second houses as holiday homes in sunnier climes: about 750,000 UK citizens bought holiday homes in Spain.[23] Some became flippers – buying and selling property quickly without necessarily improving it.[24] Others decided to buy houses in the hope that it would provide a pension in their retirement – houses were perceived to be good investments, as illustrated by the simile 'as safe as houses'.[25] Indeed, the Commission of Investigation into the Banking Sector in Ireland stated in its report that the purchase of a second home by Irish people during the boom was perceived as 'a no-brainer'.[26] Many people in all four economies entered the property market on a buy-to-let basis. In the United Kingdom, the number of buy-to-let mortgages rose from 0.12 million to 1.16 million between 2000 and 2008. The middle class effectively became the new landlord class.

David Callaghan was a typical middle-class investor during the boom.[27] Just as prices were peaking, in the autumn of 2007, he spent £650,000 on a luxury house just outside Newry, a city on the northern side of the Irish border. He got a £485,000 mortgage to do so. He also borrowed some more money to invest in a one-bedroom buy-to-let property in Belfast. Callaghan, like many borrowers across Ireland, Spain, the UK and the United States, soon found it impossible to cover his huge mortgage payments. He was forced to sell his luxury house for only £240,000 and his buy-to-let investment at 50 per cent below the purchase price. As a result, he was delinquent on his mortgages.

Mortgage delinquencies started rising in the United States in 2006 and accelerated in 2007.[28] From March 2007 onwards, mortgage lenders started to announce losses and high delinquencies on subprime mortgages. Several lenders failed. As a result, the mortgage securitisation market around the globe had almost ground to a halt by the summer of 2007. Then, in August 2007, the interest rate on the interbank market (the so-called LIBOR) increased and banks effectively stopped lending to one another – they did not know who was holding the soon-to-be-toxic MBSs.

The clogging up of the securitisation machine and the freezing of the interbank market had a major impact on Northern Rock, then the leading British mortgage bank. On 13 September 2007, it received liquidity assistance from the Bank of England. However, when news of this leaked out, its depositors mounted a run on the bank which ended only when Chancellor Alistair Darling guaranteed its deposits. This was Britain's first bank run in over 150 years. On 17 February 2008, Northern Rock was nationalised. About one month later, the US bank Bear Stearns was rescued by the Federal Reserve and taken over by JP Morgan for only a fraction of what its market value had been the previous week.

Over the next few months, mortgage delinquencies continued to soar, MBSs continued to default and banks reported ever larger losses. On 7 September 2008, the US Treasury placed Fannie Mae and Freddie Mac, two government-sponsored entities (GSEs) that had been established to increase the available mortgage finance for affordable homes, into conservatorship and injected substantial capital funds into them because of their perilous financial condition.[29] Then on 15 September Lehman Brothers filed for bankruptcy. The government refused to bail it out, believing that it was not a systemic threat and that it needed to be allowed to fail in order to reduce the moral hazard problem associated with bailing out banks. However, it appears that Hank Paulson and the Bush administration were more motivated by the prospect of a bipartisan backlash against another bailout, which they feared would be dubbed 'socialism' by those on the right and 'bailing out their friends on Wall Street' by those on the left. Allowing it to fail allowed them to rescue the system. Ultimately, Lehman was sacrificed so that Wall Street could live.[30] The following day AIG, an American multinational insurance company, received a bailout loan of $85 billion from the Federal Reserve.

AIG Financial Products had used AIG's AAA credit rating since 1998 to make money as a derivatives dealer. Its chief activity in this sphere was the issuance of credit default swaps guaranteeing the MBSs and CDOs held by banks and investors. In return for a stream of payments, it agreed to reimburse investors in the event of default.[31] This business had grown from a notional amount insured of $20 billion in 2002 to $533 billion in 2007.[32] The default of many MBSs and CDOs meant that AIG was having to pay out substantial sums on its credit default swaps – sums that it had made little provision for. The failure of AIG would have had major consequences for the solvency of many financial institutions that had bought credit default swaps from it.

Following the collapse of Lehman Brothers and AIG, the US Treasury and Federal Reserve came up with a plan to stave off the implosion of the banking system: the Troubled Assets Relief Plan (TARP). The TARP authorised expenditures of $700 billion to help the Treasury buy or insure 'toxic' assets (i.e. mortgages, MBSs and CDOs) from banks. After being initially voted down by Congress on 29 September, it was signed into law on 3 October. Within a matter of weeks, the poorly thought out and hastily put together TARP programme would be changed to provide capital, guarantees and direct support to banks. On 15 October, the US Treasury announced the TARP Capital Purchase Program, which allowed it to take up to $250 billion from TARP and inject it as capital into troubled banks. In the announcement, the Treasury stated that 9 major financial institutions had already agreed to receive capital injections.[33] A further 42 institutions participated in the programme.

Following its nationalisation of Northern Rock earlier in 2008, the UK Treasury put together a rescue package to deal with another large mortgage bank, the Bradford and Bingley, on 27 September 2008. Then, on 8 October 2008, the UK government announced three measures to relieve the ongoing financial crisis. First, it extended the Special Liquidity Scheme, whereby the Bank of England, indemnified by the Treasury, swapped Treasury bills for a bank's illiquid assets for up to 3 years. Second, the government established a fund which could be used to inject capital into banks. Third, it guaranteed interbank lending to enable banks to refinance their maturing debts. As a result of the crisis, £132.85 billion of cash was directly injected into UK banks between 2007 and 2011 and, at its peak, the Treasury's contingent liabilities were just over £1 trillion, which was 82.4 per cent of GDP.[34]

In late September and early October 2008, major banks in Belgium, France, Germany, Italy, the Netherlands, Sweden and Switzerland received capital injections and loan guarantees from their governments. Many European banks required rescue because they had invested in the AAA-rated subprime MBSs and CDOs created in the United States.[35] Some also got into trouble because of the problems on the global inter-bank market. At this stage, the Federal Reserve played a crucial role in providing dollar liquidity for European banks through its swap line facility, whereby it provided dollars to the ECB and Bank of England to help banks that had raised a lot of funding in dollars.[36]

The Irish government announced on 30 September 2008 that it was taking the very unusual step of guaranteeing virtually all the existing and future liabilities of its six domestic banks until September 2010.[37] The gross liabilities it would cover amounted to €375 billion – twice Ireland's gross national product.[38] Subsequently, on 14 December 2008, the government announced a €10 billion recapitalisation programme for Irish banks. On 15 January 2009, the now-notorious Anglo Irish Bank, which had financed a good deal of property development and speculation in Ireland, was nationalised. This was followed by the establishment of the National Asset Management Agency (NAMA) in 2009, a scheme designed to purchase about €90 billion of bad property loans from banks.

As NAMA progressed through 2009 and into 2010, it became clear that the scale of the loan losses was much greater, and therefore the recapitalisation of Irish banks would be costlier than expected. However, the international markets were more concerned about the ability of the Irish state to cover its liability guarantee and meet the ever-growing costs of fixing its banking system. This triggered large outflows of foreign money from Irish banks.[39] At the same time, the yield on Ireland's sovereign debt soared. Not only did Irish banks need bailing out, but so did Ireland. In late November 2010, the European Union and the International Monetary Fund (IMF) provided a bailout package of €85 billion (which equated to about 53 per cent of Ireland's GDP) to help recapitalise the Irish banking system.

Between 10 and 13 October 2008, the Spanish government, in order to relieve the refinancing pressures of the country's savings banks (*cajas*), established an asset purchase scheme and a debt guarantee scheme for new debt issues. Then in June 2009, it established a special purpose vehicle, the Fund for the Orderly Restructuring of the Banking Sector, which could borrow up to €100 billion to address the insolvency of many *cajas*.[40] This was carried out mainly by merging *cajas* and providing asset guarantees for those who bought insolvent ones. By the end of the restructuring process, Spain's 45 *cajas* had become 17. However, the restructuring process simply created large systemic entities where there had been none. In addition, the debt guarantee inextricably linked the creditworthiness of the Spanish government to that of the banking system. In the midst of the Eurozone crisis, where Ireland, Greece and Portugal had already received IMF and EU bailouts, this meant that in June 2012, Spain was in the situation that Ireland had been in 18 months before. International markets questioned the credibility of the government's guarantee of the banking system and as a result Spain received a €100 billion credit line from the European Union to resolve its banking woes.

CAUSES

When we looked through the ashes of the Australian Land Boom of 1888, we saw that financial markets played a major role in homes and land becoming marketable objects of speculation. The same was true in the 2000s, except the scale and global scope was so much larger. The principal reason for the increased marketability of houses was the greater availability of mortgage finance to much wider sections of the population than ever before. Furthermore, the securitisation of mortgages created highly marketable instruments which allowed investors from around the globe to speculate billions of dollars on homes in the United States, Spain and the UK.

This increase in the marketability of homes can be seen from the fact that the sales of existing homes more than doubled during the bubble. The popping of the bubble, however, had a major effect on the number of house sales. House sales in England and Wales in 2008, 2009 and 2010 were 50 per cent lower than they had been on average between 2001 and 2007.[41] In Northern Ireland, after 51,000 sales in 2006 and 38,000 in 2007, the average number of sales per annum between 2008 and 2012 (inclusive) was only 14,800.[42] In the United States, existing home sales averaged 4.3 million per annum between 2008 and 2012 (inclusive), having been about 7.1 in 2005 and 6.5 million in 2006.[43]

A bubble is not possible without the fuel of money and credit. In the case of the housing bubble, the metaphorical fuel was available in tanker loads. Economies such as China, Japan and Germany, with their export-led growth policies, recycled the earnings from their exports by sending large amounts of capital to the likes of Ireland, Spain, the United States and the United Kingdom.[44] In the case of the United States, it was estimated that just over 60 per cent of the increase in mortgage funds can be directly attributed to this money flowing in from overseas.[45]

The Eurozone had large sums of capital flowing from core nations, such as Germany, France and the Netherlands, to the infamous PIIGS (Portugal, Ireland, Italy, Greece and Spain). Most of the capital directed to Ireland and Spain was channelled through their banking systems and was used to finance the housing booms in those countries. Indeed, the adoption of the euro resulted in deeper integration of the euro-based wholesale funding market, making it much easier for Irish and Spanish banks to raise finance from other countries. This money was then lent to domestic property developers and homebuyers.[46]

One popular view of the 2008 crisis was that the flood of capital from overseas lowered the real interest rate across developed economies. However, some economists have dismissed the role of global imbalances in driving down interest rates and have suggested that loose monetary policy and low central bank interest rates were more of a problem.[47] The interest rates of the Eurozone were set to suit the core economies and, as a result, were too low for economies like Ireland and Spain. The Federal Reserve kept interest rates low after the dot-com bust and 2001 recession in order to stimulate the economy by encouraging housing starts and home sales with low mortgage rates.[48] In one sense this worked too well, because low interest rates prompted US consumers to buy houses in an unprecedented fashion.

Low interest rates, however, would not have been such a problem had they not been accompanied by such a dramatic extension of mortgage credit. The ratio of residential loans to GDP in the European Union as a whole was 36.4 in 2007; the equivalent figures for Ireland, Spain, the United Kingdom and the United States were 71.4, 59.8, 74.8 and 63.4 respectively.[49] The ratio of mortgage debt to GDP in these four countries was higher than in any other country in the world, and they all had a relatively high proportion of lower-income households with mortgages.[50] In the United States, mortgage debt climbed from $5.3 trillion in 2001 to $10.5 trillion in 2007 and mortgage debt per household rose from $91,500 in 2001 to $149,500 in 2007.[51] To put this in context, mortgage debt in the United States rose almost as much in 6 years as it had in the period from 1776 to 2000! Similarly, in Ireland, the total mortgage debt went from €34 billion in 2001 to €123 billion in 2007, which meant that mortgage debt per household increased from about €27,000 to €87,000.[52]

How was such a large increase in mortgage debt possible? As discussed above, banks and mortgage lenders substantially reduced their lending standards. The simplest way of doing this was to relax the down payment constraint on mortgages – the loan-to-value ratio. This enabled credit-constrained lower-income households to enter the housing market for the first time.[53] In the case of the United States, the subprime sector grew from 7.6 per cent of mortgage originations in 2001 to 23.5 per cent in 2006.[54] The median loan-to-value ratio of subprime mortgages originating in the United States rose from 90 per cent in 2005 to 100 per cent in the first half of 2007.[55] When comparing countries that experienced a housing bubble with those that did not, the relaxation of lending standards and securitisation is the common factor: it occurred in the United States, the United Kingdom, Ireland and Spain, but not to anywhere near the same extent in other major economies.[56]

Homes had become marketable objects of speculation and the banking system was supplying seemingly unlimited amounts of leverage to potential speculators. But to what extent did speculation exist and how widespread was it? During the housing boom, more and more people began to see houses as investments, not so much for the rental income they would produce as for their potential capital appreciation. Indeed, economists Karl Case and Robert Shiller suggest that viewing housing as an investment is a defining characteristic of a housing bubble.[57] The official report into the Irish banking crisis talks of speculators 'piling into residential and other real estate projects' and suggests that rising prices induced speculative purchases.[58] Similarly, many new builds in Spain were acquired by investors.[59]

Speculators also played a role in the US housing boom and were blamed by the popular press for the bubble.[60] Across metropolitan areas investor ownership of property was closely correlated with excess house price appreciation. In addition, there is strong evidence that the acceleration of private-label mortgage securitisation in the United States brought many flippers into the market, whose speculation had a major effect on house prices and transaction volume before the crash in 2007.[61] In an interview with the Financial Crisis Inquiry Commission in the United States, Angelo Mozilo, the former long-serving CEO of a financial corporation that collapsed during the crisis, talked of a gold rush mentality that turned ordinary people into speculators. In his evidence, he stated that 'housing prices were rising so rapidly – at a rate that I'd never seen in my 55 years in the business – that people, regular people, average people got caught up in the mania of buying a house, make $50,000 . . . and talk at a cocktail party about it'.[62]

One of the reasons people became speculators during the US boom was that they were optimistic about future house price growth.[63] A 2003 survey of people in four US metropolitan areas who had purchased houses found that they tended to buy for future price increases rather than the pleasure of living in the home.[64] Over 90 per cent of those surveyed expected house prices to at least treble in price over the next decade. These long-term expectations played a major role in raising US housing demand.[65] Those who did not wish to buy physical property could still speculate on the housing market via MBSs and CDOs. As the report of the US's Financial Crisis Inquiry Commission put it, 'a mortgage on a home in south Florida might become part of dozens of securities owned by hundreds of investors – or parts of bets owned by hundreds more'.[66]

What role did the media play in stimulating speculation? As in the dot-com boom, television played a major part by shaping the popular narrative about house prices and property investment. Docusoaps about people looking for new homes or relocating to sunnier climes began to feature in the United Kingdom in 2000 with *Location, Location, Location.*[67] The show's presenters, Phil Spencer and Kirstie Allsopp, helped buyers find the perfect home that matched their budget. The show spawned a series of spin-offs and rival shows such as *Homes Under the Hammer* and *To Buy or Not to Buy.* In the United States, *House Hunters*, which first aired in 1999, followed a similar format to *Location, Location, Location.* Twenty specials and spin-offs of the show were created throughout the 2000s.[68] *Property Ladder*, which first went out in the United Kingdom in 2001, followed amateur property developers as they tried to make a profit from buying and developing property. In the United States, *Flip That House* introduced to the viewing public the idea of property as an investment.

The official report into Ireland's banking crisis expressed the view that the media had a major effect on people's perceptions, discussions and actions with regard to the housing boom. It went on to state that the media 'enthusiastically supported households' preoccupation with property ownership'.[69] Irish newspapers became unwitting conduits for external economic experts from the financial sector who were cheerleaders for the property boom.[70] This view is supported by a cross-country study of reporting before and after the global financial crisis.[71] Because advertising revenue from traditional sources was falling, Irish papers also grew dependent on the lucrative (and increasing) income from the advertising of housing, new builds and real-estate services, who appear to have pressured them into covering the boom in a particular way.[72] The same pressures were present in Spain, where they were compounded by the government indirectly or implicitly commanding the media not to impede the boom.[73] In the UK, the number of articles covering the housing market increased by 300 per cent between 2000 and 2008, while the BBC News website increased its coverage tenfold.[74] The optimism of newspapers appears to have played a role in propagating the housing booms by stimulating speculation.

Unlike the assets at the centre of other bubbles, housing markets are very difficult if not impossible to short sell. This means that the speculation pushing house prices up could not be countered by speculators

betting on a fall in house prices. A small number of investors documented in Michael Lewis's *The Big Short* shorted the housing market by buying
credit default swaps on MBSs, which paid out when the MBSs defaulted.
In order to make these trades, however, these investors had to navigate
complex regulations, were ostracised by colleagues and in some cases
risked their jobs as fund managers by going against the herd – perhaps
explaining why there were so few of them.[75]

What was the spark that converted ordinary people into property
speculators? The answer to this question can be found in government
housing policies. At the end of the 1990s, Western democracies faced
a major challenge. Wealth inequality had grown inexorably since the
1970s, as the economic gains of globalisation bypassed the lower classes
of society. As well as undermining the stability of democracies, politicians
needed the votes of those who had seen their incomes and prospects
stagnate. Many democracies, particularly those of a more social democratic bent, used fiscal measures to deal with inequality, providing social
housing and generous entitlement programmes. Ireland, Spain, the
United Kingdom and the United States, however, took a different
approach, using housing policy to encourage the bottom-income quintiles to buy houses, while incentivising the financial sector to lend to these
quintiles. In all four countries, this strategy was adopted by the main
parties of both the left and right wing.

The taxes and growth generated by the housing boom enabled local
and national governments to spend more on health, welfare and education, without needing to raise taxation.[76] In 2006, the tax take in Ireland
from house sales was about 17 per cent of total tax revenue – a decade
earlier, it had constituted only 4 per cent of total tax revenue.[77] The UK's
Parliamentary Commission on Banking Standards stated that successive
administrations during the boom were 'dazzled by the economic growth
and tax revenues promised from the banking sector'.[78] This made governments very reluctant to burst the bubble; if anything they wanted to
keep the party going for as long as possible.

The Clinton and Bush administrations had a very explicit housing
policy – they wanted to increase the number of low-income homeowners,
particularly among minorities. For example, in 2002, Bush stated that his
administration wanted by 2010 to increase the number of minority

homeowners by 5.5 million.[79] The ostensible reason for this was that homeownership gave people greater independence, hope and a stake in the future of the country, making for better citizens and stronger communities.[80]

How was this policy goal implemented? In 1992 Congress passed the Federal Housing Enterprises Financial Safety and Soundness Act. This legislation required the Department of Housing and Urban Development (HUD) to mandate affordable housing goals for Freddie Mac and Fannie Mae. After 1992, this was primarily achieved by creating a secondary mortgage market via securitisation. HUD increased the funding that the GSEs could lend to low-income buyers from 42 to 50 per cent in 2000, rising to 56 per cent in 2004.[81] By 2007, 20 per cent had to be lent to very low-income individuals. These mandates had two effects. First, the GSEs had to lower their underwriting standards substantially to meet these mandates. Second, because Freddie and Fannie set the national underwriting standards through buying conforming loans, they dragged down the underwriting standards of private lenders.[82]

As well as HUD's mandates for the GSEs, from the 1990s onwards, the 1977 Community Reinvestment Act (CRA), which had up to then been moribund, became a key part of the drive for affordable housing. The CRA was originally passed to prevent redlining, i.e. the systematic denial of mortgage loans to districts with high ethnic minority populations. Later, when US banks wanted to merge after the removal of branching restrictions, they first had to gain the approval of the Federal Reserve Board. One of the tests applied by the Federal Reserve was good citizenship, i.e. banks' service to their local communities – part of which consisted of compliance with the CRA. Consequently, as part of the creation of large megabanks, there were commitments of about $3.5 trillion dollars of CRA lending between 1993 and 2007.[83]

The Financial Crisis Inquiry Commission could not come to a unanimous view on the causes of the crisis in the United States. The majority finding was that the HUD's mandates and CRA had little to do with the boom and subsequent crash.[84] However, Peter Wallison's dissenting view was that government homeownership policies had been the chief cause of the crisis.[85] He pointed to the data to make his point. By

2008, 27 million mortgages (50 per cent of all mortgages) in the United States were subprime or Alt-A (between prime and subprime) loans. The GSEs guaranteed 12 million of these, the Federal Housing Association guaranteed a further 4.8 million and private banks guaranteed 2.2 million under the CRA.

These particular mechanisms did not exist in Ireland, Spain or the United Kingdom. However, the housing policy among most politicians in these three economies was to increase owner-occupation.[86] In Spain and Ireland there was a long-standing bias in government policy towards ownership, meaning that these two countries had some of the highest homeownership rates in the Western world.[87] Concomitantly, they also had the lowest rates of social housing. After various fiscal crises in the 1980s caused the demise of direct government support for homeownership and social housing, the governments of Spain and Ireland increasingly relied on their deregulated financial systems to provide homes for those on low incomes.[88]

Similarly, the stated policy of successive UK governments from 1980 onwards was to encourage homeownership among the lower classes. In passing the 1980 Housing Bill, which gave social housing occupants the right to buy their home, Michael Heseltine, the then Secretary of State for the Environment, stated that 'there is in this country a deeply ingrained desire for home ownership. The Government believe that this spirit should be fostered'.[89] This spirit was still being fostered 25 years later. As Lord Turner, the head of the UK's financial regulator during the crisis, put it, if the Financial Services Authority had acted to curb the expansion of bank credit in the 2000s, politicians would have accused them of 'holding back the extension of mortgage credit to ordinary people' and 'preventing the democratisation of home ownership'.[90]

Banks got on board with the affordability mandate of their governments because the financial system was deregulated, meaning that they could lend to subprime and less-than-prime borrowers. As well as facing no restrictions on their lending activity from bank supervisors, banks did not have to hold much in the way of regulatory capital against mortgages. Almost no capital had to be held against mortgage-backed securities which carried a AAA credit rating from one of the three credit-rating agencies.[91] In fact, the regulatory system across the developed world at the time encouraged banks to hold the securities of the GSEs and other MBSs rather than originated mortgages or commercial loans.

This is not to say that the GSEs, banks and property developers were innocent bystanders being led astray by the government. According to the Parliamentary Commission on Banking Standards, politicians in the United Kingdom tended to succumb to bank lobbying.[92] In Ireland and Spain, there was a deep and unhealthy symbiotic relationship between property developers, banks and politicians, which strengthened as the housing boom progressed.[93] Irish property developers became the 'sugar daddy' of politicians, and Irish banks used their growing influence to press for light-touch regulation.[94]

In the United States, the lobbying efforts of the real estate and financial industry are part of the public record. This industry influenced politicians via campaign contributions and direct lobbying efforts. In real terms, between 1992 and 2008, its campaign contributions increased threefold and were inclined to flow to whichever party controlled Congress.[95] Between 1999 and 2008, the industry became one of the leading contributors to campaign war chests, giving more than $1 billion.[96] In terms of reported lobbying efforts, this industry spent a staggering $2.7 billion during these 9 years, a near-threefold increase over the previous period.[97] During these years, Fannie and Freddie, in terms of dollars spent, were the second and third largest lobbying institutions in the sector.[98] According to the Financial Crisis Inquiry Commission, these efforts exerted pressure on legislators to weaken regulatory constraints. A study of the effect of lobbying on the legislative outcomes of regulation bills in Congress found that lobbying caused legislators to switch their stance in favour of deregulation.[99]

CONSEQUENCES

The housing bubble of the 2000s is a perfect example of an economically and socially destructive bubble. When the bubble burst, the fall in GDP per capita across all four economies was substantial (Table 10.3). Notably, Spain's GDP per capita continued to fall until 2013, by which time it was 10.6 per cent below its 2007 level.[100] In each case it took a long

TABLE 10.3 *Post-bubble economic malaise in Ireland, Spain, United Kingdom and United States*[101]

	Fall in GDP per capita between 2007 and 2009 (%)	Year when GDP per capita returned to 2007 levels	Unemployment rate (%)			Youth unemployment rate (%)	
			Q1 2007	Q4 2009	Peak (Year)	2007	Peak
Ireland	11.2	2014	5.70	13.59	15.88 (2012)	9.15	30.75
Spain	4.9	2018	8.09	18.83	26.25 (2013)	18.10	55.48
United Kingdom	6.1	2015	5.48	7.70	8.19 (2011)	14.25	21.25
United States	4.8	2014	4.50	9.93	9.93 (2009)	10.53	18.42

time for GDP per capita to return to its 2007 level – over a decade in the case of Spain. The recession in the United Kingdom was the longest of the previous two centuries, and only the recession of the 1920s was deeper.

One indicator of the human cost of the post-bubble recession was the very high unemployment rates, particularly among young people and especially in Ireland and Spain. As can be seen from Table 10.3, at their post-crisis peak, youth unemployment rates, which measure unemployment in the 15–24 age bracket, ranged from 18.4 per cent in the United States to 55.5 per cent in Spain. The young were paying the price for a housing bubble in which they had not participated. Another indicator of the human cost, self-reported well-being, declined sharply during the financial crisis, with reports of higher levels of stress and anxiety.[102]

The collapse of the housing bubble had a major effect on families: many became homeless and had to interrupt their children's education.[103] In the United States, 8 million homes were foreclosed and about \$7 trillion in home equity was erased.[104] In 2011, 11 million properties (23 per cent of all mortgaged properties) in the United States had negative equity, rising to 70 per cent of homeowners in some areas with less salubrious zip codes.[105] In the United Kingdom, 8 per cent of mortgage holders had negative equity in 2011, representing some £250 billion of wealth wiped out since 2007. However, there were great regional differences: in parts of northern England and Northern Ireland, 19 to 28 per cent of mortgage holders had negative equity.[106] By 2014, things deteriorated even further for Northern Ireland, when it was esti-mated that 41 per cent of mortgages were in negative equity.[107] By 2012, 37 per cent of Irish households with a mortgage had negative equity and €43 billion in home equity had been erased by the crash.[108]

Given that the policy of governments in the four economies was to extend homeownership to the poor and address inequality, it is helpful to explore how the housing boom and bust affected homeownership rates and inequality. In Ireland, Spain, the United Kingdom and the United States between 2005 and 2015, homeownership rates fell by 8.2, 8.1, 5.7 and 5.2 per cent.[109] These steep falls did not occur in other economies. Even on its own narrow terms, the policy of extending homeownership was a total failure: in the case of Ireland, the United Kingdom and the United States, homeownership rates in 2015 were below those in 1990. The fall in house prices in the United States and elsewhere disproportio-nately affected poor homeowners and wiped out most of their wealth.[110] In other words, the credit-fuelled housing boom ultimately amplified the inequality it was supposed to address.

The housing boom and bust left behind ghost estates, with vacant properties, husks of houses, soil heaps, stationary cranes, and abandoned diggers and cement mixers.[111] In October 2011 there were 2,879 unfin-ished housing estates in Ireland; in 777 of these, the majority of the units were either vacant or incomplete.[112] Ghost estates stand as monuments not to human folly or irrational exuberance, but as memorials to the folly of governments who thought that easy credit and homeownership were the answers to deeper social and economic problems. Unfortunately, in contrast to other memorials, these will not be preserved to warn future generations.

Central banks around the globe continued to use extraordinary mea-sures to address the global financial crisis for the following decade and more. Interest rates were held at close to zero for the next 10 years, historically without precedent. In addition, central banks engaged in what was euphemistically called quantitative easing, whereby they created money to buy government bonds and other securities. The combination of quantitative easing and low interest rates distorted financial markets and may have resulted in overvalued equity and housing markets as investors reached for yield.

The most significant effects of the housing bubble and subsequent financial crisis, however, may yet result from the political fallout. The incompetence and corruption that led to the crisis, coupled with the utter failure of the political system to hold any of those responsible to account, resulted in a widespread loss of faith in the political classes. As in the aftermath of the Great Depression, many voters turned to populist and nationalist politicians. The election of Donald Trump and Brexit both have their roots in the housing bubble of the 2000s. This may ultimately prove to be the most substantial and long-lived effect of the Subprime Bubble.

The Subprime Bubble taught us many lessons. Most notably, we were reminded that bubbles do have major negative economic, social and political consequences – not all bubbles are benign or socially useful. Three things combined to make the Subprime Bubble so destructive. It had a political spark. It had seemingly endless amounts of fuel provided by poorly regulated banks. And it turned an economically crucial asset, the family home, into a highly marketable object of speculation. Another lesson of the Subprime Bubble is that, although central banks were powerless to prevent the boom from occurring, they played a major role in the clean-up operation after the bursting of the boom. However, in so doing, they saved reckless banks and distorted asset markets with their extraordinary monetary policy. The long-term effects of this clean-up might therefore make the next bubble more likely – and more dangerous.

CHAPTER 11

Casino Capitalism with Chinese Characteristics

When the economy is doing well, the stock market drops. When the economy is doing poorly, the stock market shoots up. It seems like when the economy is doing well, we all go to work and earn money. When the economy is doing poorly, we all gather in the village entrance to gamble.

Anonymous social media post[1]

Against all reason, everyone was pumping stocks in China because the government advised them to buy stocks.

Marshall Meyer[2]

Barely 20 years old and poorly regulated, the [Chinese] stock market still has more in common with the gambling casinos of Macau than with global exchanges in western capitals such as New York, London or Tokyo.

David Pilling[3]

THE FIRST BUBBLES WHICH WE LOOKED AT IN THIS BOOK, those of 1720, occurred in aristocratic regimes. Bubbles were invented in this era by the ruling elite in the struggle for internal legitimacy and empire. Fast forward 300 years and the rulers of China, an autocratic regime, were struggling to build an empire and secure internal legitimacy. To do so, they created two bubbles in under a decade. China's rulers had learned from past bubbles that in order to have a bubble, there needs to be marketability, speculation and leverage. In the space of 20 years, China went from having almost no marketability to heavily controlled marketability and then near-free marketability. At the same time, China went from having virtually no middle class to having the world's largest middle class. This middle class, looking to provide for their future, became the new speculating class. Finally, by introducing huge amounts of credit into financial markets in the form of margin trading, China then allowed investors to speculate with other people's money. The playbook from nearly three centuries of bubble experiences was played out in China in just over a decade.

In May 2015, we experienced one of China's bubbles at first hand during a visit to the city of Shenzhen to meet alumni of our university. At this time, China was in the grip of what appeared to be an investment mass hysteria. During a dinner with a former PhD student who was working as an asset manager for one of China's leading investment banks, we were told of how stock prices were divorced from reality and how many new dubious technology companies were floating on the Shenzhen Stock Exchange. Everyone in Shenzhen was talking about the stock market – even the taxi drivers and bellhops.

The growth of the new China is encapsulated in the city of Shenzhen. In 1978, it was a small town with about 30,000 residents; by 2015, it had over 11 million inhabitants. What had caused this transformation? In 1978, under the leadership of the reformist Deng Xiaoping, the Chinese government initiated its policy of 'socialism with Chinese characteristics', which gradually introduced markets into the existing communist structure. As part of this reform, Shenzhen was designated a special economic zone in which economic activities were largely driven by market forces, leaving it free to attract foreign investment, technology and companies. The main purpose of the zone was to produce manufactured goods for export.

When Deng Xiaoping first came to power, China was an economic backwater, with a GDP per capita less than one-thirteenth that of Western Europe. But its subsequent economic transformation was unparalleled in economic history. Its GDP grew at an average of 9.7 per cent per annum between 1978 and 2015, compared to 2.7 per cent per annum in the United States, making it the second largest economy in the world. Its real GDP per capita in 1978 was about \$156, but, by 2015, it had reached \$8,069 – a 51-fold increase.[4] This economic growth resulted in an unprecedented reduction of poverty. Nearly 90 per cent of the Chinese population in 1981 were living below the poverty line (defined as $1.90 per day at 2011 prices). In 2015 only 0.7 per cent of the population lived below this threshold. Similarly, infant mortality fell from 52.6 per 1,000 live births in 1978 to 9.2 in 2015. China's astounding economic development resulted in the creation of the world's largest middle class, which is estimated to consist of 400 million people.

The reform and opening-up policy of Deng Xiaoping moved pragmatically and gradually – summarised by Xiaoping himself as 'crossing the river by touching stones' in a famous speech that he made before the Communist Party Plenary in 1978. As well as setting up special economic zones, farmers were given land cultivation rights and were empowered to make their own decisions. The management of state-owned enterprises (SOEs) was decentralised from central to local governments and SOE managers were given more autonomy.[5] The 1980s saw the rise of town- and village-owned enterprises (TVEs) – market-oriented businesses which were typically under the control of local authorities. These enterprises were labour-intensive and benefited from the large increase in labour supply that followed the agricultural reforms. TVEs in the 1980s played a major role in China's growth.[6]

The first step towards a more capitalistic system was taken in 1990 when China began to incorporate and privatise the SOEs and TVEs. When SOEs were converted to limited liability corporations, shares were issued to their own employees and other SOEs. The government, both central and local, maintained large ownership stakes in these corporations either directly or indirectly through state-controlled 'legal persons' (i.e. companies or institutions). Some shares were also issued to the public, and so the Shanghai and Shenzhen Stock Exchanges were created in 1990 and 1991 respectively. These reforms thus introduced some marketability, but it was limited and highly regulated.

The subsequent development of the Chinese stock market can be seen from Figure 11.1. Between 1990 and 2005, the number of companies listed on these two exchanges rose from just 8 to 1,341. However, even in 2005, the largest shareholder in 63.7 per cent of these companies was the state, either in the guise of the central or local government, or as central or local government legal persons.[7] Even when the largest owner was an

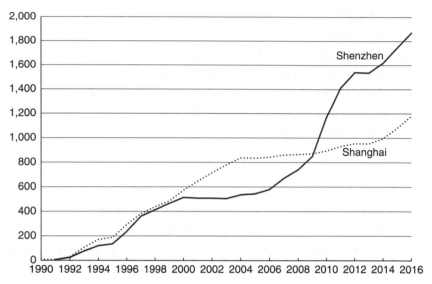

Figure 11.1 Number of listed companies on Shanghai and Shenzhen stock exchanges, 1990–2016[8]

individual or a non-government legal person, the state was usually the second largest owner or had a substantial stake in the company. Up until 2005, the shares owned by the state and by non-state legal persons were not tradeable on the stock exchanges – only the 'A' shares owned by individuals could be traded. Legal persons and the state could transfer their shares only with the express permission of the China Securities Regulatory Commission (CSRC). This meant that in 2005, 62 per cent of shares in listed corporations were almost untradeable.[9]

In December 2001, China took a major step towards integrating into the global economy when it joined the World Trade Organization. As part of the terms of its accession, however, its listed companies were banned from receiving state aid and exposed to foreign competition.[10] In an effort to iron out inefficiencies at these companies before they were out-competed, the government announced a further round of privatisation in which non-tradeable shares were converted into tradeable ones, allowing the state to transfer more of its ownership into private hands. However, this reform was abandoned when investors, fearing that an increase in the quantity of tradeable shares would undermine the value of their holdings, began to panic sell.

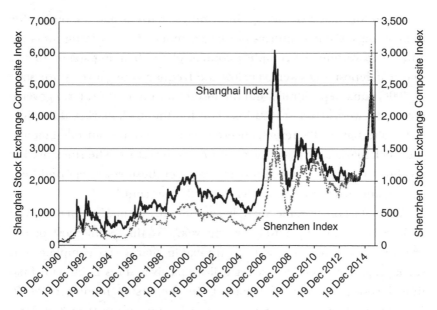

Figure 11.2 Shanghai Stock Exchange Composite Index and Shenzhen Stock Exchange Composite Index, 1990–2015[11]

After 2001, the stock market performed abysmally: the Shenzhen stock index, shown in Figure 11.2, fell by 52.7 per cent between July 2001 and July 2005. This failure was particularly stark in the context of China's spectacular economic growth, which averaged 10.5 per cent per annum between 2003 and 2005. In response, in 2005 the government attempted once again to make non-tradeable shares tradeable. This time, however, the reform was accompanied by measures to prevent the panic selling that had derailed their earlier effort. Non-tradeable shareholders were required to compensate tradeable shareholders for adverse price effects, usually through a transfer of shares.[12] A lock-up period of 1 year was placed on non-tradeable shares, during which they could not be sold, and limits were placed on how many could be sold in the 2 years after the expiry of the lock-up period.[13] But in order for this second round of privatisation to be successful, the authorities also needed to manufacture an ebullient stock market.

They thus set about attracting money to the stock market to push up prices, a task which turned out to be quite straightforward. The absence of a developed social security system meant that people had to make provision for their own old age, but Chinese citizens had few outlets for their savings. Capital controls prevented money from moving overseas, and the government's complete control of the banking system meant that real deposit rates were very low and frequently negative. At the start of 2006, bank deposit rates and the discount rate on short-term government debt were at a post-1991 low. This left the stock market as the only viable alternative. Therefore, cheered on by the state-controlled media, the stock market attracted more and more investors. The stock market was buoyed further as 2006 progressed when businesses reported high profits, and economic growth reached 12.7 per cent.[14]

At the start of 2007, the Shanghai and Shenzhen markets were up 130 and 98 per cent respectively on the year. By this point most of the transition from non-tradeable to tradeable shares was complete, but stock prices continued to rise regardless, partly as a result of many first-time investors entering the market. In the first 4 months of 2007, 10 million new retail investors opened accounts, more than had done so in the previous 4 years combined.[15] Many new investors were complete novices: the *New York Times* reported that shopkeepers, maids, farmers and watermelon hawkers gave up their jobs to become day traders.[16] Some estimates suggest that one in ten citizens was directly involved in stock trading and that the 7 per cent of Chinese citizens' savings invested in the stock market in 2005 had risen to over 30 per cent by the end of 2007.[17] Many investors had bizarre investment philosophies, choosing stocks at random or because a stock price had reached a 'lucky' number.[18] For some, the stock market was the only legal outlet for a gambling habit, since casinos and betting were illegal.

At the end of May, Zhou Xiaochuan, the head of China's central bank, warned that the market was overvalued and raised interest rates. This was quickly followed by an increase in the stamp duty on share trading in an effort to dampen trading activity. However, after several sharp falls, the state-controlled media reassured investors by hinting at state action to support shares if need be.[19] The market once again began to climb. By October 2007, the Shanghai index had risen by 412 per cent since the end of 2005, while the Shenzhen index had risen by 425 per cent.

Thereafter, however, the stock market began a precipitous decline, steadily losing value over the next year despite several attempts by the government to prop it up or let it deflate gently. By the end of July 2008, well before the world knew the extent of the problems in US, UK and EU banks, the Shanghai and Shenzhen markets had fallen by 53 and 43 per cent from their levels in October 2007. The chaos of the subsequent global financial crises undoubtedly contributed to their further falls – by the end of October 2008, the two markets had fallen 71 and 68 per cent respectively from their peaks.[20] These falls may also have been accentuated by the end of the lock-ups on the billions of formerly non-tradeable shares.

The stock market crash had little immediate effect on the Chinese economy, of which the stock market was a relatively small part. There was no financial crisis: banks were not heavily exposed to the crash, and even if they had been, they were safely under the ownership of a government that was never going to allow them to fail. There was, however, a consequence for the funding of new firms and new projects: investors' disenchantment with the stock market made it much more difficult to raise equity finance. As a result, new technology firms struggled to get off the ground, while most established companies reverted to debt finance.[21]

Following the global financial crisis in 2008, the Chinese authorities, fearing a fall in the Western demand for Chinese exports, engaged in a massive stimulus programme whereby banks and shadow banks began lending to corporations, small businesses and individuals.[22] This has been described by some economists as one of the greatest relaxations of monetary policy ever undertaken.[23] As a result, China's non-government debt rose from 116 per cent of GDP in 2007 to 227 per cent in 2014. By 2014, the Chinese authorities were worried about the level of debt and the precarious nature of the shadow banking system, as well as the inability of banks to lend to businesses. They were also concerned about a slowing economic growth rate (7.4 per cent in 2014 and 6.9 per cent in 2015) and the threat that this posed to their political legitimacy and stability.[24]

To address these issues, the authorities engaged in further stimulus by engineering another stock market bubble. First, at the third plenum of the 18th Communist Party Conference in November 2013, President Xi announced plans to liberalise the banking system and stock market in order to give market allocation a decisive role. These plans largely consisted of overhauling corporate governance at public companies and reducing the role of local government in running them.[25] The government then reformed the stock market to reduce trading costs and encourage companies to seek a stock market listing.[26] It also set up the Shanghai–Hong Kong Connect, introduced in November 2014, which effectively invited foreign investors to invest in China. Finally, monetary policy was eased even further, starting with the reduction of the central bank's benchmark rate in November 2014. The monetary stimulus was given further impetus in February 2015 when the required reserve ratio for banks was reduced. The benchmark rate was cut again at the start of March the same year.

In order to attract retail investors, the state-controlled press, including the *People's Daily*, ran laudatory editorials extolling the virtues of the stock market, explaining how its performance was a sign of present and future economic prosperity, and describing stocks as 'carriers of the China dream'.[27] This propaganda mill went into overdrive to encourage people to put their savings into the stock market.[28] For example, when the stock market fell 8 per cent on 10 December 2014, the *China Securities Journal* came out strongly with the view that the bull market had much further to go.[29] When the Shanghai Stock Exchange Composite Index broke through the 4,000-points level in April 2015, the *People's Daily* ran an editorial suggesting that this was only the beginning of a bull market.[30] The state even reached into the social media domain, by paying internet commentators (purportedly RMB 3.50 or $0.50 per post) to comment favourably on the economy and stock market.[31]

As can be seen from Figure 11.2, the Shanghai and Shenzhen stock markets started to rise in July 2014, accelerating in response to the interest rate cut of November 2014. When the two indexes peaked on 12 June 2015, the Shanghai market had appreciated by 152 per cent since the end of June 2014, while the Shenzhen market had appreciated by 185 per cent.

The rise of stock prices lowered financing costs for listed companies and enabled them to repair their balance sheets by issuing more equity and reducing their debt. This has led some commentators to refer to the 2015 bubble as the world's largest debt-to-equity swap.[32] However, rising stock prices also revived the moribund new issue market – the CSRC permitted IPOs, which had been accumulating since 2011, to go ahead.[33]

Figure 11.1 shows that the number of listed firms on the Shanghai market grew from 953 in 2013 to 1,182 by 2016, while the number of listed firms on the Shenzhen market grew from 1,536 to 1,870. This was accompanied by a substantial rise in the number of corporate securities, which went from 2,786 to 9,647 in Shanghai and 2,328 to 4,481 in Shenzhen.[34] As a result of new IPOs and seasoned equity offerings, the number of shares on the Shanghai market grew from 2.5 to 3.3 trillion between 2013 and 2016, and on the Shenzhen market it went from 0.8 trillion to 1.6 trillion. The increase in companies and stock issues was primarily driven by new technology companies and attempts by SOEs in non-essential sectors to restructure, merge and divest to private shareholders.

New IPOs often generated a great deal of excitement. For example, the shares in the Beijing Baofeng Technology Company, an internet video platform, were 291 times oversubscribed in March 2015, and its first-day return was 44 per cent – the maximum first-day increase permitted by the regulator.[35] Thereafter its stock price increased by 10 per cent every day for 2 months, 10 per cent being the maximum daily increase permitted by the CSRC. Its share price increased 42-fold in those 2 months. In an attempt to cash in on excitement about new technology, 80 listed companies changed their name in the first 5 months of 2015 to give themselves more of a hi-tech aura.[36] For example, Kemian Wood Industry shifted from wooden floors to online gaming and was rebranded as Zeus Entertainment.[37] It was later accused of fabricating stories in order to inflate its share price. Similarly, a hotel was rebranded as a high-speed rail network, a ceramics manufacturer as a clean-energy company and a fireworks manufacturer as a peer-to-peer lender.

The first indication that the bubble would soon burst came on 28 May, when the Shanghai market fell by 6.5 per cent, its largest 1-day fall in 15 years, and the Shenzhen market fell by 5.5 per cent. These falls would have been greater had it not been for the rule that individual stocks on the Shanghai and Shenzhen markets could fall by no more than 10 per cent in any given day – 260 stocks on the Shanghai market hit that limit on 28 May.[38] But the market recovered quickly, reaching an all-time high on Friday 12 June. The following Monday, however, the rout began, and the Shanghai and Shenzhen composite indexes fell by 13.3 and 12.7 per cent respectively in one week.

Three events had converged to trigger the crash. First, regulators had moved to clamp down on out-of-control margin lending, fearing that the market was excessively leveraged. Second, at the start of June, monetary policy was tightened, presaging an increase in the Shanghai Inter-Bank Offering Rate. Third, on 10 June, the international index provider MSCI declined to include Chinese shares, thus preventing a potential $50 billion of foreign funds from flowing into the Chinese stock market.[39]

Front-page commentaries in the state-controlled press urged investors not to panic, and at the beginning of the following week the markets steadied.[40] However, this stabilisation was short-lived, and the Shanghai and Shenzhen markets fell by 7.4 and 7.9 per cent respectively on Friday 26 June; on the Shanghai market, 2,049 stocks hit the 10 per cent limit.[41] By this date, the two markets had fallen by nearly 20 per cent in two weeks. The following day, the central bank responded with the extraordinary step of cutting its benchmark interest rate by 0.25 per cent and its required reserve ratio by 0.5 per cent.

Even these measures, however, were still insufficient to stop the sell-off: when the markets reopened on Monday 29 June, Shanghai fell 3.3 per cent and Shenzhen 7.9 per cent. The CSRC responded by introducing a series of measures aimed at encouraging people to buy stocks. It allowed investors to use their homes and other real assets as collateral to borrow money to invest in stocks, it pledged to crack down on market manipulators, it lowered settlement fees on the two stock exchanges, and it threatened to punish negative reporting in the media.[42] But at the end of the week, the Shanghai and Shenzhen markets had fallen by a further 12.1 and 16.2 per cent respectively, and were 28.6 and 33.2 per cent below their 12 June peaks.

Between the market's close on Friday 3 July and its reopening on Monday 6 July, the CSRC made a further attempt to arrest the stock market's rapid decline.[43] First, it suspended forthcoming IPOs. Second, in order to supply capital markets with liquidity, it announced that the China Securities Finance Corporation (CSF), a state-owned lender to securities companies, would have its capital quadrupled to RMB 100 billion and would have access to funds from the central bank to buy shares on the open market. This transformed the CSF into an asset manager tasked with buying stocks to stabilise the market. Third, it announced a restriction on futures trading, a clampdown on 'malicious shorting' and punishments for negative news media reporting. Fourth, the CSRC persuaded 21 leading brokerages and 25 major mutual funds to use both their funds and influence to stabilise the market.

Yet even these measures were ineffective: after a short-lived rebound on the Monday, the market continued its precipitous fall, potentially endangering the wider Chinese financial system. China's Premier Li Keqiang and Vice-premier Ma Kai intervened at this juncture to throw the weight of the Party behind the rescue effort.[44] After the market closed on 8 July, a co-ordinated series of measures was announced. First, the central bank categorically stated that it would provide liquidity to the CSF to buy shares. Second, the CSF started purchasing small stocks as well as blue chips. Third, large shareholders and senior managers, many of whom had cashed out heavily in the months before the bubble burst, were ordered to buy back 10 to 20 per cent of shares sold in the previous 6 months.[45] Fourth, the bank regulator announced that it would allow banks to make loans with stocks as collateral. Fifth, the insurance regulator increased the proportion of assets that insurance companies could invest in stocks. Sixth, the Ministry of Finance promised to do whatever it took to protect market stability. Seventh, the Ministry of Public Security announced that it was going to prosecute 'evil' short sellers. Eighth, state-owned enterprises were ordered not to sell shares, and 292 committed themselves to buying their own stocks. Finally, the government used its propaganda machine to talk up stocks. The *People's Daily* ran an editorial declaring that 'after the rain and storms, rainbows appear'.[46] On 10 July, the graduands of Tsinghua University, one of China's most prestigious universities, were instructed to chant loudly at the start of their graduation ceremony, 'Revive the A shares, benefit the people, revive the A shares, benefit the people.'[47]

The result of all these measures was that by the end of July the market had recovered some of its losses. The Chinese authorities soon found, however, that it was much easier to inflate a bubble than to prevent it from bursting. In late August and early September, partly as a result of restrictions on 'evil' short sellers drying up liquidity, the market began its final descent.[48] By 15 September, 3 months after its peak, the Shanghai market was down 46.8 per cent and the Shenzhen market 56.6 per cent. These broad composite indexes, however, mask the severity of the crash for smaller and newer stocks, many of which temporarily suspended trading during the crash.

Just as in 2007, the crash of the Chinese stock market did not result in a financial crisis. It also appears to have had little effect on the real economy. Growth did slow after 2015, but it was slowing well before the stock market crash. If anything, the bubble may have helped China hit its growth target in 2015 and temporarily conceal the fact that economic growth was slowing down.[49] However, the politically driven bubble and heavy-handed efforts to avert the crash called into question the credibility of China's efforts to start using free markets to allocate capital.

Another similarity with 2007 was the entry of millions of novices into the stock market. Ordinary Chinese citizens, encouraged by government propaganda and a belief that the government would not let the market collapse, ploughed their savings into stocks. To meet this demand, brokerage offices popped up around the country, with several firms struggling to process the huge demand for new trading accounts.[50] By 2015 there were about 90 million individual investors – more than there were members of the Communist Party. Because institutional investors and professional money managers were uncommon in China, these individual investors accounted for about 90 per cent of all the daily stock market transactions in 2015.[51] The growth of interest in investment from ordinary citizens during the bubble is illustrated by the 30 million new trading accounts opened by individual investors in the first 5 months of 2015 – 12 million of them opened in May alone.[52]

Many of these novices were uneducated – surveys at the time suggested that two-thirds of investors had not completed high school.[53] Many took incredibly naive approaches to investment. One newcomer, Vector Yang, simply picked stocks the way he picked vegetables, buying the cheapest ones at random.[54] Another, Ginger Zennge, bought stocks on 15 June, the day the bubble popped, because it happened to coincide with President Xi's birthday.[55]

During the boom, there were media stories of grandmothers – the so-called 'aunties' – making large returns on the stock market. The 'aunties' gathered in brokerage offices during the day, watched the stock price charts change, ate their packed lunch and placed stock orders. One auntie, a Ms Zhang, said in 2015 that 'the Chinese stock market is full of small potatoes like us. You make 10 yuan in the stock market, it means you can have a nice meal today'.[56] The aunties were usually more sophisticated in their approach to stock picking than Vector Yang or Ginger Zengge – they relied on a mixture of rumours, numerology and feng shui to help them choose.[57] At the younger end of the spectrum, a survey by the Chinese state media estimated that 31 per cent of undergraduate students invested in stocks during the bubble, often using the money their parents had given them to live on. Like so many older investors, these undergraduates believed that 'even though there exists risks and bubbles in China's share market, the state is able to maintain its health to prevent the collapse'.[58]

CAUSES

Both the 2007 and 2015 bubbles were created and sustained by the government, but the reasons for the inception of the bubble were different on each occasion. In 2007, the Chinese authorities were attempting to further privatise listed companies by converting their non-tradeable state-owned shares into tradeable ones that could be sold to private shareholders. In order to persuade individual investors to purchase these shares, the state manufactured a bubble in stocks. In 2015, the issue facing the Chinese state was a different one – how to unwind the huge stimulus it had launched following the global financial crisis in 2008 while keeping economic growth above the politically acceptable 7 per cent level.

Engineering the 2007 bubble was easy, because the repressed financial system had given China's middle classes very little choice over what to do with their abundant savings – they could either deposit their money in a government-owned bank that paid interest below the rate of inflation, or they could invest in stocks.[59] Although margin finance had not yet been legalised, in 2007 China's Banking Regulatory Commission suggested that individuals had been using car and home loans and credit card borrowings to invest in the stock market.[60]

However, given that Chinese investors had been duped once before, the amount of credit necessary to inflate the market after 2007 had to be much greater. Margin trading was permitted in China for the first time in 2010; after a pilot period, the number of constituent securities which could be sold on margin increased from 90 to 280 at the end of December 2011.[61] Restrictions on which individuals could obtain margin loans were weakened after 2011, and the huge credit stimulus following the global financial crisis meant that brokerages had all the liquidity they could want.[62] In addition, interest rate cuts by the central bank and deposit rates below inflation encouraged savers to search for higher returns elsewhere.

By 2014, licensed security companies were permitted to grant margin loans on a leverage ratio of 2:1, i.e. every investor could borrow RMB 200 to buy stocks for every RMB 100 in hand. Individuals could obtain margin loans only if they had cash or securities worth RMB 500,000 (about $70,000 at the time) and if they had had a share trading account for 6 months or more. However, the run-up to 2014 saw the rise of unofficial or shadow margin lending through peer-to-peer online lending companies and money-matching firms. Shadow margin lenders were particularly popular with small investors because they imposed no requirements or capital thresholds. In addition, investors could use unofficial margin finance to buy shares that were not on the approved CRSC list of stocks suitable for margin lending. They also allowed investors to borrow more: the maximum leverage ratio at shadow margin lenders was typically 5:1. In order to compete, official brokerages lowered the qualification criteria for opening margin accounts.[63]

The scale of margin lending in 2015 was unprecedented in the history of stock markets – it was estimated that it supported between 20 and 25 per cent of China's stock market capitalisation.[64] Between October 2014 and June 2015, the amount of margin loans increased fourfold, from RMB 698 billion ($104 billion) to RMB 2.7 trillion ($404 billion).[65] The shadow margin lending sector was small until the stock market started rising in 2014, but by the peak of the bubble, it constituted between 55 and 75 per cent of all margin lending.[66] The proliferation of margin calls explains why the market fell so quickly in 2015 and why government attempts to shore the market up were largely fruitless. Just as in the United States in 1929, the fact that the bubble was fuelled by margin lending made the crash much more rapid and dramatic.

Marketability changed fundamentally in China in both the 2007 and 2015 bubbles; the entire basis of the 2007 bubble had been a large-scale conversion of non-tradeable shares into tradeable shares. In early 2014, trading costs were substantially reduced after President Xi's announcement at the third plenum. The number of brokerage offices subsequently mushroomed, making it much easier for Chinese citizens to buy and sell shares. Furthermore, as in the United States in the 1920s, the widespread availability of margin lending and the rise of unofficial margin lending from 2014 onwards made stocks much more marketable to a wider cross-section of people. The effect of increased marketability and the excitement generated during the bubbles can be seen from Figure 11.3, which shows the average daily turnover value on the two stock exchanges. In the year before each bubble there was an increase in turnover value, and during each bubble there was a large increase in the volume of trading.

Speculation was rife in the Chinese stock market in both 2007 and 2015. As documented above, millions of novice investors were drawn into the market during the boom phase of the two bubbles, many of them

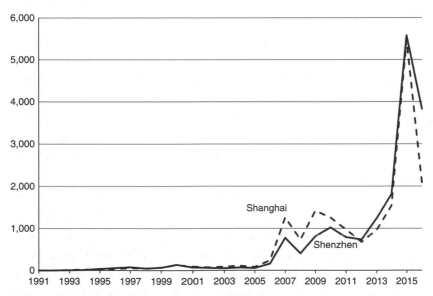

Figure 11.3 Average daily turnover value (RMB 100 million) on the Shanghai and Shenzhen stock exchanges, 1991–2016[67]

pure momentum traders.[68] In 2014 and 2015, their entrance into the market was facilitated by the wide availability of margin finance.[69] The large number of retail investors, who constituted 80 to 85 per cent of stock market investment at the time, meant that these momentum traders had a substantial effect on the movements of the Chinese stock markets. Restrictions on the Internet and news media gave the state substantial control over the information available to investors, making it much easier for the state to engineer price increases.[70] Just as the democratisation of speculation in the mid-1840s in the UK created a huge bubble in railway stocks, so the democratisation of speculation in China, particularly in the 2015 bubble, resulted in a bubble almost unprecedented in its magnitude.

In 2007, speculating in the opposite direction was effectively impossible because short selling was illegal.[71] These short-sale constraints enabled momentum traders to push stock prices higher without informed traders being able to correct prices.[72] By 2014, the State Council of China had permitted short selling in an effort to improve the efficiency of the stock market, but only on 280 blue-chip securities.[73] These 280 securities were a small fraction of the 9,354 corporate securities listed on the Shanghai and Shenzhen markets in 2015, so for most stocks there were still significant short-sale constraints.

In many senses, Chinese citizens tended to view the Shanghai and Shenzhen stock exchanges as casinos. During 2015, margin loans meant that large swathes of China's new and growing middle class could now take a punt on the stock market. The casino capitalism criticised by the likes of John Maynard Keynes in the 1930s was alive and well in China.

China's bubbles are some of the best examples of the bubble triangle in operation. They show that marketability and speculation are key, and that the scale of bubbles is very much determined by the amount of fuel available in the form of leverage. They are also clear examples of how and why governments create bubbles. Unlike some other bubble episodes, however, the Chinese bubbles were not followed by a recession or widespread unrest. One reason for this was that the sheer involvement of the state in the economy was unparalleled, which allowed the government to allocate losses across society. Furthermore, the principal banks were owned by the government and therefore had the full backing of the state and its financial power. There was therefore no risk of them failing.

In many ways, the Chinese bubbles resembled the very first bubbles of 1720. In both cases the bubbles were deliberately engineered to aid the conversion of illiquid government debt into liquid equity. In 1720, an economically dominant French state that controlled the media found it impossible to prevent a bubble from bursting, despite attempting to introduce a series of increasingly draconian measures. In 2015, the Chinese government found itself in exactly the same position. In 1720, the French and British governments used John Law and the South Sea directors as scapegoats in an effort to avoid taking responsibility for the crash. In 2015, the Chinese Communist Party did exactly the same thing, laying the blame for the bubble at the feet of Xiao Gang, the boss of the CSRC. Gang was forced to publicly confess his failings and was dismissed from his role in early 2016.[74] History had repeated itself – perhaps as tragedy, perhaps as farce.

CHAPTER 12

Predicting Bubbles

The Bank had not kindled the fire, but, instead of attempting to stop the progress of the flames, it supplied fuel for maintaining and extending the conflagration.

Thomas Tooke[1]

WHEN WE STARTED WRITING THIS BOOK IN THE SUMMER of 2016, the monetary environment suggested that another bubble would develop soon. Interest rates were almost zero, and the historically low returns on traditional assets, especially government bonds, made them unappealing to investors. As banks recovered from the effects of the financial crisis, credit was becoming more widely available. The continuing development of the Internet meant that the marketability of financial assets was increasing. Although levels of speculation appeared to be relatively low, the bubble triangle suggested that a spark could change this very quickly.

A spark soon arrived in the form of blockchain technology: an encryption technique that allowed virtual assets known as cryptocurrencies to circulate without being managed by any central authority. The most widely known cryptocurrency was bitcoin. To its advocates, bitcoin was the money of the future: it could not be devalued through inflation by a central bank, you could spend it on anything without having to worry about government interference or taxes, and it cut out the middleman, namely commercial banks. A bitcoin did not represent anything of value – its worth lay entirely in the fact that it was, for some (mostly illicit) purposes, a superior medium of exchange.[2]

In August 2016, one bitcoin was trading at $555; in the next 16 months its price rose by almost 3,400 per cent to a peak of $19,783.[3] This was accompanied by a promotion boom, as a mix of cryptocurrency enthusiasts and opportunistic charlatans issued their own virtual currencies in the form of initial coin offerings, or ICOs. These coins had, on the face of it, no intrinsic value – to entitle their holders to future cash flows would have violated laws against issuing unregistered securities – but they nevertheless attracted $6.2 billion of money from investors in 2017 and a further $7.9 billion in 2018.[4]

By December 2017, however, it had become clear that bitcoin was hardly being used as a currency at all. It had promised freedom from middlemen, but trading it without a third party was cumbersome unless the user was expert in cybersecurity. Its popularity exposed the inability of its system to process large numbers of transactions, resulting in long delays in transferring bitcoins and substantial transaction costs. The impossibility of reversing mistakes made it impractical, and its volatility made it useless as a store of value or unit of account. And its much-vaunted decentralisation meant that no one had the power to fix these considerable drawbacks. It was simply a speculative asset, and when investors began to cash out, bitcoin crashed. In the 7 weeks following its peak, it fell by 65 per cent, reaching $6,698 in February 2018. After a temporary recovery, it collapsed again. On 17 December 2018, exactly one year after its peak, one bitcoin was valued at $3,332 – a fall of 83 per cent.[5] Other cryptocurrencies fared even worse: Invictus Capital's CRYPTO20 index, which tracked the value of the 20 largest cryptocurrencies, fell by over 93 per cent.[6]

The bubble triangle presents a framework that applies just as well to the 2017 cryptocurrency bubble as it does to any of the financial bubbles over the past 300 years. But how good will it be at predicting future bubbles?

The three sides of the bubble triangle all need to be present for a bubble to happen. In terms of money and credit, bubbles are much more likely to happen when there are low yields on traditional assets, low interest rates and unconstrained credit provision. Indeed, deregulation of financial markets can ultimately result in a greater likelihood of bubbles occurring because it removes limits on the amount of fuel that can be created. Bubbles are also much more likely when marketability increases due to legal or regulatory changes, financial innovation or technological improvements. Speculators are always present in financial markets, but an increase in their number or an increase in the number of amateurs can increase the probability of a bubble because there is an increase in momentum trading. Bubbles start when investors and speculators react to new technology or political initiatives. Ultimately, the ability to predict bubbles chiefly comes down to being able to predict these sparks.

What do the various political sparks of major historical bubbles have in common? There appears to be no common pattern or grand socio-economic theory which explains why political sparks are created. Several of our bubbles have no politicians lining their own pockets. The political regimes in which historical bubbles occur range from absolutist monarchies to full franchise democracies. All we can say is that the incentives faced by the various governments in each episode resulted in the deliberate manufacture of bubbles or the introduction of policies which would necessarily create bubbles. This absence of common factors makes politically sparked bubbles difficult, but not impossible, for investors, citizens or the news media to predict.

Why is it that the same set of policies can produce a bubble in one instance but not in another? Our explanation is that the other elements of the bubble triangle are missing. It could be that financial markets are underdeveloped and so assets have limited marketability or there are a limited number of public companies. There could also be legal or cultural restrictions on speculation. Alternatively, the banking system, financial institutions and the capital markets might be so underdeveloped or heavily constrained that there is not enough money and credit to fuel a bubble.

Technological sparks are also difficult to predict because one must foresee what the effect of the technology will be, how people will react to it and whether it will catch on. In addition, one must understand the narrative surrounding the new technology and whether this makes it compelling to investors. Not all major technologies are associated with stock market bubbles. The development of steam technology, for example, occurred in an environment where the law was hostile to the company form and the stock market was underdeveloped, which severely hampered marketability. Steam technology was thus developed by small partnerships and private entrepreneurs.

Unlike steam, the new fourth industrial revolution technologies – biotech, nanotechnology and artificial intelligence – have been developed by companies, not individual entrepreneurs. However, unlike during the dot-com and other technology bubbles, the funding for these companies comes from venture capitalists (VCs) and institutional investors rather than stock markets. Notably, press commentators have referred to the 'tech unicorn bubble', a unicorn being a VC-backed company with a valuation greater than $1 billion. One study found that the average unicorn was overvalued by about 50 per cent above its fair value, and some were overvalued by more than 100 per cent.[7] Although private investors may have substantially overpaid for the unicorns, by our definition – an upward movement of prices that then collapses – this would not be described as a bubble.

The bubble triangle can also help predict whether bubbles will be useful or destructive. Table 12.1 considers bubbles along two dimensions – the spark and leverage.[8] Four of our historical bubbles are in the top right box, having a political spark and a bubble fuelled by bank leverage. Far from being useful, each of these bubbles had a devastating and prolonged effect on the economy and wider society. This implies that the combination of a political spark and bank leverage creates bubbles that cause great economic harm. The two bubbles in the bottom left box had few negative effects on the economy or

TABLE 12.1 *Bubble sparks and leverage*

Political spark	China (2007)	First emerging market bubble South Sea Bubble Railway Mania China (2015)	Mississippi Bubble Australian Land Boom Subprime Bubble Japanese Bubble
Technological spark	Bicycle Mania Dot-Com Bubble	Wall Street Bubble	
	Low capital-market leverage	High capital-market leverage	Bank leverage

wider society. Indeed, both were instrumental in generating investment in a new transformative technology which benefited and even liberated society.

In the episodes in the middle two boxes, the extent of the economic damage depended on how exposed the financial system was to the capital-market leverage generated during the bubble. For those which threatened the financial system, the wider social benefit may have been bought at too high a price for society to afford. The South Sea Bubble, however, may be history's only useful political bubble, putting Britain on a much firmer fiscal and military footing without any repercussions for the banking system.

If the bubble triangle is good at predicting bubbles, then it needs to be able to explain why bubbles have recently been occurring more frequently. More than a century separated the first and second financial bubbles, and after the Wall Street Crash there were no major bubbles for over 50 years. However, since 1990 a major bubble has occurred, on average, once every 6 years. These patterns can be explained by fluctuations in the degree to which credit and marketability were regulated. After the bubbles of 1720, marketability was regulated to the point where forming a company with tradeable shares was virtually impossible. This effectively removed the marketability side of the bubble triangle. The liberalisation of incorporation law, the development of stock markets and the growing middle classes joining the ranks of speculators over the next century increased the likelihood of bubbles, by ensuring that all three sides of the triangle were present. Similarly, after the Wall Street Crash, the regulation of financial markets, the stringent regulation of banks and the deglobalisation of capital both restricted marketability and limited the potential fuel for bubbles. However, the globalisation of capital and deregulation of banking since the 1970s has led to an unprecedented extension of credit and increase in debt. In addition, the deregulation of financial markets has made trading much cheaper and easier, greatly increasing the marketability of financial assets. The global economy has essentially become a giant tinderbox, susceptible to any spark that may come its way.

The question also arises as to whether more recent changes in financial markets will make bubbles more or less likely in the future. Two of the major changes in financial markets over the past two decades are the rise of algorithmic and high-frequency trading and asset management. Algorithmic trading is where buy and sell trades are automatically executed by computers based on pre-programmed instructions, and high-frequency trading is a type of algorithmic trading that can execute a large volume of trades in mere fractions of a second. Algorithmic and high-frequency trading are obvious increases in marketability, suggesting that they may make bubbles more likely. Recent experience has shown that such trading has the potential to move stock markets a great deal in a very short space of time: on 6 May 2010, the Dow Jones Industrial Average dropped 10 per cent in a matter of minutes, recovering these losses almost immediately. Algorithmic and high-frequency trading played a major role in this 'flash crash' and one can see how it has the potential to exacerbate price movements during bubbles.

Some economists believe that bubbles will become less likely in the future, because the rise of the asset management industry means that amateurish individuals with many behavioural flaws are being replaced by sophisticated investors.[9] But recent history suggests otherwise. The Japanese Bubble was largely driven by institutional investors, and they also played a large role during the Dot-Com Bubble. During the housing bubble, it was chiefly institutions that invested in subprime mortgage-backed securities. Indeed, the rise of passive asset management, whereby funds track stock indexes, means that sectors or assets that are rising in price because of a bubble will attract even more funds than they ordinarily would. In other words, the rise of passive asset management has the potential to pour even more fuel on bubble fires in the future.

WHAT SHOULD GOVERNMENTS DO?

Bubbles can be very costly for society but, as we have seen, they also can bestow benefits. This complicates government plans to lean against bubbles. Government policy is further complicated by the fact that governments are, as we have seen, often responsible for sparking the bubble in the first place. In terms of policy, we ask two questions. First, what are a government's options during a bubble that is sparked by new technology? Second, how might a government prevent itself from, or be prevented from, creating a socially destructive bubble?

During a technology bubble, the government can attack any area of the bubble triangle, but it is easiest for them to tighten monetary policy or macroprudential standards to reduce the money and credit which are fuelling the bubble. However, such policies are not without their dangers.[10] It is difficult to identify with confidence whether or not there is a technology bubble or, if there is one, when it will burst.[11] Ben Bernanke, former Chair of the Federal Reserve, has suggested that central banks should intervene only in the very unlikely circumstance that they have greater foresight than other market participants.[12] Bernanke also suggests that too aggressive an approach to dealing with bubbles can actually do more harm than good. If a central bank hikes up interest rates or aggressively contracts the money supply to shrink a bubble, it may succeed only at the expense of substantial falls in economic output.[13] For this reason, central bankers have often been reluctant to prick bubbles (i.e. act aggressively and decisively in raising interest rates) and have even been reluctant to adopt a more gradual approach of 'leaning against the wind'.[14] This reluctance may well have been shaped by historical episodes where central banks did take action, with detrimental consequences. The deliberate pricking of the stock market boom in 1927 by the German central bank, for example, hit Germany at a key point in its post-hyperinflation recovery, affecting investment and tipping the economy into a severe depression.[15] This depression was then instrumental in the rise of National Socialism.

For governments, it is very costly to remove oxygen (marketability) or reduce heat (speculation) during a potential technological bubble; therefore these options are very rarely chosen. However, controls on marketability and speculation can be used as a method of preventing bubbles occurring *ex ante*. The post-1980 period has seen the emergence of a political consensus that increased marketability is an unmitigated positive. But this book covers 300 years, and, for 260 of those, bubbles were very rare events – largely because societies and their political leaders understood that marketability is a double-edged sword. What would policies that restricted marketability look like? Restrictions on securitisation and derivative securities would prevent mortgages, loans and houses from becoming highly marketable securities. The European Shareholder Rights Directive contains several policies which are designed to discourage corporate short-termism, such as additional voting rights, tax incentives, loyalty dividends or loyalty shares for long-term shareholders. These policies would have the added benefit of reducing the marketability of shares, and may also reduce speculation. Another policy that would reduce marketability is a financial transaction tax on each trade of a share or a house. Such a policy could discourage the formation of bubbles from the outset if the tax rate was high enough. It would be equivalent to throwing sand in the gears of the trading system.[16] John Maynard Keynes also suggested that such a tax would limit the influence of speculators upon stock markets.[17]

If leaning against technology bubbles is impractical, then governments and central banks can simply clean up the mess from the collapse of the bubble by soothing the pain of its bursting.[18] The bursting of bubbles usually coincides in the first instance with liquidity and funding difficulties for financial market participants. Central banks can provide liquidity through the lender of last resort function or through central bank purchases of securities on the open market.[19] The lender of last resort ultimately 'stands ready to halt a run out of real and illiquid financial assets into money by making more money available'.[20] After the bursting of the dot-com technology bubble, the Federal Reserve eased monetary policy. However, this action may have created a moral hazard problem and therefore increased the likelihood of another bubble.

What can governments do about political bubbles? Since a political bubble is generally created because it serves the government's interest, the government itself is unlikely to end it. A government might try to commit to not creating a bubble in the future by passing laws placing constraints on one or more sides of the bubble triangle. But the government would retain the power to repeal these laws, so such commitments are unlikely to be credible. One cannot simply trust a government to keep its own hands tied.

An alternative route would be for the government to aim to prevent only the more economically destructive political bubbles. As Table 12.1 shows, the political bubbles that caused the most damage – the

Mississippi, Australian, Japanese and Subprime bubbles – were those which were fuelled by bank debt rather than by capital markets. This suggests that one way to limit the damage from a political bubble is to implement bank regulation which limits the growth of credit, forces banks to hold large liquid reserves and directs bank credit away from speculative activities such as stocks and real estate. One might also attempt to create firewalls which separate institutions involved in bubbly assets from the banking system. Of course, governments have a range of political incentives, and regulation may end up serving these incentives rather than the needs of the economy.[21] For example, bank regulation might be used as a tool to encourage credit to flow towards politically connected borrowers and firms. Governments of democracies may also be under pressure to remove bank regulations so that credit flows more freely to all citizens, not only the wealthy elite. As was the case with the Subprime Bubble of the 2000s, such deregulation brings with it the possibility of excessive credit creation and a concomitant bubble.

THE ROLE OF THE FOURTH ESTATE

Since the government is unlikely to constrain itself, who can hold it to account? One possibility is that the news media might act as a check on political bubbles by bringing them to the attention of citizens. The news media has the potential to be extremely influential. Alexis de Tocqueville wrote that 'only a newspaper can deposit the same thought in a thousand minds at once'; in the era of television and the Internet, the news media can now plant the same thought in a million or more minds at once.[22] Recent research by economists analysing the text of newspapers suggests that the news media move financial and housing markets and drive market sentiment.[23] During bubbles, the media may publicise price rises through colourful reports about early investors growing rich, or shape public opinion with new-paradigm theories seeking to justify high asset prices.[24] Robert Shiller argues that the news media are 'fundamental propagators of speculative price movements through their efforts to make news interesting to their audience'.[25]

What are the incentives of journalists and the news media, and can they be trusted by investors and citizens? Venal journalism, where newspapers and journalists are paid or are induced to spread false news or puff stocks, has existed since newspapers started discussing financial matters. In the case of the Mississippi and Chinese bubbles, state control of the press very much dictated what they could print and, as a result, they printed pieces which puffed the bubbles. During the Bicycle Mania, it was common for promoters to pay both the mainstream and financial press to print articles recommending shares in their companies. The specialised trade press during the Railway and Bicycle Manias had a strong incentive to inflate the bubble, because their very existence depended upon its continuation.

On the other hand, the media might have an incentive to develop reputations as purveyors of truth and exposers of financial folly. Building such a reputation is costly, but the payoff in terms of future readership and credibility is potentially huge. During the nineteenth-century bubbles in the UK, newspapers such as *The Times*, *The Economist* and the *Financial Times* often published editorials which clearly stated that there was a bubble. It is not a coincidence that, unlike many of their contemporaries, these three publications are still around today.

However, this reputation as a financial watchdog can easily be undermined, for four reasons. First, news media reporting is shaped by consumer demands.[26] In the news media market, readers may demand a positive slant on financial markets. Competition forces newspapers to give readers what they want and may ultimately marginalise voices of dissent. Second, journalists need information to report on financial markets, but information is sometimes so complex that journalists do not have the time to process and understand it. This appears to have been the case during the Subprime Bubble, particularly with regards to esoteric assets such as mortgage-backed securities. It also appears to have been the case during the South Sea Bubble: the scheme is still difficult to understand even with the benefit of 300 years of hindsight.

Third, journalists often build *quid pro quo* relationships with their sources where, in return for a positive spin on a favoured company, government or individual, they get access to private information.[27] During a boom, the public's high level of interest in the market makes these relationships even more valuable to newspapers, giving them even more of an incentive to puff the bubble asset.[28] This was the case during the 1920s bubble when, rather than undertaking the difficult task of valuing assets for themselves, the major American newspapers based most financial news stories on the heavily biased opinions of high-profile bankers. Fourth, the incentives of the news media can be distorted by advertising revenue. If they become over-reliant on advertising revenue which is linked to the boom in asset prices, then their incentive is not to prick the bubble, but to puff it. This conflict of interest existed during the Subprime Bubble when the revenue from property advertisements was welcomed by the traditional news media just as it faced an existential threat from the Internet. It also existed for the railway periodicals which carried advertisements of new railway schemes in the 1840s, and for the Australian press during the land boom of the 1880s.

The role of the media in bubbles therefore largely depends on the incentives that they face. Increasingly, the nature of the news media is shifting in a direction that makes it very difficult for informed voices to be heard above the noise. This problem was clearly illustrated by the Bitcoin Bubble, during which many well-informed sceptics were limited to writing self-published books and running personal blogs with small readerships.[29] The average investor was much more likely to encounter cranks, uninformed journalists repeating the misinformation of cranks, bitcoin holders trying to attract new investors to increase its price and advertisements for bitcoin trading platforms. In addition, the pressure on the business models of the news media makes investigative financial journalism costlier to support. More fundamentally, the move away from the written word to television financial news, docusoaps and social media may corrode the ability of investors to think clearly and understand the complexities of the financial system.[30]

CAVEAT INVESTOR

Governments are typically unwilling to prick technology bubbles, and are often reluctant to tie their own hands to prevent themselves from creating political bubbles. The incentives for the fourth estate mean that it cannot be relied on to prick bubbles either. What then can citizens and investors do in the face of bubbles? Does our study of bubbles offer investors insights in terms of timing bubbles so that they can get in early and sell at the peak? Or do our historical bubbles simply offer salutary lessons in how to spot bubbles and avoid them?

The lessons from the ashes of past bubbles for amateur investors are particularly pertinent. During bubbles, amateur investors often rush into the market, whether for stocks or houses. In nearly every bubble episode, there are instances of what George Akerlof and Robert Shiller call 'phishing for phools' – attempts to persuade people to part with their money and put it into some nebulous scheme.[31] The main takeaway from this book for amateur investors is that they are better off sitting out bubbles in stocks and particularly in houses. Get-rich-quick investments are always enticing, but typically only highly experienced investors and insiders profit from a bubble, generally at the expense of newcomers. Nevertheless, investors can benefit after the bubble has burst because asset prices have a tendency to overcorrect, meaning that investors can acquire such assets at bargain prices.

Riding or shorting bubbles will be out of reach for most investors. Riding a bubble requires investors to sell near the top, but markets are notoriously difficult to time. This means that unless an investor has very deep pockets, shorting bubbles is out of the question, because the longer the duration of the bubble, the costlier it is to hold a short position.

How should investors approach technology bubbles? Since the returns on technology shares are extremely uncertain, perhaps the best way to think about them is as lotteries.[32] Most will produce a large negative return, but a few will generate huge profits for shareholders. If an investor had invested $100 in Amazon's IPO in 1997 and held it until its 20th anniversary in 2017, the stake would have been worth about $49,000, 155 times what investing in the S&P 500 would have earned.[33]

The chief lesson for investors from our book is that they need to act like fire-safety inspectors, examining each situation to see if the elements of the bubble triangle are present and looking out for political or technological sparks. This will require investors to think long and hard about the incentives of politicians and the structure of the political system. Our ultimate clarion call is that investors need to understand much more than the intricacies of finance and economics – sociology, technology, psychology, political science and, most importantly, history are required to inform the mental models of investors.[34] The bubble triangle has been sinking investors since 1720. Lest we forget.

Acknowledgements

This book was conceived in the spring of 2016. We were both intrigued by bubbles and we wanted to write a book which told the story of the global history of bubbles and helped us understand their causes. Our curiosity about bubbles was shared by Cambridge University Press and our editor Michael Watson.

Queen's University Belfast kindly provided Will with a 2-year postdoctoral position and John with a sabbatical to help us write the book. Thanks to Nola Hewitt-Dundas, our Head of School, and Paddy Johnston, the late Vice-Chancellor of Queen's, for all their support in this regard. Thanks also to the University of Melbourne and Yale University for hosting John during his sabbatical and providing stimulating environments to read, think and write about bubbles. The fellowship afforded to John and his family by McKinnon RPCA and Cambridge RPCNA during his sabbatical visits was very much appreciated.

We are both privileged to be members of the Queen's University Centre for Economic History – our colleagues and students as well as visitors to the Centre create a unique environment in which to work. We have benefited from comments, conversations and feedback from many colleagues who were extremely generous with their time. Thanks to the following for their feedback: Graeme Acheson, Robin Adams, Michael Aldous, Stephen Billington, David Bogle, Alan de Bromhead, Graham Brownlow, Chris Colvin, Christopher Coyle, Áine Doran, Áine Gallagher, Will Goetzmann, Richard Grossman, Alan Hanna, Charlie Hickson, Bill Janeway, Lyndon Moore, Russell Napier, David Paulson, Andrea Quinn, Yuxin Sun, Clive Walker and Laura Wurm.

ACKNOWLEDGEMENTS

Gareth Campbell, Oscar Gelderblom, Naomi Lamoreaux and James Taylor participated in a roundtable workshop on an early version of the manuscript and we are indebted to them for the valuable advice they provided. Ryan Harty very generously agreed to design a graphic for the bubble triangle. Michael Watson at the Press has been a very encouraging and helpful editor and provided us with extensive feedback on an early draft. Eve Richards provided valuable proofreading and encouragement on an early draft.

Early overviews and portions of the book were presented at the Bank of England, United Arab Emirates University and Yale University. Thanks to Olly Bush, Kelly Goodman, Jose-Antonio Espin-Sanchez, Mallory Hope, Naomi Lamoreaux, Peter Oyelere, Fabian Schrey, Francesca Trivellato and Sam Woods for their suggestions and comments.

This book would not have been written without the love and support of our families. We dedicate this book to them.

Notes

CHAPTER 1: THE BUBBLE TRIANGLE

1. Anon., *The South Sea Bubble*, pp. 160–1.
2. Radio address given by President Obama on 10 August 2013 – reported by Bloomberg.
3. Harris, 'Handel the investor', 533.
4. HM Land Registry Open Data, 'UK House Price Index, Northern Ireland'.
5. Scherbina and Schlusche, 'Asset price bubbles'; Farhi and Panageas, 'The real effects of stock market mispricing'.
6. On the destructiveness of banking crises, see Friedman and Schwartz, *The Great Contraction*; Bernanke, 'Nonmonetary effects'; Calomiris and Mason, 'Consequences of bank distress'; Dell'Ariccia, Detragiache and Rajan, 'The real effect of banking crises'. For estimates of the costs of banking crises, see Hoggarth, Reis and Saporta, 'Costs of banking system instability'; Laeven and Valencia, 'Resolution of banking crises'.
7. Deaton, 'The financial crisis'.
8. Eatwell, 'Useful bubbles'.
9. Olivier, 'Growth-enhancing bubbles'. See also Martin and Ventura, 'Economic growth with bubbles'.
10. Janeway, *Doing Capitalism*, p. 237.
11. Zimmer, 'The "bubble" that keeps on bubbling'.
12. Garber, *Famous First Bubbles*, p. 124.
13. Engsted, 'Fama on bubbles', 2; Fama, 'Two pillars of asset pricing', 1,475.
14. Engsted, 'Fama on bubbles'.
15. Kindleberger, *Mania, Panics, and Crashes*, p. 16.
16. Garber, *Famous First Bubbles*, p. 4.
17. On the relationship between trading volume and bubbles, see Barberis et al., 'Extrapolation and bubbles'; Greenwood, Shleifer and You, 'Bubbles for Fama'; Hong and Stein, 'Disagreement and the stock market'; and Scheinkman, *Speculation, Trading and Bubbles*.
18. Allen and Gale, 'Bubbles and crises'; 'Bubbles, crises, and policy'; 'Asset price bubbles'; Allen, 'Do financial institutions matter?'
19. Allen and Gale, 'Bubbles and crises'; Minsky, *Stabilizing an Unstable Economy*; Kindleberger, *Manias, Panics and Crashes*.

20. Bagehot, 'Investments', *Inquirer*, 31 July 1852. John Bull was a popular nineteenth-century personification of the UK in political satires, meant to represent a straightforward common-sense Englishman.

21. Kaldor, 'Speculation', 1.

22. O'Hara, 'Bubbles', 14; Blanchard and Watson, 'Bubbles'.

23. Abreu and Brunnermeier, 'Synchronization risk', 'Bubbles and crashes'; Brunnermeier and Nagel, 'Hedge funds'; Xiong and Yu, 'Chinese warrants bubble'.

24. Haruvy and Noussair, 'The effect of short selling'; Ofek and Richardson, 'Dotcom mania'; Scheinkman and Xiong, 'Overconfidence'; Shleifer and Vishny, 'The limits of arbitrage'.

25. Quinn, 'Squeezing the bears'.

26. Brunnermeier, 'Bubbles'; Gjerstad and Smith, 'Monetary policy', 274.

27. Perez, 'The double bubble'.

28. Hickson and Thompson, 'Predicting bubbles'.

29. Later writers appear to have embellished this with the result being the well-known aphorism attributed to Newton – that he 'could calculate the motions of the heavenly bodies, but not the madness of people' – see Odlyzko, 'Newton's financial misadventures'.

30. Kindleberger, *Mania, Panics, and Crashes*; Galbraith, *A Short History of Financial Euphoria*; Shiller, *Irrational Exuberance*; Akerlof and Shiller, *Animal Spirits*.

31. Akerlof and Shiller, *Animal Spirits*; Barberis, Shleifer and Vishny, 'A model of investor sentiment'; Daniel, Hirshleifer and Subrahmanyam, 'Investor psychology'; Lux, 'Herd behaviour'.

32. Barberis, Shleifer and Vishny, 'A model of investor sentiment'; Daniel, Hirshleifer and Subrahmanyam, 'Investor psychology'.

33. Lux, 'Herd behaviour'.

34. Donaldson and Kamstra, 'A new dividend forecasting procedure'; Garber, *Famous First Bubbles*; Pástor and Veronesi, 'Technological revolutions'.

35. Dale, Johnson and Tang, 'Financial markets can go mad'; Garber, *Famous First Bubbles*; Shiller, *Irrational Exuberance*.

36. Opp, 'Dump the concept of rationality'.

37. These criteria are very close to those used by Goetzmann, 'Bubble investing' and Greenwood et al., 'Bubbles for Fama'.

38. Greenwood et al., 'Bubbles for Fama'.

39. See Posthumus, 'The tulip mania'.

40. Goldgar, *Tulipmania*.

41. Garber, 'Tulipmania'; Garber, *Famous First Bubbles*.

42. Thompson, 'The tulipmania'.

43. Mackay, *Memoirs of Extraordinary Popular Delusions*, 2nd edition.

44. Goldgar, *Tulipmania*, p. 6.

45. Goldgar, *Tulipmania*, pp. 6–7.

46. Englund, 'The Swedish banking crisis'; Moe, Solheim and Vale, 'The Norwegian banking crisis'; Nyberg, 'The Finnish banking crisis'; Radlet et al., 'The East Asian financial crisis'.

47. Radlet et al., 'The East Asian financial crisis'; Mishkin, 'Lessons from the Asian crisis'.
48. Radlet et al., 'The East Asian financial crisis', 38; Aumeboonsuke and Tangjitprom, 'The performance of newly issued stocks in Thailand'.
49. On the justification for this approach to economic history, see Lamoreaux, 'The future of economic history'.

CHAPTER 2: 1720 AND THE INVENTION OF THE BUBBLE

1. Swift, 'The Bubble'.
2. Ceballos and Álvarez, 'Royal dynasties'.
3. Dickson, *The Financial Revolution*, pp. 79–80. GDP estimates from Hills, Thomas and Dimsdale, 'The UK recession'. Britain at this time used the Julian calendar, which was approximately 11 days behind the Gregorian calendar used on the Continent. For consistency, all dates in this chapter have been converted to the Gregorian calendar.
4. Hart, Jonker and van Zanden, *A Financial History*, pp. 70–1.
5. Stasavage, *Public Debt*, p. 106, 132.
6. Dale, *The First Crash*, pp. 56–7; Velde, 'John Law's system', 6–7.
7. Historical literature on Law includes: Blaug, *Pre-Classical Economists*; Hamilton, 'John Law'; Mackay, *Extraordinary Popular Delusions*, 2nd edition, chapter 1; Murphy, *John Law*; Neal, *'I Am Not Master of Events'*. The lowbrow romantic novel referenced is Emerson Hough's *The Mississippi Bubble: How the Star of Good Fortune Rose and Set and Rose Again, by a Woman's Grace, for One John Law of Lauriston*.
8. Dale, *The First Crash*, p. 58; Hamilton, 'John Law'; Law, *Money and Trade Considered*; Schumpeter, *History of Economic Analysis*, pp. 294–5.
9. Davis, 'An historical study', 23.
10. Dale, *The First Crash*, p. 59; Davis, 'An historical study', 26; Velde, 'John Law's system', 18.
11. Velde, 'John Law's system', 20.
12. The company's original name was 'The Company of the West', but we have used the term 'Mississippi Company' for consistency with previous research.
13. Murphy, *John Law*, p. 166; Velde, 'Was John Law's system a bubble?', 105.
14. Velde, 'Was John Law's system a bubble?', 107.
15. Dale, *The First Crash*, p. 66; Velde, 'Was John Law's system a bubble?', 105.
16. Carswell, *South Sea Bubble*, p. 88.
17. Darnton, 'An early information society', 6; Velde, 'John Law's system', 110; Velde, 'Government equity', 10.
18. *Sources*: Murphy, *John Law*, p. 208; *Gazette d'Amsterdam*, 1719–20.
    Notes: Vertical lines indicate the dates of subscriptions to Mississippi Company shares.
19. Murphy, *John Law*, pp. 221–3.
20. Murphy, *John Law*, pp. 227–30, 237–8.
21. Velde, 'John Law's system', 30.
22. Dale, *The First Crash*, pp. 128–30; Murphy, *John Law*, p. 266
23. Velde, 'John Law's system', 36–9.

24. Dickson, *Financial Revolution*, pp. 92–3.
25. Neal, *The Rise of Financial Capitalism*, p. 94.
26. Dale, *The First Crash*, p. 75.
27. Kleer, 'Riding a wave', 266.
28. Anderson, 'The origin of commerce', 8–9.
29. Kleer, 'Folly of particulars', 176.
30. House of Commons, *The Several Reports*.
31. Kleer, 'Folly of particulars'; Kleer, 'Riding a wave'.
32. Carswell, *South Sea Bubble*; Paul, *South Sea Bubble*.
33. Dale, *The First Crash*, pp. 98–101; Dickson, *Financial Revolution*, pp. 144–5.
34. Dale, *The First Crash*, p. 6.
35. Dickson, *Financial Revolution*, p. 108; Hoppit, 'Myths', 150.
36. Dale, *The First Crash*, pp. 98–101; Dickson, *Financial Revolution*, pp. 144–5.
37. Dale, *The First Crash*, pp. 14–16.
38. Paul, 'The "South Sea Bubble", 1720'.
39. Dale, *The First Crash*, p. 18; Kleer, 'Riding a wave', 274–5; Wilson, *Anglo-Dutch Commerce*, p. 104.
40. Hutcheson, *Some Calculations*.
41. *Source*: European State Finance Database.
42. Chancellor, *Devil Take the Hindmost*, p. 65.
43. Dickson, *Financial Revolution*, pp. 134, 168–9.
44. Dickson, *Financial Revolution*, pp. 159–60.
45. House of Commons, *An Act for Making*.
46. Dickson, *Financial Revolution*, p. 185.
47. Dickson, *Financial Revolution*, pp. 172–4; *Statutes at Large*, pp. 299, 354–8.
48. Hoppit, 'Myths', 143–5.
49. *Source*: European State Finance Database.
50. Frehen et al., 'New evidence', 594–6.
51. Velde, 'John Law'; Gelderblom and Jonker, 'Public finance', 25.
52. *Sources*: Yale International Center for Finance, South Sea Bubble 1720 Project, https://som.yale.edu/faculty-research/our-centers-initiatives/international-center-finance/data/historical-southseasbubble, last accessed 18 February 2019.
    Notes: Price-weighted index of 23 Dutch companies, with the index set to 100 on 1 April 1720.
53. Gelderblom and Jonker, 'Mirroring', 9–10.
54. Gelderblom and Jonker, 'Mirroring', 11–12.
55. Neal, *The Rise of Financial Capitalism*, p. 79.
56. Condorelli, 'The 1719–29 stock euphoria', 25, 52.
57. Hutcheson, *Several Calculations*, p. 64.
58. Neal, *The Rise of Financial Capitalism*; Temin and Voth, 'Riding'.
59. *Whitehall Evening Post*, 24–26 March 1720.
60. Hutcheson, *Several Calculations*; Hutcheson, *Some Calculations*.
61. Kleer, 'Riding a wave', 278.

62. Hoppit, 'Myths', 164.
63. Defoe, *Anatomy*; Swift, 'The Bubble'.
64. Hoppit, 'Myths', 159–62.
65. Garber, 'Famous first bubbles', 46–7, 52.
66. Velde, 'Was John Law's system a bubble?', 114–19.
67. Dale, *The First Crash*, pp. 114–17; Hutcheson, *Some Calculations*.
68. Dale, *The First Crash*, pp. 158–9.
69. Hamilton, 'Prices and wages', 78.
70. Bonney, 'France'; Bordo and White, 'A tale of two currencies'; Ferguson, *The Ascent of Money*, p. 127.
71. *Daily Post*, 7 January 1721, pp. 2–4; *London Journal*, 7 January 1721, p. 2; *Weekly Journal or British Gazetteer*, 14 January 1721, p. 4.
72. Hoppit, 'Myths', 154–5.
73. Broadberry et al., *British Economic Growth*; Hoppit, 'Myths', 152–7.
74. Carlos, Maguire and Neal, 'A knavish people . . . '; Carlos, Maguire and Neal, 'Financial acumen'; Carlos and Neal, 'The micro-foundations'; Dickson, *Financial Revolution*, p. 282; Wilson, *Anglo-Dutch Commerce*, pp. 104–5.
75. Frehen, Goetzmann and Rouwenhorst, 'New evidence'.
76. Hoppit, 'Myths', 158.
77. Murphy, 'Corporate ownership', 195.
78. Harris, 'The Bubble Act'; Turner, 'The development', 127.
79. Frehen, Goetzmann and Rouwenhorsts, 'New evidence', 588.

CHAPTER 3: MARKETABILITY REVIVED: THE FIRST
EMERGING MARKET BUBBLE

1. McCulloch, *A Dictionary*, pp. 187–8.
2. This poem was entitled *An Incantation* and was sung by the Bubble Spirit – letter to the Editor of *The Times*, 18 April 1826, p. 2.
3. Ward, *The Finance of Canal Building*, p. 164. The absence of reported price data and the very thin market for canal shares also makes it very difficult to assess the extent of the boom in canal share prices in this era.
4. Day, *A Defence of Joint Stock Companies*.
5. Davenport-Hines, 'Wilks, John'.
6. *The Times*, 20 September 1826, p. 2.
7. *The Times*, 19 October 1826, p. 2.
8. Davenport-Hines, 'Wilks, John'.
9. Hills, Thomas and Dinsdale, 'The UK recession in context', Data Annex.
10. Tooke, *A History of Prices*, p. 148.
11. Randall, *Real del Monte*, p. 33.
12. Fenn, *British Investment in South America*, p. 61.
13. Costeloe, 'William Bullock'.
14. *Source:* English, *A Complete View of Joint Stock Companies*.

15. Prospectus of the Anglo-Mexican Mining Association in English, *A General Guide to the Companies*, pp. 4–8.
16. English, *A Complete View of Joint Stock Companies*, p. 30.
17. *Sources*: Anon., *The South Sea Bubble*, pp. 171–9; *Report of the Select Committee on Joint Stock Companies*, 1844, Appendix 4, pp. 334–9.
18. Gayer, Rostow and Schwartz, *Growth and Fluctuation*, Vol. I, pp. 377–410.
19. Head, *Rough Notes Taken During Some Rapid Journeys Across the Pampas*, pp. 303–4.
20. Cited in Dawson, *The First Latin American Debt Crisis*, p. 101.
21. Excerpt in Anon., *The South Sea Bubble*, pp. 160–1.
22. Francis, *History of the Bank of England*, Vol. II, p. 3. Francis recalls seeing this prospectus at the time and refers to it as jocularity emanating from the Stock Exchange. Subsequent accounts such as King, *History of the London Discount Market*, p. 36; Andreades, *History of the Bank of England*, p. 250; Chancellor, *Devil Take the Hindmost*, p. 105, have reported it as being a real rather than satirical prospectus.
23. *Sources*: Authors' calculations based on biweekly editions of *Wetenhall's Course of the Exchange*, 1824–6; Campbell et al., 'What moved share prices?'

     Notes: These indexes of capital appreciation are weighted – the previous month's market capitalisation is used as a weight for this month's return. The foreign mining index contains all the foreign mining companies listed in *Wetenhall's Course of the Exchange* between August 1824, when the first foreign mining company was quoted, and December 1826. The new non-mining index contains all companies that listed between August 1824 and December 1826. The blue-chip index is based on the 30 largest stocks by market capitalisation on the London stock market from 1824 to 1826. The constituents of the index are based on the 30 largest stocks at the end of December in the previous year. We assume that shares are issued at their par value and incur a -100 per cent return if they delist, which is consistent with bankruptcy proceedings reported in the press at the time. The indexes are set equal to 100 in August 1824. We use the last reported price of the month and in the very rare instance where no price is reported, we use the previous month's share price. Returns of individual companies are adjusted to take account of any calls on capital.
24. Wright, *History of the Reigns of George IV and William VI*, p. 56.
25. Draft of unsent letter, c. April 1825, Disraeli, *Letters, 1815–1834*, p. 28.
26. *The Times*, 7 February 1825, p. 3.
27. See Harris, *Industrializing English Law*, p. 252.
28. Emden, *Money Powers of Europe*, p. 38.
29. Harris, 'Political economy', 688.
30. *The Times*, 15 March 1825, p. 2.
31. Disraeli, *An Inquiry into the Plans, Progress and Policy*, pp. 82–90.
32. Harris, *Industrializing English Law*, p. 245.
33. Hunt, *The Development of the Business Corporation*, p. 45.
34. Tooke, *A History of Prices*, p. 159.
35. Dawson, *The First Latin American Debt Crisis*, p. 113.
36. *The Times*, 10 May 1826, p. 3.

37. See, for example, Randall, *Real del Monte.*
38. Head, *Rough Notes Taken During Some Rapid Journeys Across the Pampas,* pp. 278–81.
39. See, for example, Ward, *Mexico in 1827.*
40. Fenn, *British Investment in South America,* p. 60.
41. *Morning Chronicle,* 10 March 1825, p. 2 and 21 March 1825, p. 2.
42. *The Times,* 23 November 1824, p. 3.
43. *The Times,* 12 April 1824, p. 3; 15 April 1824, p. 2; 5 May 1824, p. 4; 1 June 1824, p. 3.
44. *The Times,* 31 October 1825, p. 3; 27 March 1826, p. 2; 20 September 1826, p. 2.
45. Chancellor, *Devil Take the Hindmost,* p. 106.
46. Anon., *Remarks on Joint Stock Companies,* p. 5.
47. Rippy, 'Latin America', 125.
48. *The Times,* 15 April 1824, p. 2.
49. Taylor, *Statements Respecting the Profits of Mining,* p. 55.
50. *Report of the Select Committee on Joint Stock Companies, 1844,* Q. 2345, 2354–5.
51. McCulloch, *A Dictionary,* p. 188.
52. Francis, *Chronicles and Characters of the Stock Exchange,* pp. 263–4.
53. Disraeli, *Letters, 1815–1834,* p. 27 – draft of an unsent letter to Robert Messer, his stockbroker.
54. *The Times,* 15 April 1824, p. 2.
55. Martineau, *A History of the Thirty Year's Peace,* Vol. II, p. 7; Tooke, *A History of Prices,* p. 150. See also Hunt, *The Development of the Business Corporation,* p. 33 and Gayer, Rostow and Schwartz, *Growth and Fluctuation,* Vol. I, p. 378.
56. Hyndman, *Commercial Crises of the Nineteenth Century,* pp. 27–8. See also Anon., *Remarks on Joint Stock Companies,* p. 4.
57. Fenn, *British Investment in South America,* p. 98; *The Times,* 25 March 1825, p. 3.
58. Acheson, Turner and Ye, 'The character and denomination', 868.
59. Campbell, Turner and Ye, 'The liquidity of the London capital markets'.
60. Neal, 'The financial crisis', p. 60; Committee of Secrecy on the Bank of England Charter, P.P. 1831–2 VI, Evidence of J. Horsley Palmer, q. 606.
61. Hawtrey, *A Century of Bank Rate,* p. 14; Gayer et al., *Growth and Fluctuation,* Vol. I, p. 185.
62. See Committee of Secrecy on the Bank of England Charter, P.P. 1831–2 VI, Appendix 6.
63. Committee of Secrecy on the Bank of England Charter, P.P. 1831–2 VI, Evidence of George W. Norman, q. 2666; William Beckett, q. 1392; and John Wilkins, q. 1638; Turner, *Banking in Crisis,* p. 69.
64. Tooke, *A History of Prices,* p. 179.
65. Committee of Secrecy on the Bank of England Charter, P.P. 1831–2 VI, Evidence of Thomas Tooke, qq. 3852, 3857.
66. Select Committee on Banks of Issue, P.P. 1840 IV, Evidence of Thomas Tooke, q. 3762.
67. Clapham, *The Bank of England,* Vol. II, p. 94; Committee of Secrecy on the Bank of England Charter, P.P. 1831–2 VI, Evidence of George W. Norman, q. 2557; Evidence of Vincent Stuckey, q. 1186; Samuel J. Loyd, q. 3466; George Grote, q. 4646; John Easthope, q. 5795. Hilton, *Corn, Cash and Commerce,* p. 202, suggests that the boom was precipitated by a lack of co-ordination between the government and Bank of England.

68. Committee of Secrecy on the Bank of England Charter, P.P. 1831–2 VI, Evidence of William Ward, q. 1992; Jeremiah Harman, q. 2330; George W. Norman, q. 2667; John Richards, q. 5019; and Thomas Tooke, q. 3852, 3911.
69. Michie, *Money, Mania and Markets*, p. 35. Indeed, *The Times*, 1 July 1825, p. 3, warned against the practice.
70. See the prospectuses in English, *A General Guide to the Companies*.
71. Emden, *Money Powers of Europe*, p. 39; Gilmore, 'Henry George Ward', 36–7; Chancellor, *Devil Take the Hindmost*, p. 100.
72. Jenks, *The Migration of British Capital*, p. 53.
73. Harris, 'Political economy', 686–7.
74. *The Times*, 7 February 1825, p. 3.
75. *The Times*, 27 August 1825, p. 3.
76. Powell, *The Evolution of the Money Market*, p. 326.
77. Pressnell, *Country Banking*, p. 487.
78. *The Times*, 20 December 1825, p. 2. See also *The Times*, 16 December 1825, p. 2.
79. Committee of Secrecy on the Bank of England Charter, P.P. 1831–2 VI, Appendix 101.
80. Turner, *Banking in Crisis*, pp. 53–4.
81. Gayer, Rostow and Schwartz, *The Growth and Fluctuation*, Vol. I, p. 191; Committee of Secrecy on the Bank of England Charter, P.P. 1831–2 VI, Evidence of N. M. Rothschild, qq. 4895–6.
82. Stuckey, 'Thoughts on the improvement', 424.
83. Committee of Secrecy on the Bank of England Charter, P.P. 1831–2 VI, Evidence of John Richards, q. 5006 and Jeremiah Harman, q. 2262.
84. Committee of Secrecy on the Bank of England Charter, P.P. 1831–2 VI, Evidence of N. M. Rothschild, q. 4897.
85. In practice, partnerships would have been very small even without this regulation, because partnership law forbade the separation of ownership and control. See Turner, *Banking in Crisis*, pp. 103–8; Acheson, Hickson and Turner, 'Organizational flexibility'.
86. *The Times*, 8 December 1825, p. 2; Pressnell, *Country Banking*, p. 491.
87. Collins and Baker, *Commercial Banks and Industrial Finance*; Turner, *Banking in Crisis*.
88. Emden, *Money Powers of Europe*, p. 61; Taylor, 'Financial crises and the birth of the financial press'.

CHAPTER 4: DEMOCRATISING SPECULATION: THE GREAT RAILWAY MANIA

1. William Makepeace Thackeray, *The Speculators*.
2. Letter written by Charles Dickens in 1845 – see Dickens, *The Letters of Charles Dickens*, p. 361.
3. *The Economist*, 'The beauty of bubbles', 20 December 2008. See also Campbell, 'Myopic rationality'; Kostal, *Law and English Railway Capitalism*, p. 29; Odlyzko, 'Collective hallucinations'.

4. Mackay, *Memoirs of Extraordinary Popular Delusions*, 3rd edition, p. 84. Interestingly, Mackay, despite being the great chronicler and student of manias and bubbles, was not so perceptive during the Railway Mania – he did not think that there had been a bubble until well after it burst (Odlyzko, 'Charles Mackay's own popular delusions').

5. The English translation of *Das Kapital* rather unfortunately translates this phrase as the 'great railway swindle' (Marx, *Capital*, p. 538). However, this is inaccurate (McCartney and Arnold, 'The railway mania', 836).

6. Jackman, *The Development of Transportation*, p. 522; Kostal, *Law and English Railway Capitalism*, p. 16; Turner, 'The development of English company law'.

7. Francis, *A History of the English Railway*, p. 140.

8. Authors' calculations based on data from *Wetenhall's Course of the Exchange*, 1834–7.

9. Simmons, *The Railway in England and Wales*, p. 24; Odlyzko, 'Collective hallucinations'.

10. Federal Reserve Economic Data, 'Mileage of New Railway Lines Authorized by Parliament for Great Britain'.

11. Cleveland-Stevens, *English Railways*, p. 102.

12. Cleveland-Stevens, *English Railways*, p. 155.

13. Junner, *The Practice before the Railway Commissioners*, p. xix; Lewin, *Railway Mania*, p. 18; Casson, *The World's First Railway System*, p. 277.

14. *The Economist*, 6 July 1844, p. 962.

15. *Railway Times*, 9 November 1844, p. 1,309.

16. *Sources*: Campbell, 'Myopic rationality'; Campbell, 'Deriving the railway mania'; Campbell and Turner, 'Dispelling the myth'; *Railway Times* (1843–50) and *Wetenhall's Course of the Exchange* (1843–50).

    Notes: The All-Railway index includes all railway shares. The Non-Railways blue-chip index includes the 20 largest non-railways by market capitalisation. Capital gains for each stock are weighted by the previous week's market capitalisation to produce weekly market indexes of capital appreciation. Each index is set equal to 1,000 in the first week of January 1843.

17. Aytoun, 'How we got up the Glenmutchkin Railway'.

18. Anon., *The Railway Speculator's Memorandum Book*, p. 7; Reed, *Investment in Railways*, p. 89.

19. Anon., *A Short and Sure Guide*, p. 10; Kostal, *Law and English Railway Capitalism*, pp. 76–7.

20. Lewin, *The Railway Mania*, p. 17; *Railway Times*, 19 July 1845, p. 1,208.

21. Casson, *The World's First Railway System*, p. 277.

22. *Railway Times*, 25 April 1846, p. 578.

23. *The Times*, 17 November 1845, p. 4. This figure probably underestimates the extent of promotion because 335 companies not on this list went on to petition Parliament – *The Times*, 14 January 1846, p. 6.

24. See *Railway Times*, 4 October 1845, p. 1,768.

25. *Sources*: Campbell and Turner, 'Managerial failure', 1,252 and Campbell, Turner and Walker, 'The role of the media in a bubble', 479.

    Notes: The word count of promotion adverts was obtained by scanning in all the company adverts in the *Railway Times* and running the scans through the *Linguistic*

Inquiry and Word Count software. The Railway share index includes all railway shares. Capital gains for each stock are weighted by the previous week's market capitalisation to produce weekly market indexes of capital appreciation. The stock index is set equal to 1,000 in the first week of January 1843.

26. Return of the Number of Newspaper Stamps at One Penny, P.P. 1852, XLII.
27. Campbell, Turner and Walker, 'The role of the media in a bubble'.
28. *The Economist*, 4 October 1845, pp. 950–3
29. *The Times*, 1 July 1845, p. 4; 30 July 1845, p. 4; 17 November 1845, p. 4.
30. Brown, *Victorian News*, pp. 27–9, 50; Simmons, *The Victorian Railway*, p. 240.
31. *The Times*, 18 October 1845, p. 5
32. Simmons, *The Railway in England and Wales*, p. 40.
33. Tuck, *The Railway Shareholder's Manual.*
34. *Railway Times*, Editorials from 18 October 1845 to 13 December 1845, pp. 1,962, 2,057, 2,137, 2,185, 2,233, 2,281, 2,313, 2,345 and 2,377.
35. Campbell, Turner and Walker, 'The role of the media in a bubble'.
36. *The Economist*, 25 October 1845, p. 1,029.
37. *The Economist*, 15 November 1845, p. 1,126.
38. Lambert, *The Railway King*, p. 167.
39. *The Economist*, 8 November 1845, p. 1,109
40. Smith, *The Bubble of the Age.*
41. York and North Midland Railway, *Report of the Committee of Investigation*; *Railway Times*, 28 April 1849, p. 441; *Railway Times*, 14 July 1849, p. 690; *Railway Times*, 27 October 1849, p. 1,086.
42. Arnold and McCartney, 'It may be earlier than you think'; Reports of the Select Committee of House of Lords on Audit of Railway Accounts, P.P. 1849, XXII.
43. The Abandonment of Railways Act (1850).
44. Clifford, *A History of Private Bill Legislation*, p. 89.
45. *Sources*: Gross capital formation is from Mitchell, 'The coming of the railway', p. 335; and nominal GDP is from Mitchell, *British Historical Statistics*, p. 831. Paid-up capital of British railways is from the authors' calculations based on data from *Wetenhall's Course of the Exchange*, 1831–70 and Acheson et al., 'Rule Britannia'.

      Notes: The paid-up capital of British railways is based upon the end-of-year value of those railways listed on the London Stock Exchange.
46. Acheson et al., 'Rule Britannia', 1,117.
47. Campbell, Turner and Ye, 'The liquidity of the London capital markets'.
48. Killick and Thomas, 'The provincial stock exchanges', 103; Thomas, *The Provincial Stock Exchanges*, pp. 28–69; Michie, *The London Stock Exchange*, p. 117.
49. Thomas, *The Provincial Stock Exchanges*, p. 50; Killick and Thomas, 'The provincial stock exchanges', 104.
50. *The Economist*, 13 April 1844, p. 674.
51. *Railway Times*, 4 May 1884, p. 510.
52. Campbell, 'Deriving the railway mania'.
53. Anon., 'History of Bank of England', 515; Campbell and Turner, 'Dispelling the myth'.

54. Williamson, 'Earnings', 474.

55. Broadbridge, 'The sources of railway share capital', 206.

56. Taylor, 'Business in pictures', p. 118; Michie, *Guilty Money*, pp. 23–9.

57. Francis, *A History of the English Railway*, p. 195; Spencer, *Railway Morals*, p. 14; Anon., 'History of Bank of England', 512; Broadbridge, 'The sources of railway share capital', 204; Lee, 'The provision of capital', 39; Kindleberger, *Mania, Panics and Crashes*, p. 25; Michie, *Money, Mania and Markets*, p. 96.

58. Odlyzko, 'Collective hallucinations', 4–5.

59. Return of Railway Subscribers, (P.P. 1845, XL); Return of Railway Subscribers (P.P. 1846, XXXVIII).

60. Casson, *The World's First Railway System*, p. 278.

61. Lewin, *The Railway Mania*, p. 18.

62. Gale, *A Letter to the Right Hon. the Earl of Dalhousie*, p. 5.

63. *The Economist*, 21 October 1848, p. 1,187.

64. McCartney and Arnold, 'Capital clamours for profitable investment'.

65. *Railway Times*, 9 March 1844, p. 285.

66. Esteves and Mesevage, 'The rise of new corruption'.

67. Spencer, *Railway Morals*, p. 14.

68. Campbell and Turner, 'Dispelling the myth', 19.

69. Dobbin, *Forging Industrial Policy*, p. 175; *Railway Times*, 23 August 1845, p. 1,321.

70. Gordon, *Passage to Union*, pp. 17–22.

71. Dobbin, *Forging Industrial Policy*, pp. 40–2.

72. The US railroad system expanded greatly in the 1850s, but the extent of the asset price reversal was much smaller in the US than in Britain. See Pástor and Veronesi, 'Technological revolutions', 1,475.

73. Gale, *A Letter to the Right Hon. the Earl of Dalhousie*, pp. 9–15.

74. Campbell and Turner, 'Managerial failure'.

75. *The Economist*, 4 November 1848, p. 1,241; Jackman, *The Development of Transportation*; p. 599.

76. Letter written by Charlotte Brontë in 1849 – see Brontë, *The Letters of Charlotte Brontë*, p. 267.

77. Secret Committee of the House of Lords on Causes of Commercial Distress, P.P. 1847–8 I, Evidence of James Morris and H. J. Prescott, q. 2674. See also *The Times*, 1 October 1847, p. 6.

78. Campbell, 'Deriving the railway mania', p. 22.

79. *The Economist*, 20 November 1847, p. 1,334.

80. Eatwell, 'Useful bubbles'.

81. Lardner, *Railway Economy*, p. 49.

82. Hawke, *Railways and Economic Growth*; Leunig, 'Time is Money'.

83. Leunig, 'Time is money'.

84. Casson, 'The efficiency of the Victorian British railway network'.

85. Crafts, Mills and Mulatu, 'Total factor productivity growth'.

CHAPTER 5: OTHER PEOPLE'S MONEY: THE AUSTRALIAN LAND BOOM

1. Cork, 'The late Australian banking crisis', 177.
2. Cannon, *The Land Boomers*, p. 43.
3. Davison, *The Rise and Fall of Marvellous Melbourne*.
4. See Butlin, 'The shape of the Australian economy'; Kelley, 'Demographic change'.
5. Davison, *The Rise and Fall of Marvellous Melbourne*, p. 12.
6. Cannon, *The Land Boomers*, p. 24.
7. *Australasian Insurance and Banking Record*, Vol. XXII, 1888, p. 3.
8. *Sources*: Butlin, *Investment in Australian Economic Development*, pp. 11–13; Butlin, *Australian Domestic Product*, pp. 6–7, 33, 424.

    Notes: GDP and GDP per capita figures are in constant prices based on 1911.
9. *Australasian Insurance and Banking Record*, Vol. XXI, 1887, p. 1.
10. *Australasian Insurance and Banking Record*, Vol. XXIII, 1889, p. 314.
11. Boehm, *Prosperity and Depression*, p. 152.
12. *Sources*: Butlin, *Investment in Australian Economic Development*, p. 143.
13. Butlin, *Investment in Australian Economic Development*, p. 261; Davison, *The Rise and Fall of Marvellous Melbourne*, pp. 77–8.
14. Butlin, *Investment in Australian Economic Development*, p. 266; Wood, *The Commercial Bank of Australia*, p. 142.
15. *Australasian Insurance and Banking Record*, Vol. XII, 1888, p. 140.
16. House of Were, *The History of J. B. Were and Son*, p. 127.
17. *Australasian Insurance and Banking Record*, Vol. XII, 1888, p. 351.
18. Cannon, *The Land Boomers*, p. 25.
19. Daly, *Sydney Boom Sydney Bust*, pp. 148–9.
20. Silberberg, 'Rates of return on Melbourne land investment'.
21. Stapledon, 'Trends and cycles', 315.
22. Daly, *Sydney Boom Sydney Bust*, pp. 148–9.
23. *Sources*: Knoll, Schularick and Steger, 'No place like home', based on data in Stapledon, 'Trends and cycles', and Butlin, *Investment in Australian Economic Development*.

    Notes: This house price index is set equal to 100 in 1870.
24. Boehm, *Prosperity and Depression*, p. 251.
25. Weaver, 'A pathology of insolvents', 125.
26. *Australasian Insurance and Banking Record*, Vol. XII, 1888, p. 140.
27. *Sources*: Authors' calculations based on the share price tables in the *Australasian Insurance and Banking Record*, a monthly publication which reported the mid-month share prices of companies traded on the Stock Exchange of Melbourne.

    Notes: This index of capital appreciation is a weighted index, where the previous month's market capitalisation is used as a weight for this month's return. The index contains all companies listed in the *Australasian Insurance and Banking Record*'s monthly table of mortgage property and investment companies. We assume that shares are issued at their par value and a -100 per cent return when stocks delist. We use the mid-point of the bid-ask spread when both are reported, otherwise we use the bid or ask prices. The index is set equal to 100 in December 1887.

28. *Australasian Insurance and Banking Record,* Vol. XIII, 1889, pp. 28–9.

29. Cannon, *The Land Boomers,* p. 25; *Australasian Insurance and Banking Record,* Vol. XIII, 1889, pp. 28–9.

30. Hall, *The Stock Exchange of Melbourne,* p. 164; *Australasian Insurance and Banking Record,* Vol. XIII, 1889, p. 721.

31. *Sources:* Authors' calculations based on the share price tables in *Australasian Insurance and Banking Record,* a monthly publication which reported the mid-month share prices of companies traded on the Stock Exchange of Melbourne. The number of transactions on Stock Exchange of Melbourne are from Hall, *The Stock Exchange of Melbourne,* p. 162.

    Notes: To calculate market capitalisation, we use the mid-point of the bid-ask spread when both are reported, otherwise we use the bid or ask prices. The number of transactions data is for the year ending 30 September.

32. *Australasian Insurance and Banking Record,* Vol. XIII, 1889, pp. 28–9.

33. Boehm, *Prosperity and Depression,* p. 254.

34. *Australasian Insurance and Banking Record,* Vol. XII, 1888, p. 811.

35. *Australasian Insurance and Banking Record,* Vol. XII, 1888, p. 811.

36. Wood, *The Commercial Bank of Australia,* p. 143; Boehm, *Prosperity and Depression,* p. 255; *Australasian Insurance and Banking Record,* Vol. XIII, 1889, p. 149.

37. Wood, *The Commercial Bank of Australia,* p. 147.

38. Boehm, *Prosperity and Depression,* pp. 159–60.

39. *Australasian Insurance and Banking Record,* Vol. XIII, 1889, p. 639 and Vol. XIV, 1890, p. 1.

40. Hall, *The Stock Exchange of Melbourne,* p. 123; *Australasian Insurance and Banking Record,* Vol. XIII, 1889, p. 639.

41. Butlin, *Investment in Australian Economic Development,* p. 428.

42. Cannon, *The Land Boomers,* p. 26.

43. Peel, *The Australian Crisis of 1893.*

44. Boehm, *Prosperity and Depression,* p. 256; Bailey, 'Australian borrowing in Scotland'.

45. *Australasian Insurance and Banking Record,* Vol. XIII, 1889, p. 802.

46. *Australasian Insurance and Banking Record,* Vol. XV, 1891, pp. 561–2; Vol. XVI, 1892, p. 866.

47. Sykes, *Two Centuries of Panic,* p. 147.

48. *Australasian Insurance and Banking Record,* Vol. XIV, 1890, p. 78.

49. *Australasian Insurance and Banking Record,* Vol. XVI, 1892, p. 97.

50. *Australasian Insurance and Banking Record,* Vol. XVI, 1892, pp. 247–8.

51. *Australasian Insurance and Banking Record,* Vol. XVI, 1892, pp. 80, 317; Cannon, *The Land Boomers,* p. 56.

52. Cannon, *The Land Boomers,* p. 130.

53. Cork, 'The late Australian banking crisis', 179.

54. Cannon, *The Land Boomers,* pp. 130–3.

55. Boehm, *Prosperity and Depression,* p. 256.

56. Boehm, *Prosperity and Depression,* p. 252.

57. *Sources*: Calculations based on banks' balance sheets, which are in Butlin, *The Australian Monetary System*; Butlin, *Investment in Australian Economic Development*, p. 161.

    Notes: The capital ratio equals the sum of capital plus shareholder reserves plus profit and loss reserves divided by the sum of total deposits and note issue. The liquidity ratio equals the sum of bank holdings of coins and bank notes divided by total assets.

58. Hickson and Turner, 'Free banking gone awry', 158.

59. Ellis, 'The Australian banking crisis'; Cork, 'The late Australian banking crisis'; Cannon, *The Land Boomers*, p. 109; Boehm, *Prosperity and Depression*, pp. 219, 252; Wood, *The Commercial Bank of Australia*, p. 143.

60. Boehm, *Prosperity and Depression*, pp. 216–17.

61. Butlin, *Investment in Australian Economic Development*, p. 264.

62. Boehm, *Prosperity and Depression*, p. 215.

63. Cannon, *The Land Boomers*, p. 36; Boehm, *Prosperity and Depression*, p. 252.

64. *Bankers' Magazine*, 'Australia's dark day', Vol. LV, 1893, p. 902. Notably, among developed economies 100 years later, gambling expenditure per capita was highest in Australia – see Public Inquiry into the Australian Gambling Industry.

65. Cork, 'The late Australian banking crisis', 178.

66. *Australasian Insurance and Banking Record*, Vol. XIII, 1889, pp. 28–9; Cannon, *The Land Boomers*, p. 97.

67. Cork, 'The late Australian banking crisis', 179. See also Boehm, *Prosperity and Depression*, p. 224.

68. *Australasian Insurance and Banking Record*, Vol. XII, 1888, p. 351; Vol. XIII, 1889, pp. 28–9, 314.

69. House of Were, *The History of J. B. Were and Son*, pp. 125–6.

70. Dowd, 'Free banking in Australia'; Hickson and Turner, 'Free banking gone awry'; Merrett, 'Australian banking practice'; Merrett, 'Preventing bank failure'; Pope, 'Free banking in Australia'.

71. Butlin, *The Australian Monetary System*, p. 89.

72. Report of the Royal Commission on Banking Laws, p. vi.

73. 52 Vict., No. 1002.

74. Report of the Royal Commission on Banking Laws, p. viii.

75. *Australasian Insurance and Banking Record*, Vol. XIII, 1889, p. 217; Blainey and Hutton, *Gold and Paper*, p. 83.

76. Cannon, *The Land Boomers*, p. 49.

77. Cannon, *The Land Boomers*, p. 61.

78. *The Economist*, 25 March 1893, p. 364.

79. Coghlan, *Labour and Industry*, p. 1673.

80. Merrett, 'Preventing bank failure', 126.

81. *Australasian Insurance and Banking Record*, Vol. XVII, 1893, p. 236.

82. Coghlan, *Labour and Industry*, p. 1,743.

83. Coghlan, *Labour and Industry*, p. 1,747.

84. In 1892, the 'Big Three' controlled 31.0 per cent of all the assets of the banking system.

85. Coghlan, *Labour and Industry*, pp. 1,677–8.

86. Shann, *An Economic History of Australia*, p. 330.
87. *The Economist*, 13 May 1893, pp. 555–6; Cork, 'The late Australian banking crisis', 188.
88. 'Some lessons of the Australian crisis' in *Bankers' Magazine*, Vol. LVI, 1893, p. 660.
89. Coghlan, *Labour and Industry*, p. 1,745.
90. Hickson and Turner, 'Free banking gone awry'.
91. Davison, *The Rise and Fall of Marvellous Melbourne*, p. 15.
92. Butlin, *Investment in Australian Economic Development*, p. 143; Cannon, *The Land Boomers*, p. 48.
93. Fisher and Kent, 'Two depressions', 14.
94. Haig, 'New estimates', 23.
95. Boehm, *Prosperity and Depression*, pp. 313–14.
96. Blainey and Hutton, *Gold and Paper*, p. 255.
97. Butlin, *Investment in Australian Economic Development*, p. 143
98. Cannon, *The Land Boomers*, pp. 37–43; Gollan, *The Commonwealth Bank*, pp. 36–8

CHAPTER 6: WHEELER-DEALERS: THE BRITISH BICYCLE MANIA

1. Grew, *The Cycle Industry*, pp. 71–2.
2. *Money*, 'The history of panics', 30 May 1896.
3. Harrison, 'The competitiveness', 287.
4. Harrison, 'The competitiveness', 289.
5. Rubinstein, 'Cycling', 48–50.
6. Quinn, 'Technological revolutions', 17.
7. *Cradle of Inventions*.
8. Stratmann, *Fraudsters*.
9. *The Times*, 'Queen's Bench Division', 28 July 1898.
10. *Financial Times*, 'The cycle share market', 25 April 1896.
11. Stratmann, *Fraudsters*.
12. Prices obtained from the *Birmingham Daily Mail* and *Financial Times* respectively.
13. *Financial Times*, 'The cycle trade boom', 22 April 1896.
14. *Financial Times*, 'Cyclomania', 27 April 1896.
15. *Financial Times*, 'The cycle market', 22 May 1896.
16. *Source*: Quinn, 'Technological revolutions', 19.
17. *Source:* Birch, *Birch's Manual*.
18. *Money*, 'The growth of goodwill', 25 November 1896.
19. *Money*, 'Cycle promotions', 20 June 1896.
20. *The Times*, 'Queen's Bench Division', 30 June 1899.
21. *Financial Times*, 'Accles, Ltd.', 6 June 1896; 'Prospectus promise and report performance', 30 December 1897.
22. National Archives (Kew), BT31 Files, Accles Ltd., Summary of Capital and Shares.
23. *Financial Times*, 'Prospectus promise and report performance', 30 December 1897.
24. *The Times*, 'Queen's Bench Division', 30 June 1899.
25. *The Times*, 'Queen's Bench Division', 28 July 1898.

26. *Manchester Times*, 'The action by "Commerce Limited"', 28 January 1898.

27. *The Economist*, 'The cycle boom', 16 May 1896.

28. *The Economist*, 'Cycle company promotion', 27 June 1896.

29. *Money*, 'Cycle promotions', 20 June 1896.

30. *Money*, 'The cycle cataclysm', 20 June 1896.

31. *Money*, 'Lawson's latest', 23 May 1896.

32. *Cycling*, 'Financial', 9 January 1897.

33. *Cycling*, 'Financial', 12 June 1897; 'Financial', 11 September 1897.

34. *Cycling*, 'Financial', 27 March 1897, 10 April 1897, 1 May 1897, 8 May 1897, 15 May 1897, 29 May 1897, 5 June 1897.

35. *Scotsman*, 'The Beeston Tyre Rim Company (Limited)', 4 May 1896.

36. Quinn, 'Technological revolutions', 33.

37. *Financial Times*, 'The cycle outlook', 1 May 1897; 'Cycle shares and American over-production', 6 July 1897.

38. *Financial Times*, 'The cycle outlook', 1 May 1897.

39. *Financial Times*, 25 October 1897, 30 December 1897.

40. Quinn, 'Technological revolutions'.

41. Harrison, 'The competitiveness'.

42. Lloyd-Jones and Lewis, 'Raleigh', 82.

43. Gissing, *The Whirlpool*, pp. 130, 174.

44. Acheson, Campbell and Turner, 'Who financed', 617.

45. *Sources:* National Archives (Kew), BT31 Files, Summaries of Capital and Shares; Acheson, Campbell and Turner, 'Who financed'; Braggion and Moore, 'Dividend policies'.

 Notes: The table summarises the self-reported occupations of shareholders before and after the March 1897 crash in a sample of 25 cycle companies.

 * indicates the average proportion of capital contributed by directors to the companies in Braggion and Moore, 'Dividend policies'. Company directors also listed an occupation, and so the analysis of their capital contribution in the table is also conducted separately.

46. *Money*, 'The growth of goodwill', 25 November 1896.

47. Quinn, 'Technological revolutions', 9.

48. Acheson, Campbell and Ye, 'Character and denomination', 869.

49. Acheson, Campbell and Ye, 'Character and denomination'.

50. Bank of England, *A Millennium of Macroeconomic Data*.

51. *The Economist*, 'The "boom" in cycle shares', 25 April 1896; *Financial Times*, 'The cycle market', 22 May 1896.

52. National Archives (Kew), BT31 Files, Concentric Tube, Summary of Capital and Shares, 3 September 1896.

53. *The Economist*, 'The "boom" in cycle shares', 25 April 1896.

54. Kynaston, *The London Stock Exchange*, 142–3.

55. Quinn, 'Squeezing the bears'.

56. *Bath Chronicle*, 'Hints to small investors', 1 October 1896.

57. Quinn, 'Squeezing the bears', 18.

58. Kennedy and Delargy, 'Explaining Victorian entrepreneurship', 55–7.
59. Van Helten, 'Mining', 163–73.
60. Parsons, 'King Khama', 11–12.
61. Acheson, Coyle and Turner, 'Happy hour', 3–5.
62. Acheson, Coyle and Turner, 'Happy hour', 16.
63. Grew, *The Cycle Industry*, pp. 71–5; Harrison, 'The competitiveness'; Millward, 'The cycle trade'.
64. Geary and Stark, 'Regional GDP', 131.
65. Bank of England, *A Millennium of Macroeconomic Data*.
66. Boyer and Hatton, 'New estimates'.
67. Quinn, 'Technological revolutions'.
68. *Financial Times*, 'The cycle share market', 30 April 1897.
69. *Money*, 'Cycles and banks', 31 July 1897.
70. Van Helten, 'Mining', 172; Parsons, 'King Khama', 11–12.
71. Acheson, Campbell and Turner, 'Who financed?', 617.
72. Harrison, 'The competitiveness', 287, 294.
73. Harrison, 'The competitiveness', 297.
74. Harrison, 'The competitiveness', 301–2.
75. Schumpeter, *Capitalism, Socialism and Democracy*, pp. 82–5.
76. Rubinstein, 'Cycling', pp. 48–50; *Guardian*, 'Freewheeling to equality', 18 June 2015; *Independent*, 'How the bicycle set women free', 9 November 2017.
77. Vivanco, *Reconsidering the Bicycle*, p. 33.

CHAPTER 7: THE ROARING TWENTIES AND THE WALL STREET CRASH

1. Fitzgerald, *The Great Gatsby*, p. 3.
2. Fisher, 'The debt-deflation theory', 341.
3. Jordá, Schularick and Taylor, 'Macrofinancial history'.
4. Kang and Rockoff, 'Capitalizing patriotism', 46–52.
5. Hilt and Rahn, 'Turning citizens into investors', 93.
6. Kang and Rockoff, 'Capitalizing patriotism', 57.
7. Hilt and Rahn, 'Turning citizens into investors', 94.
8. Archival Federal Reserve Economic Data; Federal Reserve Economic Data.
9. White, 'The stock market boom', 69.
10. Federal Reserve Economic Data; Basile et al., 'Towards a history', 44.
11. White, 'Lessons', 10.
12. White, 'Lessons', 24–9.
13. *Source:* Federal Reserve Economic Data.
    Notes: Annual data.
14. Goetzmann and Newman, 'Securitization', 24, 28; White, 'Lessons', 30.
15. Gjerstad and Smith, *Rethinking Housing Bubbles*, p. 102.
16. White, 'Lessons', 44.
17. Turner, *The Florida Land Boom*.

18. Frazer and Guthrie, *The Florida Land Boom*.
19. Crump, 'The American land boom', *Financial Times*, 10 November 1925.
20. Vanderblue, 'The Florida land boom', 254.
21. Zuckoff, *Ponzi's Scheme*.
22. Costigliola, 'The United States', 490; Edwards, 'Government control'.
23. Costigliola, 'The United States', 495.
24. Eichengreen, *Hall of Mirrors*, p. 55; Wigmore, *The Crash*, pp. 198–200.
25. Goetzmann and Newman, 'Securitization', 23.
26. Voth, 'With a bang'; Flandreau, Gaillard, and Packer, 'Ratings performance', 6.
27. Klein, *Rainbow's End*, p. 57.
28. The DJIA was reasonably representative of the performance of the overall stock market at this time. The S&P All Common Stock index rose by 141 per cent during the same period.
29. White, 'The stock market boom', 73.
30. Klein, *Rainbow's End*, p. 84,
31. Nicholas, 'Stock market swings', 221.
32. *Source:* Bloomberg.
33. Federal Reserve Economic Data.
34. White, 'The stock market boom', 74.
35. Eichengreen, *Hall of Mirrors*, pp. 59–60.
36. White, 'The stock market boom', 75–6.
37. *Source:* Federal Reserve Economic Data.
    Notes: Includes issues by railroad, industrial, public utility and financial companies, but not issues by banks, trusts or insurance companies. Includes refunds and issues by foreign corporations in the United States.
38. Wigmore, *The Crash*, pp. 26, 660.
39. Noyes, *Forty Years*.
40. *New York Times*, 'Topics in Wall Street', 1 September 1929.
41. Klein, *Rainbow's End*, p. 186.
42. Gentzkow et al., 'Circulation'; Klein, *Rainbow's End*, p. 151.
43. Wigmore, *The Crash*, pp. 4–5; Federal Reserve Economic Data.
44. Klein, *Rainbow's End*, p. 201.
45. Klein, *Rainbow's End*, pp. 207–9.
46. Wigmore, *The Crash*, p. 7.
47. *New York Daily Investment News*, 'Stock market crisis over', 25 October 1929.
48. *New York Times*, 'Worst stock crash stemmed by banks', 25 October 1929.
49. Wigmore, *The Crash*, p. 13.
50. *New York Times*, 'Stock prices slump', 29 October 1929.
51. *New York Daily News*, 'Avoid speculative buys', 25 October 1929; 'Market fireworks ended', 28 October 1929; '9,212,000-share turnover', 29 October 1929.
52. Klein, *Rainbow's End*, p. 226.
53. Brooks, *Once in Golconda*, pp. 86–7.
54. Klein, *Rainbow's End*, p. 239.

55. *New York Times*, 25 October 1929.
56. Huertas and Silverman, 'Charles E. Mitchell'.
57. Choudhry, 'Interdependence'.
58. Le Bris and Hautcoeur, 'A challenge', 182–3.
59. Frennberg and Hansson, 'Computation', 22.
60. Voth, 'With a Bang'.
61. *Barclays' Equity Gilt Study*, 2016, p. 74.
62. Hilt and Rahn, 'Turning citizens into investors', 93.
63. Klein, *Rainbow's End*, pp. 53–6, 147.
64. Jones, 'A century of stock market liquidity', 43.
65. Klein, *Rainbow's End*, p. 84, 146.
66. Eichengreen and Mitchener, 'The Great Depression', 10; White, 'The stock market boom', 69; Wigmore, *The Crash*, p. 660.
67. White, 'The stock market boom', 75.
68. White, 'Lessons', 19.
69. Minutes of the Board of Governors of the Federal Reserve System, 1928.
70. Galbraith, *The Great Crash*, 46.
71. *New York Times*, 'Topics in Wall Street', 21 August 1929.
72. Chancellor, *Devil Take the Hindmost*, pp. 201–2; Klein, *Rainbow's End*, pp. 149–50.
73. Hausman, Hertner and Wilkins, *Global Electrification*, p. 26.
74. Hounshell, *From the American System*.
75. White, 'Stock market boom', 73.
76. Klein, *Rainbow's End*, pp. xvii–xviii.
77. *New York Times*, 'Topics in Wall Street', 13 March 1928.
78. White, 'The stock market boom', 78–80.
79. James, '1929', 29.
80. Romer, 'The Great Crash'.
81. Gjerstad and Smith, *Rethinking Housing Bubbles*, p. 94; Olney, *Buy Now, Pay Later*, p. 108.
82. Jordá, Schularick and Taylor, 'Macrofinancial history'.
83. Eichengreen, *Golden Fetters*, pp. 258–9.
84. Bernanke, 'Nonmonetary effects', 259; Eichengreen and Hatton, 'Interwar unemployment'; Jordá, Schularick and Taylor, 'Macrofinancial history'.
85. Eichengreen, *Golden Fetters*.
86. Eichengreen and Hatton, 'Interwar unemployment', 6; Jordá, Schularick and Taylor, 'Macrofinancial history'.
87. Fishback, Haines and Kantor, 'Births, deaths, and New Deal relief'; Schubert, *Twenty Thousand Transients*.
88. De Bromhead, Eichengreen and O'Rourke, 'Political extremism'.
89. Bernstein, *The Great Depression*; Friedman and Schwartz, *A Monetary History*.
90. Bernanke, 'Nonmonetary Effects'; Eichengreen, *Golden Fetters*; Friedman and Schwartz, *A Monetary History*.
91. Nicholas, 'Stock market swings'.

92. Janeway, *Doing Capitalism*, pp. 155–6.
93. Wigmore, *The Crash*, p. 28.
94. Romer, 'The Great Crash'.

CHAPTER 8:   BLOWING BUBBLES FOR POLITICAL PURPOSES:

JAPAN IN THE 1980S

1. Wood, *The Bubble Economy*, pp. 9–10.
2. Securities Act of 1933; Securities Exchange Act of 1934, pp. 3, 82.
3. Totman, *A History of Japan*, p. 454.
4. Takagi, 'Japanese equity market', 544–5.
5. Totman, *A History of Japan*, pp. 458–9; World Development Indicators, 'GDP (constant LCU) for Japan'.
6. Tsuru, *Japan's Capitalism*, p. 182.
7. Federal Reserve Economic Data, 'Exchange rate to U.S. dollar for Japan'.
8. Lincoln, 'Infrastructural deficiencies'.
9. Plaza Accord, para. 18.
10. Frankel and Morgan, 'Deregulation and competition', 584.
11. Federal Reserve Economic Data, 'Discount rate for Japan'; 'Total credit to households and NPISHs, adjusted for breaks, for Japan'; World Development Indicators, 'GDP (constant LCU) for Japan'.
12. Federal Reserve Economic Data, 'M3 for Japan, national currency, annual, not seasonally adjusted'.
13. Federal Reserve Economic Data, 'Interest rates, government securities, treasury bills for Japan'.
14. Wood, *The Bubble Economy*, p. 49.
15. Dehesh and Pugh, 'The internationalization', 149.
16. Oizumi, 'Property finance', 199.
17. *Source:* Land Institute of Japan.
    Notes: Average land price index for Tokyo ward, Yokohama, Nagoya, Kyoto, Osaka and Kobe. Index is set to 100 in 2010.
18. Dehesh and Pugh, 'The internationalization', 153; Oizumi, 'Property finance', 202; Plaza Accord, para. 18.
19. Dehesh and Pugh, 'The internationalization', 154; Tsuru, *Japan's Capitalism*, p. 163.
20. Noguchi, 'Land prices', 13–14; Stone and Ziemba, 'Land and stock prices', 149.
21. Takagi, 'The Japanese equity market', 557–8.
22. Takagi, 'The Japanese equity market', 558, 563, 568.
23. *Source:* Bloomberg.
    Notes: Contains all companies listed in the First Section of the Tokyo Stock Exchange.
24. Dehesh and Pugh, 'The internationalization', 157; Takagi, 'The Japanese equity market', 559.
25. Wood, *The Bubble Economy*, p. 26.

26. Stone and Ziemba, 'Land and stock prices', 149.
27. Hebner and Hiraki, 'Japanese initial public offerings'; Jenkinson, 'Initial public offerings', 439; Takagi, 'The Japanese equity market', 552; Warrington College of Business IPO Data, 'Japan, 1980–2018'.
28. Federal Reserve Economic Data, 'Discount rate for Japan'.
29. Dehesh and Pugh, 'The internationalization', 158; Mitsui Fudosan, 'New home sales'; Oizumi, 'Property finance', 210.
30. See, for example, Cargill, 'What caused Japan's banking crisis?', 46–7; Okina, Shirakawa and Shiratsuka, 'The asset price bubble'; Wood, *The Bubble Economy*, p. 12.
31. Frankel and Morgan, 'Deregulation and competition', 582; Takagi, 'The Japanese equity market', 549, 559.
32. Laurence, *Money Rules*, p. 150; Reading, *Japan: The Coming Collapse*, p. 177.
33. Takagi, 'Japanese equity market', 550–1, 553; Tesar and Werner, 'Home bias', 481.
34. Shiller, Kon-ya and Tsutsui, 'Why did the Nikkei crash?'
35. Shiller, Kon-Ya and Tsutsui, 'Why did the Nikkei crash?', 161
36. Tsuru, *Japan's Capitalism*, pp. 161–2.
37. Oizumi, 'Property finance', 203; Zimmerman, 'The growing presence', 10.
38. Noguchi, 'The "bubble"', 296.
39. Wood, *The Bubble Economy*, pp. 38–9.
40. Hirayama, 'Housing policy', 151–4.
41. Oizumi, 'Property finance', 202.
42. Dehesh and Pugh, 'The internationalization', 157; Oizumi, 'Property finance', 202.
43. Murphy, *The Real Price*, p. 154.
44. Wood, *The Bubble Economy*, p. 124.
45. *Harvard Business Review*, 'Power from the ground up: Japan's land bubble', May–June 1990.
46. Dehesh and Pugh, 'The internationalization', 153–4; Takagi, 'The Japanese equity market', 558–9.
47. Wood, *The Bubble Economy*, p. 19.
48. Murphy, *The Real Price*, p. 152.
49. Shiller, Kon-Ya and Tsutsui, 'Why did the Nikkei crash?', 161.
50. Wood, *The Bubble Economy*, p. 91.
51. Although the standard Japanese definition of a recession at this time was growth below 3 per cent, in order to remain consistent with other chapters, we use the term to mean negative growth for two successive quarters.
52. Federal Reserve Economic Data, 'General government net lending/borrowing for Japan', 'Discount rate for Japan'; World Development Indicators, 'GDP (constant LCU) for Japan'.
53. Hoshi and Patrick, 'The Japanese financial system', 14.
54. Nakaso, 'The financial crisis in Japan', 6–9.
55. Nakaso, 'The financial crisis in Japan', 9–11, 55; *Japan Times*, 'Government nationalizes Long-Term Credit Bank of Japan', 23 October 1998.
56. Nakaso, 'The financial crisis in Japan', 6.

57. Hoshi and Kashyap, 'Japan's financial crisis'; World Development Indicators, 'GDP (constant LCU) for Japan'.
58. Federal Reserve Economic Data, 'Real gross domestic product for the U.S.'
59. Federal Reserve Economic Data, 'Unemployment rate: aged 15–64: all persons for Japan'; World Development Indicators, 'GDP (constant LCU) for Japan'.
60. Federal Reserve Economic Data, 'Constant GDP per capita for Japan', 'Constant GDP per capita for the United Kingdom'.
61. Wood, *The Bubble Economy*, p. 21.
62. *New York Times*, 'Nomura gets big penalties', 9 October 1991.
63. Shindo, 'Administrative guidance', 71–2.
64. Shiratori, 'The politics of electoral reform', 83.
65. Wood, *The Bubble Economy*, p. 69.
66. *New York Times*, 'Shin Kanemaru, 81, kingmaker in Japan toppled by corruption', 29 March 1996.
67. Yamamura, 'The Japanese political economy', 293.
68. Yamamura, 'The Japanese political economy', 295.
69. Wood, *The Bubble Economy*, pp. 69, 97–8; *New York Times*, 'Japan penalizes Nomura and big bank for payoffs', 31 July 1997.
70. Cai and Wei, 'The investment and operating performance'.
71. *Fortune*, Japan Exchange Group.
72. Janeway, *Doing Capitalism*.

CHAPTER 9: THE DOT-COM BUBBLE

1. Alan Greenspan, 'The challenge of central banking in a democratic society', 5 December 1996, www.federalreserve.gov/boarddocs/speeches/1996/19961205 .htm, last accessed 11 March 2019.
2. Versluysen, 'Financial deregulation, 13, 18–20.
3. Naughton, *A Brief History*, p. 239.
4. Cassidy, *Dot.Con*, pp. 51–2.
5. www.internetlivestats.com/total-number-of-websites/, last accessed 21 November 2019.
6. Cassidy, *Dot.Con*, p. 58
7. *Fortune*, 'Fortune checks out 25 cool companies for products, ideas, and investments', 11 July 1994; *New York Times*, 'New venture in cyberspace by silicon graphics founder', 7 May 1994.
8. *Fortune*, 'Netscape IPO 20-year anniversary: Fortune's 2005 oral history of the birth of the web', 9 August 2015.
9. Cassidy, *Dot.Con*, pp. 84–5.
10. Bransten and Jackson, 'Netscape shares touch $75 in first-day trading', *Financial Times*, 10 August 1995.
11. Cassidy, *Dot.Con*, p. 88.
12. Warrington College of Business IPO Data, 'Initial public offerings: VC-backed'.
13. Karpoff, Lee and Masulis, 'Contracting under asymmetric information'.

14. Warrington College of Business IPO Data, 'Initial public offerings: underpricing'.
15. Aggarwal, Krigman and Womack, 'Strategic IPO underpricing'.
16. Ljungvist and Wilhelm, 'IPO pricing', 724.
17. *Source:* 'Initial public offerings: Technology stock IPOs'.
    Notes: Total market value is based on the IPO's first market price.
18. *Source:* Bloomberg.
19. Fama, 'Two pillars', 1476.
20. Shiller, *Irrational Exuberance*, p. 7.
21. Data on market capitalisations and share prices are from Bloomberg.
22. New York Stock Exchange Market Data, 'The Investing Public'.
23. Brennan, 'How did it happen?', 5.
24. Shiller, *Irrational Exuberance*, p. 48.
25. Lowenstein, *Origins*, pp. 70, 85.
26. Shiller, *Irrational Exuberance*, p. 49.
27. Cramer, 'Cramer rewrites an opening debate', *The Street*, 11 February 2000.
28. *Fortune*, 'When the shoeshine boys talk stocks', 15 April 1996.
29. Wolf, 'Cauldron bubble', *Financial Times*, 23 December 1998.
30. *The Economist*, 'Bubble.com', 21 September 2000.
31. Cellan-Jones, *Dot.Bomb*, p. 6.
32. *Financial Times*, 'US Stock Markets take wholesale battering as inflation worries rise', 15 April 2000.
33. Norris, 'Another technology victim', *New York Times*, 29 April 2000.
34. Ofek and Richardson, 'DotCom mania', 1116.
35. Ofek and Richardson, 'DotCom mania', 1113.
36. Market capitalisation data obtained from Bloomberg.
37. Barnett and Andrews, 'AOL merger was "the biggest mistake in corporate history", believes Time Warner chief Jeff Bewkes', *Daily Telegraph*, 28 September 2010.
38. Bloomberg.
39. Deutsche Börse Group, 'Nemax 50'.
40. *Source:* Bloomberg.
    Notes: Each index includes only companies for which technology is the primary source of revenue, as categorised by the ICB Industry Classification Benchmark. The SX8P includes shares of the 600 largest European technology companies, and the two MSCI IT indexes include a varying number of information technology shares for their respective regions. All indexes are set equal to 100 in January 1995.
41. Jones, 'A century of stock market liquidity', 42–3.
42. US Securities and Exchange Commission, 'After-hours trading: understanding the risks'; 'Electronic communications networks'; On-line brokerage', p. 1.
43. International Monetary Fund Global Debt Database.
44. Financial Industry Regulatory Authority, *Margin Statistics*, www.finra.org/investors/margin-statistics, last accessed 20 August 2019.
45. Shiller, *Irrational Exuberance*, pp. 56–7.

46. Dhar and Goetzmann, 'Bubble investors', 21.
47. Griffin et al., 'Who drove?', 1,262–3, 1,268.
48. Greenwood and Nagel, 'Inexperienced investors'.
49. McCullough, *How the Internet Happened*, p. 168.
50. Shiller, *Irrational Exuberance*, p. 42.
51. Weber, 'The end of the business cycle?', *Foreign Affairs*, July/August 1997.
52. DeLong and Magin, 'A short note', 2–3.
53. Eaton, 'Market watch; Netscape fever: will it spread?', *New York Times*, 13 August 1995.
54. Brennan, 'How did it happen?', p. 18; Urry, 'Surfers catch the wave of a rising tide', *Financial Times*, 12 August 1995.
55. Authers, 'Profit from prophesies of doom', *Financial Times*, 23 November 2008; Kotkin, 'A bear saw around the corner', *New York Times*, 3 January 2009.
56. Grant, *The Trouble with Prosperity*, pp. 294–8.
57. DeLong and Magin, 'A short note'.
58. Lowenstein, *Origins*.
59. Brennan, 'How did it happen?', 9–11.
60. Fabbri and Marin, 'What explains the rise in CEO pay', 8; Coffee, 'A theory of corporate scandals'.
61. Coffee, 'A theory of corporate scandals', 204–5.
62. National Bureau of Economic Research, 'US Business Cycle Expansions'.
63. Kliesen, 'The 2001 recession', 28–30.
64. Griffin et al., 'Who drove?', 1,260.
65. Schuermann, 'Why were banks better off?', 6.
66. GDP data obtained from the World Bank.
67. Nehls and Schmidt, 'Credit crunch'.
68. Eatwell, 'Useful bubbles', 43.
69. Andreesen, 'Why software?', *Wall Street Journal*, 20 August 2011.
70. Rao, 'A new soft technology', *Breaking Smart*.
71. See, for example, Garber, 'Famous first bubbles'; Stone and Ziemba, 'Land and stock prices'; Donaldson and Kamstra, 'A new dividend forecasting procedure'.
72. Pástor and Veronesi, 'Technological revolutions'; Pástor and Veronesi, 'Was there a NASDAQ bubble?'.
73. Pástor and Veronesi, 'Was there a NASDAQ bubble?', 62.
74. Pástor and Veronesi, 'Technological revolutions'; Ofek and Richardson, 'DotCom mania', 1,113.
75. Ofek and Richardson, 'DotCom mania'.
76. Lamont and Stein, 'Aggregate short interest'.
77. Schulz, 'Downward-sloping demand curves'.
78. Janeway, *Doing Capitalism*, p. 193.
79. Shiller, *Irrational Exuberance*, pp. 39–70.
80. Schuermann, 'Why were banks better off?', 6; Nehls and Schmidt, 'Credit crunch', 18.

81. Case and Shiller, 'Is there a bubble?'
82. Cassidy, *Dot.Con*, p. 324.

CHAPTER 10: 'NO MORE BOOM AND BUST': THE SUBPRIME BUBBLE

1. Financial Crisis Inquiry Commission, *The Financial Crisis Inquiry Report*, p. 4.
2. McCarthy, Poole and Rosenthal, *Political Bubbles*, p. 11.
3. Channel 4 News, 'FactCheck: no more boom and bust?', 17 October 2008, www .channel4.com/news/articles/politics/domestic_politics/factcheck+no+more+boom +and+bust/2564157.html, last accessed 19 August 2019.
4. Kelly, 'On the likely extent of falls in Irish house prices'.
5. RTE, 'Ahern apologises for suicide remark', 4 July 2007, www.rte.ie/news/2007/0704/ 90808-economy/, last accessed 19 August 2019.
6. Sinai, 'House price movements', 20.
7. *Sources*: Robert Shiller's house price index – www.econ.yale.edu/~shiller/data.htm, last accessed 7 June 2018. See Shiller, *Irrational Exuberance*, pp. 11–15 for details.
8. *Sources*: Standard and Poor's CoreLogic Case-Shiller Home Price Indexes, https://us.spin dices.com/index-family/real-estate/sp-corelogic-case-shiller, last accessed 19 November 2019.

   Notes: The Composite-10 index is a market-weighted average of the following metropolitan areas: Boston, Chicago, Denver, Las Vegas, Los Angeles, Miami, New York City, San Diego, San Francisco and Washington, DC. The Composite-20 index composes all 20 of the metropolitan areas above. The National Index tracks the value of single-family housing across the United States.
9. Haughwot et al., 'The supply side of the housing boom', 70.
10. Glaesar and Sinai, 'Postmortem for a housing crash', 9.
11. Case, Shiller and Thompson, 'What have they been thinking?', 2.
12. Ruiz, Stupariu and Vilarino, 'The crisis', 1,460.
13. Jiménez, 'Building boom', 263; Dellepiane, Hardiman and Heras, 'Building on easy money', 23.
14. *Sources*: Real house price indexes for Ireland, Spain and United Kingdom are from OECD statistics. The Northern Ireland index is the nominal index provided by the Nationwide Building Society, adjusted for inflation using the Retail Price Index.

    Notes: The index for each country is set at 100 in 1973.
15. *Sources*: Data for Ireland is based on changes in the housing stock and is from the Department of Housing, Planning and Local Government; data for Great Britain and Northern Ireland is from the Office for National Statistics; data for Spain is from the European Central Bank's Statistical Data Warehouse; and data for the United States is from the US Census Bureau.

    Notes: The figure for the 1990s is the average. Great Britain excludes Northern Ireland.
16. Terraced housing in many northern cities increased in value during the boom by 100 per cent and fell by 50 per cent or more during the bust – see *Guardian*, 29 August 2015.

17. Mian and Sufi, 'The consequences'; Goodman and Mayer, 'Homeownership', 32.
18. Norris and Coates, 'Mortgage availability', 198.
19. Task Force of the Monetary Policy Committee of the European System of Central Banks, 'Housing finance', p. 43.
20. Purnanandam, 'Originate-to-distribute model'.
21. Lewis, *The Big Short*, pp. 97–8, 152.
22. *Guardian*, 29 August 2015.
23. Jiménez, 'Building boom', 263–4.
24. Honohan, 'Euro membership', 138; Connor, Flavin and O'Kelly, 'The U.S. and Irish credit crises', 67.
25. Dellepiane, Hardiman and Heras, 'Building on easy money', 29; Jiménez, 'Building boom', 263.
26. Commission of Investigation into the Banking Sector in Ireland, *Misjudging Risk*, p. ii.
27. See *Guardian*, 29 August 2015.
28. Financial Crisis Inquiry Commission, *The Financial Crisis Inquiry Report*, pp. 213–14.
29. US Treasury Department Office of Public Affairs, *Treasury Senior Preferred Stock Purchase Agreement*, 7 September 2008.
30. Ball, *The Fed and Lehman Brothers*, p. 222.
31. Although credit default swaps are sometimes viewed as credit insurance, they are unlike real insurance in that the issuer is under no requirement to hold reserves and the purchaser need have no insurable interest in the asset.
32. Financial Crisis Inquiry Commission, *The Financial Crisis Inquiry Report*, p. 140.
33. US Department of the Treasury Press Room, *Treasury Announces TARP Capital Purchase Program*, 14 October 2008.
34. Turner, *Banking in Crisis*, p. 168.
35. Claessens et al., 'Lessons and policy implications'; Hüfner, 'The German banking system'; Xiao, 'French banks'.
36. See Tooze, *Crashed*, chapter 8.
37. Whelan, 'Ireland's economic crisis', 431; Kelly, 'The Irish credit bubble', 15; Honohan, 'Resolving Ireland's banking crisis', 220–1.
38. Commission of Investigation into the Banking Sector in Ireland, *Misjudging Risk*, 77.
39. Whelan, 'Ireland's economic crisis', 432.
40. Banco de España, *Report on the Financial and Banking Crisis in Spain*, pp. 109–12.
41. Turner, *Banking in Crisis*, p. 96.
42. HM Revenue and Customs, *Annual UK Property Transaction Statistics*, 2015.
43. Figures from National Association of Realtors.
44. Rajan, *Fault Lines*, p. 6; Regling and Watson, *A Preliminary Report*, p. 19; Jiménez, 'Building boom', 264; Financial Crisis Inquiry Commission, *The Financial Crisis Inquiry Report*, p. 104; *Turner Review*, pp. 11–12.
45. Gjerstad and Smith, *Rethinking Housing Bubbles*, p. 66.
46. Regling and Watson, *A Preliminary Report*, p. 29. Ireland and Spain were the two EU countries with the widest gap between deposits from domestic non-financial sectors and loans to domestic non-financial sectors – see Task Force of the

Monetary Policy Committee of the European System of Central Banks, 'Housing finance', 43.

47. Taylor, 'The financial crisis'; Gjerstad and Smith, 'Monetary policy', 271; Taylor, 'Causes of the financial crisis', 53.

48. Financial Crisis Inquiry Commission, *The Financial Crisis Inquiry Report*, p. 88.

49. CESifo DICE Database, www.cesifo-group.de/de/ifoHome/facts/DICE/Banking-and-Financial-Markets/Banking/Comparative-Statistics.html, last accessed 19 November 2019.

50. Lam, 'Government interventions', 5; Task Force of the Monetary Policy Committee of the European System of Central Banks, 'Housing finance', 73.

51. Financial Crisis Inquiry Commission, *The Financial Crisis Inquiry Report*, p. 7.

52. Norris and Coates, 'Mortgage availability', 196.

53. Andrews and Sánchez, 'The evolution of home ownership rates'.

54. Financial Crisis Inquiry Commission, *The Financial Crisis Inquiry Report*, p. 7.

55. Mayer, 'Housing bubbles', 564, 574.

56. Mian and Sufi, 'The consequences'; *House of Debt*; Dell'Arriccia, Igan and Laeven, 'Credit booms'; Mayer, 'Housing bubbles'; Santos, '*Antes del diluvio*'; Ruiz, Stupariu and Vilarino, 'The crisis'; Norris and Coates, 'Mortgage availability'; 'How housing killed the Celtic Tiger'; Dellepiane, Hardiman and Heras, 'Building on easy money'; Turner, *Banking in Crisis*, pp. 93–9.

57. Case and Shiller, 'Is there a bubble?', 335.

58. Commission of Investigation into the Banking Sector in Ireland, *Misjudging Risk*, p. ii, 20.

59. Jiménez, 'Building boom', 263.

60. Mayer, 'Housing bubbles', 574.

61. Mian and Sufi, 'Credit supply and housing speculation'.

62. Financial Crisis Inquiry Commission, *The Financial Crisis Inquiry Report*, p. 6.

63. Glaesar, 'A nation of gamblers', 38.

64. Case and Shiller, 'Is there a bubble?', 321.

65. Case, Shiller and Thompson, 'What have they been thinking?'

66. Financial Crisis Inquiry Commission, *The Financial Crisis Inquiry Report*, p. 8.

67. Kelly and Boyle, 'Business on television', 237

68. *Washington Post*, 28 January 2016.

69. Commission of Investigation into the Banking Sector in Ireland, *Misjudging Risk*, p. 50.

70. Casey, 'The Irish newspapers'.

71. Knowles, Phillips and Lidberg, 'Reporting the global financial crisis'.

72. Mercile, 'The role of the media'.

73. Schifferes and Knowles, 'The British media', 43; Müller, 'The real estate bubble in Spain'.

74. Walker, Housing booms'; 'The direction of media influence'.

75. Glaesar, 'A nation of gamblers', 4.

76. Financial Crisis Inquiry Commission, *The Financial Crisis Inquiry Report*, p. 7; Turner, *Banking in Crisis*, p. 217; Munoz and Cueto, 'What has happened in Spain?', 212. For the

dependence of Spanish city and town finances on housebuilding, see Jiménez, 'Building boom', 266; Dellepiane, Hardiman and Heras, 'Building on easy money', 29.

77. Connor, Flavin and O'Kelly, 'The U.S. and Irish credit crises', p. 74; O'Sullivan and Kennedy, 'What caused the Irish banking crisis?', 230.

78. Parliamentary Commission on Banking Standards, *Changing Banking for Good*, p. 12.

79. Andrews and Sánchez, 'The evolution of home ownership rates', 208.

80. Béland, 'Neo-liberalism and social policy', 97–8.

81. Rajan, *Fault Lines*, pp. 35, 38.

82. Calomiris and Haber, *Fragile by Design*, pp. 234–5.

83. Wallison, 'Government housing policy', 401.

84. Financial Crisis Inquiry Commission, *The Financial Crisis Inquiry Report*, p. xxxvii.

85. Financial Crisis Inquiry Commission, *The Financial Crisis Inquiry Report*, p. 445; Wallison, 'Cause and effect'.

86. Dellepiane, Hardiman and Heras, 'Building on easy money', 29.

87. Belsky and Retsinas, 'History of housing finance', 2–3; Andrews and Sánchez, 'The evolution of home ownership rates'.

88. Norris and Coates, 'Mortgage availability', 193.

89. Hansard, *House of Commons Debate*, 15 January 1980, Vol. 976, cols 1,443–575.

90. House of Commons Treasury Committee, *Banking Crisis: Regulation and Supervision*, p. 11.

91. On the role of the three credit-rating agencies in the housing boom and bust, see White, 'The credit-rating agencies'.

92. Parliamentary Commission on Banking Standards, *Changing Banking for Good*, p. 12.

93. Dellepiane, Hardiman and Heras, 'Building on easy money', 14, 20; Kelly, 'The Irish credit bubble', 24; Connor, Flavin and O'Kelly, 'The U.S. and Irish credit crises', 73–4; Ó Riain, 'The crisis', 503.

94. Kelly, 'What happened to Ireland?', 9.

95. McCarthy, Poole and Rosenthal, *Political Bubbles*, p. 83.

96. Johnson and Kwak, *13 Bankers*, p. 5; Johnson, 'The quiet coup'; Financial Crisis Inquiry Commission, *The Financial Crisis Inquiry Report*, p. xviii.

97. Financial Crisis Inquiry Commission, *The Financial Crisis Inquiry Report*, p. xviii.

98. McCarthy, Poole and Rosenthal, *Political Bubbles*, p. 83.

99. Igan and Mishra, 'Wall Street'.

100. Based on OECD data.

101. *Source*: OECD.

102. Deaton, 'The financial crisis'.

103. Financial Crisis Inquiry Commission, *The Financial Crisis Inquiry Report*, p. 409.

104. Goodman and Mayer, 'Homeownership', 31.

105. Mian and Sufi, *House of Debt*, p. 26.

106. Purdey, 'Housing equity', 9.

107. BBC News, 'Negative equity afflicts half a million households', www.bbc.co.uk/news/business-26389009, last accessed 19 November 2019.

108. Duffy and O'Hanlon, 'Negative equity'.

109. Goodman and Mayer, 'Homeownership', 33.
110. Mian and Sufi, *House of Debt*, p. 22.
111. Kitchin, O'Callaghan and Gleeson, 'The new ruins of Ireland'; Financial Crisis Inquiry Commission, *The Financial Crisis Inquiry Report*, p. 408; Dellepiane, Hardiman and Heras, 'Building on easy money', 3; Munoz and Cueto, 'What has happened in Spain?', 209.
112. Kitchin, O'Callaghan and Gleeson, 'The new ruins of Ireland', 1,072.

CHAPTER 11: CASINO CAPITALISM WITH CHINESE CHARACTERISTICS

1. Post on Freeweibo.com as reported by the *Washington Post*, 7 November 2015.
2. Knowledge@Wharton, 'What's behind China's stock market gamble?', https://knowledge.wharton.upenn.edu/article/whats-behind-chinas-stock-market-gamble/, last accessed 19 November 2019.
3. *Financial Times*, 30 July 2015, p. 7.
4. World Bank indicators – based on current US dollars.
5. Steinfeld, *Forging Reform in China*; Zhan and Turner, 'Crossing the river'.
6. Huang, 'How did China take off?'; Zhu, 'Understanding China's growth'.
7. Zhan and Turner, 'Crossing the river', 241.
8. Allen and Qian, 'China's financial system', 535.
9. *Sources: Shanghai Stock Exchange Fact Book*, 2017, pp. 217, 220; *Shenzhen Stock Exchange Fact Book*, 1998, pp. 6–7; *Shenzhen Stock Exchange Fact Book*, 2001, pp. 6–7; *Shenzhen Stock Exchange Fact Book*, 2007, pp. 6–7; *Shenzhen Stock Exchange Fact Book*, 2008, pp. 6–7; *Shenzhen Stock Exchange Fact Book*, 2016, pp. 6–7.
10. Zhan and Turner, 'Crossing the river', 238–9.
11. *Sources*: Shanghai and Shenzhen Stock Exchanges
    Notes: The Shanghai Stock Exchange Composite Index starts on 19 December 1990 and is set at 100 on that day. The Shenzhen Stock Exchange Composite Index starts on 3 April 1991 and is set at 100 on that day. The graph above stops at the end of September 2015, when the bubble bottomed out.
12. Beltratti, Bortolotti and Caccavaio, 'Stock market efficiency', 126.
13. Liao, Liu and Wang, 'China's secondary privatization', 504–5.
14. Li, 'The emergence of China's 2006–2007 stock market bubble'.
15. *Financial Times*, 19 April 2007, p. 1.
16. *New York Times*, 2 April 2008.
17. Yao and Luo, 'The economic psychology', 684–5.
18. *Financial Times*, 7 June 2007, p. 14.
19. *Financial Times*, 7 June 2007, p. 14.
20. Yang and Lim, 'Why did the Chinese stock market perform so badly?'
21. *The Economist*, 30 May 2015, pp. 69–70.
22. Carpenter and Whitelaw, 'The development of China's stock market', 234.
23. *Financial Times*, 20 August 2015, p. 7.
24. Smith, 'Is China the next Japan?', 288.

25. Qian, 'The 2015 stock panic'.
26. *Guardian*, 8 July 2015; *Foreign Policy*, 20 July 2015.
27. *Washington Post*, 22 August 2015; Salidjanova, 'China's stock market collapse'; BBC News, 'What does China's stock market crash tell us?', www.bbc.co.uk/news/business-33540763, 22 July 2015, last accessed 19 November 2019; *The Economist*, 30 May 2015, pp. 69–70.
28. *Financial Times*, 10 June 2015; *Washington Post*, 12 May 2015; Knowledge@Wharton, 'What's behind China's stock market gamble?', https://knowledge.wharton.upenn.edu/article/whats-behind-chinas-stock-market-gamble/, last accessed 19 November 2019.
29. *The Economist*, 13 December 2014, p. 73.
30. Lu and Lu, 'Unveiling China's stock market bubble'.
31. *Washington Post*, 11 July 2015.
32. Knowledge@Wharton, 'What's behind China's stock market gamble?', https://knowledge.wharton.upenn.edu/article/whats-behind-chinas-stock-market-gamble/, last accessed 19 November 2019; *Foreign Policy*, 20 July 2015; *Financial Times*, 10 June 2015, p. 30; *Financial Times*, 26 June 2015, p. 20; *Financial Times*, 30 July 2015, p. 7.
33. Qian, 'The 2015 stock panic'.
34. *Shanghai Stock Exchange Fact Book*, 2017, pp. 217–20; *Shenzhen Stock Exchange Fact Book*, 2016, pp. 6–7.
35. Lu and Lu, 'Unveiling China's stock market bubble', 148.
36. *The Economist*, 30 May 2015, pp. 69–70.
37. *The Economist*, 30 May 2015, pp. 69–70.
38. *Financial Times*, 29 May 2015, p. 11.
39. Qian, 'The 2015 stock panic'; *Financial Times*, 20 June 2015, p. 11.
40. *Financial Times*, 20 June 2015, p. 20.
41. Qian, 'The 2015 stock panic'.
42. Salidjanova, 'China's stock market collapse', p. 3; Qian, 'The 2015 stock panic'.
43. Qian, 'The 2015 stock panic'.
44. *Financial Times*, 29 August 2015, p. 7.
45. *International Financial Law Review*, 23 September 2015.
46. *Washington Post*, 7 July 2015, 11 July 2015.
47. *Financial Times*, 10 July 2015, p. 11.
48. Qian, 'The 2015 stock panic'.
49. Salidjanova, 'China's stock market collapse', 2.
50. *Washington Post*, 22 August 2015.
51. Lu and Lu, 'Unveiling China's stock market bubble', 148.
52. *Financial Times*, 11 April 2015, p. 9; *Financial Times*, 2 July 2015, p. 10.
53. *Washington Post*, 12 May 2015, 8 July 2015.
54. *Washington Post*, 22 August 2015
55. *Financial Times*, 10 July 2015, p. 10.
56. *Washington Post*, 7 October 2015.
57. *Financial Times*, 10 July 2015, p. 11.
58. Lu and Lu, 'Unveiling China's stock market bubble', 149.
59. *Financial Times*, 31 January 2007, p. 14; *Financial Times*, 7 June 2007, p. 14.

60. *Financial Times*, 31 January 2007, p. 17.
61. Lu and Lu, 'Unveiling China's stock market bubble', 152–3.
62. *China Daily*, 11 November 2015.
63. Qian, 'The 2015 stock panic'.
64. *Washington Post*, 8 July 2015; Smith, 'Is China the next Japan?', 291.
65. Lu and Lu, 'Unveiling China's stock market bubble', 151.
66. *International Financial Law Review*, 23 September 2015.
67. *Sources: Shanghai Stock Exchange Fact Book*, 2017, pp. 217, 220; *Shenzhen Stock Exchange Fact Book*, 1998, pp. 6–7; *Shenzhen Stock Exchange Fact Book*, 2001, pp. 6–7; *Shenzhen Stock Exchange Fact Book*, 2007, pp. 6–7; *Shenzhen Stock Exchange Fact Book*, 2008, pp. 6–7; *Shenzhen Stock Exchange Fact Book*, 2016, pp. 6–7.
68. Smith, 'Is China the next Japan?', 292; *International Financial Law Review*, 23 September 2015.
69. *Financial Times*, 10 July 2015, p. 11.
70. *International Financial Law Review*, 23 September 2015.
71. Andrade, Bian and Burch, 'Analyst coverage'.
72. Xiong and Yu, 'The Chinese warrants bubble'.
73. *Shanghai Stock Exchange Fact Book*, 2016, p. 13.
74. CNBC.com, 'CSRC boss Xiao Gang criticized for China's stock market mayhem', 10 January 2016, www.cnbc.com/2016/01/10/csrc-boss-xiao-gang-criticized-for-chinas-stock-market-mayhem.html, last accessed 21 August 2019.

CHAPTER 12: PREDICTING BUBBLES

1. Tooke, *A History of Prices*, Vol. II, p. 179.
2. Foley, Karlsen and Putniņš, 'Sex, drugs and bitcoin'.
3. www.coindesk.com/price/bitcoin, last accessed 19 November 2019.
4. Securities Exchange Commission, 'In the matter of Tomahawk Exploration LLC and David Thompson Laurence', www.sec.gov/litigation/admin/2018/33-10530.pdf, last accessed 25 November 2019; ICOdata.io.
5. www.coinbase.com, last accessed 19 November 2019.
6. https://crypto20.com, last accessed 19 November 2019.
7. Gornall and Strebulaev, 'Squaring venture capital valuations with reality'.
8. The inspiration for this table comes from Janeway, *Doing Capitalism*, p. 233.
9. See Jones, 'Asset bubbles' for a discussion of how the rise of asset management industry affects the various theories of bubbles.
10. Posen, 'Why central banks should not burst bubbles'.
11. Bernanke and Gertler, 'Should central banks respond to movements in asset prices?'; Trichet, 'Asset price bubbles'.
12. Bernanke, 'Asset price "bubbles" and monetary policy'.
13. Assenmacher-Wesche and Gerlach, 'Financial structure'.
14. Trichet, 'Asset price bubbles'.
15. Voth, 'With a bang, not a whimper'.

16. Tobin, 'A proposal'.
17. Keynes, *The General Theory*, chapter 12.
18. Brunnermeier and Schnabel, 'Bubbles and central banks'.
19. For an overview of the literature, see Bordo, 'The lender of last resort' and Freixas et al., 'Lender of last resort'.
20. Kindleberger, *Manias, Panics and Crashes*, p. 146.
21. Calomiris and Haber, *Fragile By Design*.
22. de Tocqueville, *Democracy in America*, p. 600.
23. Tetlock, 'Giving content to investor sentiment'; García, 'Sentiment during recessions'; Griffin, Hirschey and Kelly, 'How important is the financial media?'; Walker, 'Housing booms'.
24. Akerlof and Shiller, *Animal Spirits*, p. 55.
25. Shiller, *Irrational Exuberance*, p. 105.
26. Gentzkow and Shapiro, 'Media bias and reputation'.
27. Dyck and Zingales, 'The bubble and the media'.
28. Dyck and Zingales, 'The bubble and the media'.
29. See, for example, Gerard, *Attack*; https://davidgerard.co.uk/blockchain/, last accessed 19 November 2019; www.coppolacomment.com/, last accessed 19 November 2019. One exception to the poor quality of news media coverage was the *Financial Times*'s Alphaville.
30. On the corrosive effect of television on public discourse, see Postman, *Amusing Ourselves to Death*.
31. Akerlof and Shiller, *Phishing for Phools*.
32. See Barberis and Huang, 'Stocks as lotteries'.
33. *Wall Street Journal*, 'Amazon's IPO at 20: That amazing return you didn't earn', 14 May 2017.
34. On this, see Hagstrom, *Investing: The Last Liberal Art*.

Bibliography

OFFICIAL REPORTS / PARLIAMENTARY PAPERS

Banco de España, *Report on the Financial and Banking Crisis in Spain, 2008–2014*, 2017.

Commission of Investigation into the Banking Sector in Ireland, *Misjudging Risk: Causes of the Systemic Banking Crises in Ireland*, 2011.

Committee of Secrecy on the Bank of England Charter (P.P. 1831–32, VI).

Financial Crisis Inquiry Commission, *The Financial Crisis Inquiry Report*, 2011.

Hansard, *House of Commons Debates*, 1980.

HM Revenue and Customs, *Annual UK Property Transaction Statistics*, 2015.

House of Commons, *An Act for Making Several Provisions to Restore the Publick Credit, Which Suffers by the Frauds and Mismanagements of the Late Directors of the South-Sea Company, And Others*, London: John Baskett, 1721.

House of Commons, *The Several Reports of the Committee of Secrecy to the Honourable House of Commons, Relating to the Late South-Sea Directors*, London: A. Moore, 1721.

House of Commons Treasury Committee, *Banking Crisis: Regulation and Supervision*, London: Stationery Office, 2009.

Minutes of the Board of Governors of the Federal Reserve System, 1928.

Parliamentary Commission on Banking Standards, *Changing Banking for Good*, London: HMSO, 2013.

Plaza Accord, 1985. www.g8.utoronto.ca/finance/fm850922.htm, last accessed 11 April 2019.

Public Inquiry into the Australian Gambling Industry: Final Report, Canberra: Productivity Commission, 1999.

Railway Subscription Contracts Deposited in the Private Bill Office of the House of Commons, Session 1837 (P.P. 1837, XLVIII).

Report of the Royal Commission on Banking Laws (Victoria Parliament 1887).

Report of the Registrar of Friendly Societies for the Year Ending 1882 (Victoria Parliament 1887).

Report of the Select Committee on Joint Stock Companies (P.P. 1844, VII).

Reports of the Select Committee of House of Lords on Audit of Railway Accounts (P.P. 1849, XXII).

Return of Railway Subscribers (P.P. 1845, XL).

Return of Railway Subscribers (P.P. 1846, XXXVIII).

Return of the Number of Newspaper Stamps at One Penny (P.P. 1852, XLII).

Secret Committee of the House of Lords on Commercial Distress (P.P. 1847–8, I).

Select Committee on Banks of Issue (P.P. 1840, IV).

The Turner Review: A Regulatory Response to the Global Banking Crisis. London: FSA, 2009.

United States Senate, *Brokers' Loans: Hearings before the Committee on Banking and Currency,* 1928.

United States Treasury Department Office of Public Affairs, *Treasury Senior Preferred Stock Purchase Agreement,* 7 Sept. 2008

NEWSPAPERS AND PERIODICALS

Australasian Insurance and Banking Record

Bankers' Magazine

Bath Chronicle

BBC News

Birmingham Daily Mail

Channel 4 News

China Daily

Cycling

Daily Post

Daily Telegraph

Financial Times

Foreign Affairs

Foreign Policy

Fortune

Gazette d'Amsterdam

Guardian

Harvard Business Review

Herapath's Railway and Commercial Journal

Independent

Inquirer

International Financial Law Review

Japan Times

Leydse Courant

London Journal

Manchester Times

Money: A Journal of Business and Finance

Morning Chronicle

New York Daily Investment News

New York Daily News

New York Times

New Yorker

Punch

Railway Times
RTE
Scotsman
The Economist
The Street
The Times
Wall Street Journal
Washington Post
Weekly Journal or British Gazetteer
Wetenhall's Course of the Exchange

ARCHIVES AND DATABASES

Archival Federal Reserve Economic Data (ALFRED)
Bank of England, *A Millennium of Macroeconomic Data*
Barclays' Equity Gilt Study, 2016.
Board of Governors of the Federal Reserve System, *Minutes*, 1928
Bloomberg
CESifo DICE Database. www.cesifo-group.de/de/ifoHome/facts/DICE/Banking-and-Financial-Markets/Banking/Comparative-Statistics.html, last accessed 19 November 2019.
Cradle of Inventions
Deutsche Börse Group, 'Nemax 50'. https://deutsche-boerse.com/dbg-en/our-company/know-how/glossary/glossary-article/NEMAX-50-248782, last accessed 25 November 2019.
European State Finance Database
Federal Reserve Economic Data (FRED)
Financial Industry Regulatory Authority Margin Statistics. www.finra.org/investors/margin-statistics, last accessed 27 November 2018.
Gentzkow, M., Shapiro, J. and Sinkinson, M. 'Circulation of US Daily Newspapers, 1924, Audit Bureau of Circulations. Ann Arbor, MI: Inter-university Consortium for Political and Social Research, 2016.
HM Land Registry Open Data. http://landregistry.data.gov.uk/, last accessed 27 March 2019.
International Monetary Fund Global Debt Database
Land Institute of Japan
Mitsui Fusodan Japanese Real Estate Statistics 2019. www.mitsuifudosan.co.jp/english/realestate_statics/, last accessed 1 April 2019.
National Archives (Kew), BT31 Files.
National Bureau of Economic Research, US Business Cycle Expansions and Contractions. www.nber.org/cycles/, last accessed 4 August 2017.
New York Stock Exchange Market Data. www.nyxdata.com/Data-Products/Facts-and-Figures, last accessed 31 July 2017.
Securities Act of 1933. http://legcounsel.house.gov/Comps/Securities%20Act%20Of%201933.pdf, last accessed 31 July 2019.

Securities Exchange Act of 1934. https://fraser.stlouisfed.org/files/docs/histor
ical/congressional/securities-exchange-act.pdf, last accessed 31 July 2019.
Shanghai Stock Exchange Fact Book, 2016, 2017.
Shenzhen Stock Exchange Fact Book, 1998, 2001, 2007, 2008, 2016.
Standard and Poor's CoreLogic Case-Shiller Home Price Indexes. https://us
.spindices.com/index-family/real-estate/sp-corelogic-case-shiller, last accessed
19 November 2019.
Statutes at Large from the Fifth to Ninth Year of King George, Cambridge: Danby
Pickering, 1765.
US Securities and Exchange Commission, After-Hours Trading: Understanding
the Risks, November 2008. www.sec.gov/reportspubs/investor-publications/
investorpubsafterhourshtm.html, last accessed 17 July 2017.
US Securities and Exchange Commission, Special Study: On-Line Brokerage:
Keeping Apace of Cyberspace, November 1999. www.sec.gov/news/studies/
cyberspace.htm, last accessed 17 July 2017.
US Securities and Exchange Commission, Special Study: Electronic Communication
Networks and After-Hours Trading, June 2000. www.sec.gov/news/studies/ecn
after.htm, last accessed 17 July 2017.
Warrington College of Business IPO Data. https://site.warrington.ufl.edu/rit
ter/ipo-data/, last accessed 17 July 2017.
World Bank
World Development Indicators
Yahoo! Finance
Yale International Center for Finance, South Sea Bubble 1720 Project
Zeno Bibliothek. www.zeno.org, last accessed 25 February 2019.

BOOKS, ARTICLES, THESES AND PAMPHLETS

Abreu, D. and Brunnermeier, M. K. 'Bubbles and crashes', *Econometrica*, **71**,
173–204, 2003.
Abreu, D. and Brunnermeier, M. K. 'Synchronization risk and delayed arbitrage',
Journal of Financial Economics, **66**, 341–60, 2002.
Acheson, G. G., Campbell, G. and Turner, J. D. 'Who financed the expansion of
the equity market? Shareholder clienteles in Victorian Britain', *Business History*,
59, 607–37, 2016.
Acheson, G. G., Coyle, C. and Turner, J. D. 'Happy hour followed by hangover:
financing the UK brewery industry, 1880–1913.', *Business History*, **58**, 725–51, 2016.
Acheson, G. G., Hickson, C. R. and Turner, J. D. 'Organizational flexibility and
governance in a civil-law regime: Scottish partnership banks during the
Industrial Revolution', *Business History*, **53**, 505–29, 2011.
Acheson, G. G., Hickson, C. R., Turner, J. D. and Ye, Q. 'Rule Britannia!: British stock
market returns, 1825–1870', *Journal of Economic History*, **69**, 1,107–37, 2009.
Acheson, G. G., Turner, J. D. and Ye, Q. 'The character and denomination of
shares in the Victorian equity market', *Economic History Review*, **65**, 862–86,
2012.

Aggarwal R. K., Krigman, L. and Womack, K. L. 'Strategic IPO underpricing, information momentum, and lockup expiration selling', *Journal of Financial Economics*, **66**, 105–37, 2002.

Akerlof, G. A. and Shiller, R. J. *Animal Spirits*, Princeton University Press, 2009.

Akerlof, G. A. and Shiller, R. J. *Phishing for Phools: The Economics of Manipulation and Deception*, Princeton University Press, 2015.

Allen, F. 'Do financial institutions matter?', *Journal of Finance*, **56**, 1,165–75, 2001.

Allen, F. and Gale, D. 'Asset price bubbles and stock market interlinkages' in W. C. Hunter, G. G. Kaufman and M. Pomerleano (eds.), *Asset Price Bubbles: The Implications for Monetary, Regulatory, and International Policies*, Cambridge, MA: MIT Press, 2005.

Allen, F. and Gale, D. 'Bubbles and crises', *Economic Journal*, **110**, 236–55, 2000.

Allen, F. and Gale, D. 'Bubbles, crises, and policy', *Oxford Review of Economic Policy*, **15**, 9–18, 1999.

Allen, F. and Qian, J. 'China's financial system and the law', *Cornell International Law Journal*, **47**, 499–553, 2014.

Anderson, A. 'An extract from The Origin of Commerce (1801)' in R. B. Emmett (ed.), *Great Bubbles*, Vol. III, London: Pickering and Chatto, 2000.

Andrade, S. C., Bian, J. and Burch, T. R. 'Analyst coverage, information, and bubbles', *Journal of Financial and Quantitative Analysis*, **48**, 1,573–605, 2013.

Andreades, A. *A History of the Bank of England*, London: P. S. King and Son, 1909.

Andrews, D. and Sánchez, A. C. 'The evolution of home ownership rates in selected OECD countries: demographic and public policy influences', *OECD Journal: Economic Studies*, 207–43, 2011.

Anon. *A Short and Sure Guide to Railway Speculation*, 7th edition, London: Effingham Wilson, 1845.

Anon. 'History of Bank of England', *The Banker's Magazine*, **12**, 508–20, 1863.

Anon. *The Railway Speculator's Memorandum Book, Ledger, and General Guide to Secure Share Dealing*, London: Simpkin, Marshall and Co., 1845.

Anon. *Remarks on Joint Stock Companies by an Old Merchant*, London: John Murray, 1825.

Anon. *The South Sea Bubble and the Numerous Fraudulent Projects to Which It Gave Rise in 1720, Historically Detailed as a Beacon to the Unwary Against Modern Schemes Equally Visionary and Nefarious*, 2nd edition, London: Thomas Boys, 1825.

Arnold, A. and McCartney, S. 'It may be earlier than you think: evidence, myths and informed debate in accounting history', *Critical Perspectives on Accounting*, **14**, 227–53, 2003.

Assenmacher-Wesche, K. and Gerlach, S. 'Financial structure and the impact of monetary policy on asset prices', *Swiss National Bank Working Paper*, No. 2008–16, 2008.

Aumeboonsuke, V. and Tangjitprom, N. 'The performance of newly issued stocks in Thailand', *International Journal of Economics and Finance*, **4**, 103–9, 2012.

Aytoun, W. E. 'How we got up the Glenmutchkin Railway, and how we got out of it', *Blackwood's Edinburgh Magazine*, **21**, 453–66, 1845.

Bailey, J. D. 'Australian borrowing in Scotland in the nineteenth century', *Economic History Review*, **12**, 268–79, 1959.

Ball, L. M. *The Fed and Lehman Brothers: Setting the Record Straight on a Financial Disaster*, New York: Cambridge University Press, 2018.

Barberis, N. and Huang, M. 'Stocks as lotteries: the implications of probability weighting for security prices', *American Economic Review*, **98**, 2,066–100, 2008.

Barberis, N., Greenwood, R., Jin, L. and Shleifer, A. 'Extrapolation and bubbles', *Journal of Financial Economics*, **129**, 203–27, 2018.

Barberis, N., Shleifer, A. and Vishny, R. 'A model of investor sentiment', *Journal of Financial Economics*, **49**, 307–43, 1998.

Basile, P. F., Kang, S. W., Landon-Lane, J. and Rockoff, H. 'Towards a history of the junk bond market, 1910–1955', *NBER Working Paper*, No. 21559, 2015.

Béland, D. 'Neo-liberalism and social policy: the politics of ownership', *Policy Studies*, **28**, 91–107, 2007.

Belsky, E. and Retsinas, N. 'History of housing finance and policy in Spain', Harvard University mimeo, 2004.

Beltratti, A., Bortolotti, B. and Caccavaio, C. 'Stock market efficiency in China: evidence from the split-share reform', *Quarterly Review of Economics and Finance*, **60**, 125–37, 2016.

Bernanke, B. S. 'Asset-price "bubbles" and monetary policy', Speech delivered at the New York Chapter of the National Association for Business Economics, New York, 15 October 2002.

Bernanke, B. S. 'Nonmonetary effects of the financial crisis in the propagation of the Great Depression', *American Economic Review*, **73**, 257–76, 1983.

Bernanke, B. S. and Gertler, M. 'Should central banks respond to movements in asset prices?', *American Economic Review*, **91**, 253–7, 2001.

Bernstein, *The Great Depression: Delayed Recovery and Economic Change in America, 1929–1939*, Cambridge University Press, 1987.

Birch, J. K. *Birch's Manual of Bicycle Companies 1897*, Westminster: Albany, 1897.

Blainey, G. and Hutton, G. *Gold and Paper, 1858–1982: A History of the National Bank of Australasia Ltd*, Melbourne: Macmillan, 1983.

Blanchard, O. and Watson, M. 'Bubbles, rational expectations, and financial markets' in P. Wachter (ed.), *Crises in the Economic and Financial Structure*, Lexington, MA: Lexington Books, 1982.

Blaug, M. *Pre-Classical Economists: John Law*, Cheltenham: Edward Elgar, 1991.

Boehm, E. A. *Prosperity and Depression in Australia 1887–1897*, Oxford: Clarendon Press, 1971.

Bonney, R. 'France and the first European paper money experiment', *French History*, **15**, 254–72, 2001.

Bordo, M. D. 'The lender of last resort: alternative views and historical experience', *Federal Reserve Bank of Richmond Economic Review*, Jan/Feb, 18–29, 1990.

Bordo, M. D. and White, E. N. 'A tale of two currencies: British and French finance during the Napoleonic Wars', *Journal of Economic History*, **51**, 303–16, 1991.

Bowles, C. *The Bubblers Medley, or A Sketch of the Times: Being Europe's Memorial for the Year 1720*, London: Carington Bowles, 1720.

Boyer, G. R. and Hatton, T. J. 'New estimates of British unemployment, 1870–1913', *Journal of Economic History*, **62**, 643–75, 2002.

Braggion, F. and Moore, L. 'Dividend policies in an unregulated market: the London Stock Exchange, 1895–1905', *Review of Financial Studies*, **24**, 2,935–73, 2011.

Brennan, M. J. 'How did it happen?', *Economic Notes*, **33**, 3–22, 2004.

Broadberry, S., Campbell, B. M. S., Klein, A., Overton, M., and van Leeuwen, B. *British Economic Growth, 1270–1870*, Cambridge University Press, 2015.

Broadbridge, S. A. 'The sources of railway share capital' in M. C. Reed (ed.), *Railways in the Victorian Economy: Studies in Finance and Economic Growth*, New York: Augustus M. Kelley, 1968.

Bromhead, A. de, Eichengreen, B. and O'Rourke, K. H. 'Political extremism in the 1920s and 1930s: do german lessons generalize?', *Journal of Economic History*, **73**, 371–406, 2013.

Brontë, C. *The Letters of Charlotte Brontë, with a Selection of Letters by Family and Friends: Vol. II, 1848–1851*, edited by M. Smith, Oxford University Press, 2000.

Brooks, J. *Once in Golconda*, New York: John Wiley and Sons, 1999.

Brown, L. *Victorian News and Newspapers*, Oxford: Clarendon Press, 1985.

Brunnermeier, M. K. 'Bubbles' in S. N. Durlauf and L. E. Blume (eds.), *The New Palgrave Dictionary of Economics*, Basingstoke: Palgrave Macmillan, 2008.

Brunnermeier, M. K. and Nagel, S. 'Hedge funds and the technology bubble', *Journal of Finance*, **59**, 2,013–40, 2004.

Brunnermeier, M. K. and Schnabel, I. 'Bubbles and central banks: historical perspectives', *Gutenberg School of Management and Economics Discussion Paper* 1411, 2014.

Butlin, N. G. *Australian Domestic Product, Investment and Foreign Borrowing 1861–1938/39*, Cambridge University Press, 1962.

Butlin, N. G. *Investment in Australian Economic Development 1861–1900*, Cambridge University Press, 1964.

Butlin, N. G. 'The shape of the Australian economy 1861–1900', *Economic Record*, **34**, 10–129, 1958.

Butlin, S. J. *The Australian Monetary System 1851–1914*, Melbourne: Ambassador Press, 1986.

Cai, J. and Wei, K. C. J. 'The investment and operating performance of Japanese initial public offerings', *Pacific-Basin Finance Journal*, **5**, 389–417, 1997.

Calomiris, C. W. and Haber, S. H. *Fragile by Design: The Political Origins of Banking Crises and Scarce Credit*, Princeton University Press, 2014.

Calomiris, C. W. and Mason, J. R. 'Consequences of bank distress during the Great Depression', *American Economic Review*, **93**, 937–47, 2003.

Campbell, G. 'Deriving the railway mania', *Financial History Review*, **20**, 1–27, 2013.

Campbell, G. 'Myopic rationality in a mania', *Explorations in Economic History*, **49**, 75–91, 2012.

Campbell, G. and Turner, J. D. 'Dispelling the myth of the naive investor during the British Railway Mania, 1845–46', *Business History Review*, **86**, 3–41, 2012.

Campbell, G. and Turner, J. D. 'Managerial failure in mid-Victorian Britain?: Corporate expansion during a promotion boom', *Business History*, **57**, 1,248–76, 2015.

Campbell, G., Quinn, W., Turner, J. D. and Ye, Q. 'What moved share prices in the nineteenth-century London stock market?' *Economic History Review*, **71**, 157–89, 2018.

Campbell, G., Turner, J. D. and Walker, C. B. 'The role of the media in a bubble', *Explorations in Economic History*, **49**, 461–81, 2012.

Campbell, G., Turner, J. D. and Ye, Q. 'The liquidity of the London capital markets', *Economic History Review*, **71**, 705–1,026, 2018.

Cannon, M. *The Land Boomers*, Melbourne University Press, 1966.

Cargill, T. 'What caused Japan's banking crisis?' in T. Hoshi and H. Patrick (eds.), *Crisis and Change in the Japanese Financial System*, New York: Springer, 2000.

Carlos, A. M. and Neal, L. 'The micro-foundations of the early London capital market: Bank of England shareholders during and after the South Sea Bubble, 1720–21', *Economic History Review*, **59**, 498–538, 2006.

Carlos, A. M., Maguire, K. and Neal, L. 'A knavish people . . . ': London Jewry and the stock market during the South Sea Bubble', *Business History*, **50**, 728–48, 2008.

Carlos, A. M., Maguire, K. and Neal, L. 'Financial acumen, women speculators, and the Royal African Company during the South Sea Bubble', *Accounting, Business & Financial History*, **16**, 219–43, 2006.

Carpenter, J. N. and Whitelaw, R. F. 'The development of China's stock market and stakes for the global economy', *Annual Review of Financial Economics*, **9**, 233–57, 2017.

Carswell, J. *The South Sea Bubble*, London: The Cresset Press, 1960.

Case, K. E. and Shiller, R. J. 'Is there a bubble in the housing market?', *Brookings Papers on Economic Activity*, 299–342, 2003.

Case, K. E., Shiller, R. J. and Thompson, A. 'What have they been thinking? Home buyer behaviour in hot and cold markets', *NBER Working Paper*, No. 18400, 2012.

Casey, C. M. 'The Irish newspapers and the residential property boom', *New Political Economy*, **24**, 144–57, 2019.

Cassidy, J. *Dot.Con: The Greatest Story Ever Sold*, London: Penguin, 2002.

Casson, M. 'The efficiency of the Victorian British railway network: A counterfactual analysis', *Networks and Spatial Economics*, **9**, 339–78, 2009.

Casson, M. *The World's First Railway System: Enterprise, Competition, and Regulation on the Railway Network in Victorian Britain*, Oxford University Press, 2009.

Ceballos, F. C. and Álvarez, G. 'Royal dynasties as human inbreeding laboratories: the Habsburgs', *Heredity*, **111**, 114–21, 2013.

Cellan-Jones, R. *Dot.Bomb: The Strange Death of Dot.Com Britain*, London: Aurum Press, 2001.

Chancellor, E. *Devil Take the Hindmost: A History of Financial Speculation*, Basingstoke: Macmillan, 1999.

Choudhry, T. 'Interdependence of stock markets: Evidence from Europe during the 1920s and 1930s', *Applied Financial Economics*, **6**, 243–9, 1996.

Claessens, S., Dell'Ariccia, G., Igan, D. and Laeven, L. 'Lessons and policy implications from the global financial crisis', *IMF Working Paper*, No. WP/10/44, 2010.

Clapham, J. H. *The Bank of England: A History*, 2 vols. Cambridge University Press, 1944.

Cleveland-Stevens, E. C. *English Railways: Their Development and their Relation to the State*, London: Routledge, 1883.

Clifford, F. *A History of Private Bill Legislation*, Vol. I, London: Butterworths, 1885.

Coffee, J. C. 'A theory of corporate scandals: Why the USA and Europe differ', *Oxford Review of Economic Policy*, **21**, 198–211, 2005.

Coghlan, T. A. *Labour and Industry in Australia: From the First Settlement in 1788 to the Establishment of the Commonwealth in 1901*, Vol. IV, Oxford University Press, 1918.

Collins, M. and Baker, M. *Commercial Banks and Industrial Finance in England and Wales, 1860–1913*, Oxford University Press, 2003.

Condorelli, S. 'The 1719–20 stock euphoria: a pan-European perspective.' *Munich Personal RePEc Archive Working Paper*, No. 82821, 2016.

Connor, G., Flavin, T. and O'Kelly, B. 'The U.S. and Irish credit crises: their distinctive differences and common features', *Journal of International Money and Finance*, **31**, 60–79, 2012.

Cork, N. 'The late Australian banking crisis', *Journal of the Institute of Bankers*, **15**, 175–261, 1894.

Costeloc, M. P. 'William Bullock and the Mexican connection', *Mexican Studies*, **22**, 275–309, 2006.

Costigliola, F. 'The United States and the reconstruction of Germany in the 1920s', *Business History Review*, **50**, 477–502, 1976.

Crafts, N. F. R., Mills, T. C. and Mulatu, A. 'Total factor productivity growth on Britain's railways, 1852–1912: a reappraisal of the evidence', *Explorations in Economic History*, **44**, 608–34, 2007.

Dale, R. *The First Crash: Lessons from the South Sea Bubble*. Princeton University Press, 2004.

Dale, R. S., Johnson, J. E. V., and Tang, L. 'Financial markets can go mad: evidence of irrational behaviour during the South Sea Bubble', *Economic History Review*, **58**, 233–71, 2005.

Daly, M. T. *Sydney Boom Sydney Bust: The City and its Property Market*. Sydney: George Allen and Unwin, 1982.

Daniel, K., Hirshleifer, D. and Subrahmanyam, A. 'Investor psychology and security market under- and overreactions', *Journal of Finance*, **53**, 1,839–85, 1998.

Darnton, R. 'An early information society: News and the media in eighteenth-century Paris', *American Historical Review*, **105**, 1–35, 2000.

Davenport-Hines, R. 'Wilks, John' in *Oxford Dictionary of National Biography*, Oxford: Oxford University Press, 2004.

Davis, A. M., 'An historical study of Law's system (1887)' in R. B. Emmett (ed.), *Great Bubbles*, Vol. II, London: Pickering and Chatto, 2000.

Davison, G. *The Rise and Fall of Marvellous Melbourne*. Melbourne University Press, 1978.

Dawson, F. G. *The First Latin American Debt Crisis: The City of London and the 1822–25 Loan Bubble*, New Haven, CT: Yale University Press, 1990.

Day, H. *A Defence of Joint Stock Companies; Being An Attempt to Shew Their Legality, Expediency, and Public Benefit*, London: Longman, Hurst, Rees and Orme, 1808.

De Tocqueville, A. *Democracy in America*, New York: Penguin, 2004 [1835].

Deaton, A. 'The financial crisis and the well-being of Americans', *Oxford Economic Papers*, **64**, 1–26, 2012.

Defoe, D. *The Anatomy of Exchange-Alley*, 2nd edition, London: E. Smith, 1719.

Dehesh, A. and Pugh, C. 'The internationalization of post-1980 property cycles and the Japanese "bubble" economy, 1986–96', *International Journal of Urban and Region Research*, **23**, 147–64, 1999.

Dell'Ariccia, G., Detragiache, E. and Rajan, R. 'The real effect of banking crises', *Journal of Financial Intermediation*, **17**, 89–112, 2008.

Dell'Arriccia, G., Igan, D. and Laeven, L. 'Credit booms and lending standards: evidence from the subprime mortgage market', *Journal of Money, Credit and Banking*, **44**, 367–84, 2012.

Dellepiane, S., Hardiman, N. and Heras J. L. 'Building on easy money: the political economy of housing bubbles in Ireland and Spain', *UCD Geary Institute Discussion Papers*, WP2103/18, 2013.

DeLong, J. B. and Magin, K. 'A short note on the size of the dot-com bubble', *NBER Working Paper*, No. 12011, 2006.

Dhar, R. and Goetzmann, W. N. 'Bubble investors: what were they thinking?', *Yale ICF Working Paper*, No. 06–22, 2006.

Dickens, C. *The Letters of Charles Dickens*. Vol. IV, *1844–1846*, edited by K. Tillotson, Oxford University Press, 1977.

Dickson, P. G. M. *The Financial Revolution in England: A Study in the Development of Public Credit, 1688–1756*. London: Macmillan, 1967.

Disraeli, B. *An Inquiry into the Plans, Progress, and Policy of the American Mining Companies*, 3rd edition, London: John Murray, 1825.

Disraeli, B. *Letters, 1815–1834*, London: University of Toronto Press, 1982.

Dobbin, F. *Forging Industrial Policy: The United States, Britain, and France in the Railway Age*, Cambridge University Press, 1994.

Donaldson, R. G. and Kamstra, M. 'A new dividend forecasting procedure that rejects bubbles in asset prices: the case of 1929's stock crash', *Review of Financial Studies*, **9**, 333–83, 1996.

Dowd, K. 'Free banking in Australia' in K. Dowd (ed.), *The Experience of Free Banking*, London: Routledge, 1992.

Duffy, D. and O'Hanlon, N. 'Negative equity in the Irish housing market: estimates using loan level data', *ESRI Working Paper*, No. 463, 2013.

Dyck, A. and Zingales, L. 'The bubble and the media', in P. Cornelius and B. Kogut (eds.), *Corporate Governance and Capital Flows in a Global Economy*, New York: Oxford University Press, 2002.

Eatwell, J. 'Useful bubbles', *Contributions to Political Economy*, **23**, 35–47, 2004.

Edwards, G. W. 'Government control of foreign investments', *American Economic Review*, **18**, 684–701, 1928.

Eichengreen, B. *Golden Fetters: The Gold Standard and the Great Depression, 1919–1939*, New York: Oxford University Press, 1992.

Eichengreen, B. *Hall of Mirrors*, New York: Oxford University Press, 2015.

Eichengreen, B. and Hatton, T. 'Interwar unemployment in international perspective', *IRLE Working Paper*, No. 12–88, 1988.

Eichengreen, B. and Mitchener, K. 'The Great Depression as a credit boom gone wrong', *BIS Working Paper*, No. 137, 2003.

Ellis, A. 'The Australian banking crisis', *Economic Journal*, **3**, 293–7, 1893.

Emden, P. H. *Money Powers of Europe in the Nineteenth and Twentieth Centuries*, London: Sampson Low, Marston and Co., 1938.

English, H. *A Complete View of the Joint Stock Companies Formed during the Years 1824 and 1825*, London: Boosey and Sons, 1827.

English, H. *A General Guide to the Companies Formed for the Working of Foreign Mines*, London: Boosey & Sons, 1825.

Englund, P. 'The Swedish banking crisis: roots and consequences', *Oxford Review of Economic Policy*, **15**, 80–97, 1999.

Engsted, T. 'Fama on bubbles', *CREATES Working Paper*, No. 2014–28, 2014.

Esteves, R. and Mesevage, G. G. 'The rise of new corruption: British MPs during the Railway Mania of 1845', University of Oxford mimeo.

Fabbri, F. and Marin, D. 'What explains the rise in CEO pay in Germany? A panel data analysis for 1977–2009', *Munich Discussion Paper*, No. 2012–12, 2012.

Fama, E. 'Two pillars of asset pricing', *American Economic Review*, **104**, 1,467–85, 2014.

Farhi, E. and Panageas, S. 'The real effects of stock market mispricing at the aggregate: theory and empirical evidence', *Harvard University Working Paper*, 2006.

Fenn, M. J. *British Investment in South America and the Financial Crisis of 1825–1826*, MA thesis, Durham University, 1969.

Ferguson, N. *The Ascent of Money: A Financial History of the World*, London: Penguin, 2009.

Fishback, P., Haines, M. R. and Kantor, S. 'Births, deaths, and New Deal relief during the Great Depression', *Review of Economics and Statistics*, **89**, 1–14, 2007.

Fisher, C. and Kent, C. 'Two depressions, one banking collapse', *Reserve Bank of Australia Research Discussion Paper*, No. 1999–06, 1999.

Fisher, I. 'The debt-deflation theory of great depressions', *Econometrica*, **1**, 337–57, 1933.

Fitzgerald, F. S. *The Great Gatsby*, New York: Scribner, 1925.

Flandreau, M., Gaillard, N. and Packer, F. 'Ratings performance, regulation and the great depression: lessons from foreign government securities', *CEPR Discussion Paper*, No. DP7328, 2009.

Foley, S., Karlsen, J. R. and Putniņš, T. 'Sex, drugs, and bitcoin: how much illegal activity is financed through cryptocurrencies?', *Review of Financial Studies*, **2**, 1798–853, 2019.

Francis, J. *A History of the English Railway: Its Social Relations and Revelations, 1820–845*, London: Longman, Brown, Green, and Longmans, 1851.

Francis, J. *Chronicles and Characters of the Stock Exchange*, London: Willoughy & Co., 1849.

Francis, J. *History of the Bank of England: Its Times and Traditions*, London: Willoughby & Co., 1847.

Frankel, A. B. and Morgan, P. B. 'Deregulation and competition in Japanese banking', *Federal Reserve Bulletin*, **78**, 579–93, 1992.

Frazer, W. J. and Guthrie, J. J. *The Florida Land Boom: Speculation, Money, and the Banks*, Westport, CT: Quorum Books, 1995.

Frehen, R. G. P., Goetzmann, W. N. and Rouwenhorst, K. 'New evidence on the first financial bubble', *Journal of Financial Economics*, **108**, 585–607, 2013.

Freixas, X., Giannini, C., Hoggarth, G. and Soussa, F. 'Lender of last resort: a review of the literature', *Financial Stability Review*, **7**, 151–67, 1999.

Frennberg, P. and Hansson, B. 'Computation of a monthly index for Swedish stock returns, 1919–1989', *Scandinavian Economic History Review*, **4** 3–27, 1992.

Friedman, M. and Schwartz, A. J. *A Monetary History of the United States, 1867–1960*, Princeton University Press, 1963.

Friedman, M. and Schwartz, A. J. *The Great Contraction 1929–1933*, Princeton University Press, 2008.

Galbraith, J. K. *A Short History of Financial Euphoria*. London: Penguin, 1990.

Galbraith, J. K. *The Great Crash 1929*, London: Penguin Books, 2009.

Gale, C. J. *A Letter to the Right Hon. the Earl of Dalhousie, President of the Board of Trade, on Railway Legislation*, London: John Murray, 1844.

Garber, P. M. 'Famous first bubbles', *Journal of Economic Perspectives*, **4**, 35–54, 1990.

Garber, P. M. *Famous First Bubbles: The Fundamentals of Early Manias*, Cambridge, MA: MIT Press, 2001.

Garber, P. M. 'Tulipmania', *Journal of Political Economy*, **97**, 535–60, 1989.

García, D. 'Sentiment during recessions', *Journal of Finance*, **68**, 1,267–300, 2013.

Gayer, A. D., Rostow, W. W. and Schwartz, A. J. *The Growth and Fluctuation of the British Economy, 1790–1850*, 2 vols. Oxford University Press.

Geary, F. and Stark, T. 'Regional GDP in the UK, 1861–1911: new estimates', *Economic History Review*, **68**, 123–44, 2015.

Gelderblom, O. and Jonker, J. 'Mirroring different follies: the character of the 1720 bubble in the Dutch Republic.' *Utrecht University Working Paper*, 2009.

Gelderblom, O. and Jonker, J. 'Public finance and economic growth: the case of Holland in the seventeenth century', *Journal of Economic History*, **71**, 1–39, 2011.

Gentzkow, M. and Shapiro, J. M. 'Media bias and reputation', *Journal of Political Economy*, **114**, 280–316, 2006.

Gerard, D. *Attack of the 50 Foot Blockchain: Bitcoin, Blockchain, Ethereum and Smart Contracts*, David Gerard (self-published), 2017.

Gilmore, N. R. 'Henry George Ward, British publicist for Mexican mines', *Pacific Historical Review*, **31**, 35–47, 1963.

Gissing, G. *The Whirlpool*. London: Penguin Classics, 2015.

Gjerstad, S. and Smith, V. L. 'Monetary policy, credit extension, and housing bubbles: 2008 and 1929', *Critical Review*, **21**, 269–300, 2009.

Gjerstad, S. and Smith, V. L. *Rethinking Housing Bubbles: The Role of Household and Bank Balance Sheets in Modeling Economic Cycles*, New York: Cambridge University Press, 2014.

Glaesar, E. L. 'A nation of gamblers: real estate speculation and American history', *American Economic Review: Papers and Proceedings*, **103**, 1–42, 2013.

Glaesar, E. L. and Sinai, T. 'Postmortem for a housing crash' in E. L. Glaesar and T. Sinai (eds.), *Housing and the Financial Crash*, University of Chicago Press.

Goetzmann, W. N. 'Bubble investing: learning from history', *NBER Working Paper*, No. 21693, 2015.

Goetzmann, W. N. and Newman, F. 'Securitization in the 1920's', *NBER Working Paper*, No. 15650, 2010.

Goldgar, A. *Tulipmania: Money, Honour, and Knowledge in the Dutch Golden Age*, Chicago University Press, 2007.

Gollan, R. *The Commonwealth Bank of Australia: Origins and Early History*, Canberra: Australian National University Press, 1968.

Goodman, L. S. and Mayer, C. 'Homeownership and the American dream', *Journal of Economic Perspectives*, **32**, 31–58, 2018.

Gordon, S. H. *Passage to Union: How the Railroads Transformed American Life, 1829–1929*, Chicago, IL: Ivan R. Dee, 1996.

Gornall, W. and Strebulaev, I. A. 'Squaring venture capital valuations with reality', *NBER Working Paper*, No. 23895, 2017.

Grant, J. *The Trouble with Prosperity*, New York: Times Books, 1996.

Greenwood, R. and Nagel, S. 'Inexperienced investors and bubbles', *Journal of Financial Economics*, **93**, 239–58, 2009.

Greenwood, R., Shleifer, A. and You, Y. 'Bubbles for Fama', *NBER Working Paper*, No. 23191, 2017.

Grew, W. F. *The Cycle Industry*, London: Sir Isaac Pitman & Sons, 1921.

Griffin, J. M., Harris, J. H., Shu, T. and Topaloglu, S. 'Who drove and burst the tech bubble?', *Journal of Finance*, **66**, 1,251–90, 2011.

Griffin, J. M., Hirschey, N. H. and Kelly, P. J. 'How important is the financial media in global markets?', *Review of Financial Studies*, **24**, 3,941–92, 2011.

Hagstrom, R. G. *Investing: The Last Liberal Art*, New York: Columbia University Press, 2013.

Haig, B. 'New estimates of Australian GDP: 1861–1948/49', *Australian Economic History Review*, **41**, 1–34, 2001.

Hall, A. R. *The Stock Exchange of Melbourne and the Victorian Economy, 1852–1900*, Canberra: ANU Press, 1968.

Hamilton, E. J. 'John Law of Lauriston: banker, gamester, merchant, chief?' *American Economic Review*, **57**, 273–82, 1967.

Hamilton, E. J., 'Prices and wages at Paris under John Law's system (1936–7)' in R. B. Emmett (ed.), *Great Bubbles*, Vol. II, London: Pickering and Chatto, 2000.

Harris, E. T. 'Handel the investor', *Music & Letters*, **85**, 521–75, 2004.

Harris, R. *Industrializing English Law: Entrepreneurship and Business Organization, 1720–1844*, Cambridge University Press, 2000.

Harris, R. 'Political economy, interest groups, legal institution, and the repeal of the Bubble Act in 1825', *Economic History Review*, **50**, 675–96, 1997.

Harris, R. 'The Bubble Act: its passage and its effects on business organization', *Journal of Economic History*, **54**, 610–27, 1994.

Harrison, A. E., 'The competitiveness of the British cycle industry, 1890–1914', *Economic History Review*, **22**, 287–303, 1969.

Hart, M., Jonker, J. and van Zanden, J. L. *A Financial History of the Netherlands*, Cambridge University Press, 1997.

Haruvy, E. and Noussair, C. N. 'The effect of short selling on bubbles and crashes in experimental spot asset markets', *Journal of Finance*, **61**, 1,119–57, 2006.

Haughwot, A., Peach, R. W., Sporn, J. and Tracy, J. 'The supply side of the housing boom and bust of the 2000s' in E. L. Glaesar and T. Sinai (eds.), *Housing and the Financial Crash*, University of Chicago Press.

Hausman, W. J., Hertner, P. and Wilkins, M. *Global Electrification: Multinational Enterprise and International Finance in the History of Light and Power, 1878–2007*, Cambridge University Press, 2008.

Hawke, G. R. *Railways and Economic Growth in England and Wales, 1840–70*, Oxford University Press, 1970.

Hawtrey, R. G. *A Century of Bank Rate*, London: Longmans, Green and Co., 1938.

Head, F. B. *Rough Notes Taken during Some Rapid Journeys across the Pampas and among the Andes*, 2nd edition, London: John Murray, 1826.

Hebner, K. J. and Hiraki, T. 'Japanese initial public offerings' in I. Walter and T. Hiraki (eds.), *Restructuring Japan's Financial Markets*, Homewood, IL: Business One Irwin, 1993.

Hickson, C. R. and Thompson, E. A. 'Predicting bubbles', *Global Business and Economics Review*, **8**, 217–26, 2006.

Hickson, C. R. and Turner, J. D. 'Free banking gone awry: the Australian banking crisis of 1893', *Financial History Review*, **9**, 147–67, 2002.

Hills, S., Thomas, R. and Dimsdale, N. 'The UK recession in context – what do three centuries of data tell us?' *Bank of England Quarterly Bulletin*, Q4, 277–91, 2010.

Hilt, E. and Rahn, W. M. 'Turning citizens into investors: promoting savings with Liberty bonds during World War I', *RSF: The Russell Sage Foundation Journal of the Social Sciences*, **2**, 86–108, 2016.

Hilton, B. *Corn, Cash and Commerce: The Economic Policies of the Tory Governments 1815–1830*, Oxford University Press, 1977.

Hirayama, Y. 'Housing policy and social inequality in Japan' in M. Izuhara (ed.), *Comparing Social Policies: Exploring New Perspectives in Britain and Japan*, Bristol: Policy Press, 2003.

Hoggarth, G., Reis, R. and Saporta, V. 'Costs of banking system instability: some empirical evidence', *Journal of Banking and Finance*, **26**, 825–55, 2002.

Hong, H. and Stein, J. C. 'Disagreement and the stock market', *Journal of Economic Perspectives*, **21**, 109–28, 2007.

Honohan, P. 'Euro membership and bank stability – friends or foes? Lesson from Ireland', *Comparative Economic Studies*, **52**, 133–57, 2010.

Honohan, P. 'Resolving Ireland's banking crisis', *Economic and Social Review*, **40**, 207–31, 2009.

Hoppit, J. 'The myths of the South Sea Bubble', *Transactions of the Royal Historical Society*, **12**, 141–65, 2002.

Hoshi, T. and Kashyap, A. K. 'Japan's financial crisis and economic stagnation', *Journal of Economic Perspectives*, **18**, 3–26, 2004.

Hoshi, T. and Patrick, H. 'The Japanese financial system: an introductory overview' in T. Hoshi and H. Patrick (eds.), *Crisis and Change in the Japanese Financial System*, New York: Springer, 2000.

Hough, E. *The Mississippi Bubble: How the Star of Good Fortune Rose and Set and Rose Again, by a Woman's Grace, for One John Law of Lauriston*, New York: Grossat and Dunlop, 1902.

Hounshell, D. A. *From the American System to Mass Production, 1800–1932: The Development of Manufacturing Technology in the United States*, London: Johns Hopkins University Press, 1985.

House of Were, *The History of the House of J. B. Were and Son and Its Founder, Jonathan Binns Were*, Melbourne: House of Were, 1954.

Huang, Y. 'How did China take off?', *Journal of Economic Perspectives*, **26**, 147–70, 2012.

Huertas, T. F. and Silverman, J. L. 'Charles E. Mitchell: Scapegoat of the Crash?', *Business History Review*, **60**, 81–103, 1986.

Hüfner, F. 'The German banking system: lessons from the financial crisis', *OECD Economics Department Working Paper*, No. 788, 2010.

Hunt, B. *The Development of the Business Corporation in England 1800–1867*, Cambridge, MA: Harvard University Press, 1936.

Hutcheson, A. *Several Calculations and Remarks Relating to the South Sea Scheme and the Value of that Stock*, London, 1720.

Hutcheson, A., *Some Calculations relating to the Proposals Made by the South-Sea Company, and the Bank of England, to the House of Commons*, London, 1720.

Hyndman, H. M. *Commercial Crises of the Nineteenth Century*, New York: Augustus M. Kelley, 1968 [first pub. 1892].

Igan, D. and Mishra, P. 'Wall Street, Capital Hill, and K Street: political influence and financial regulation', *Journal of Law and Economics*, **57**, 1,063–84, 2014.

Jackman, W. T. *The Development of Transportation in Modern England*, London: Cass, 1966.

James, H. '1929: The New York Stock Market Crash', *Representations*, **110**, 129–44, 2010.

Janeway, W. H. *Doing Capitalism in the Innovation Economy: Reconfiguring the Three-Player Game between Markets, Speculators and the State*, 2nd edition, Cambridge University Press, 2018

Jenkinson, T. J. 'Initial public offerings in the United Kingdom, the United States, and Japan', *Journal of the Japanese and International Economies*, **4**, 428–49, 1990.

Jenks, L. H. *The Migration of British Capital to 1875*, London: Thomas Nelson and Sons, 1927.

Jiménez, F. 'Building boom and political corruption', *South European Society and Politics*, **14**, 255–72, 2009.

Johnson, S. 'The Quiet Coup', *The Atlantic*, May, 2009.

Johnson, S. and Kwak, J. *13 Bankers: The Wall Street Takeover and the Next Financial Meltdown*, New York: Pantheon Books, 2010.

Jones, B. 'Asset bubbles: Re-thinking policy for the age of asset management', *IMF Working Paper*, No. WP/15/27, 2015.

Jones, C. M. 'A century of stock market liquidity and trading costs', Graduate School of Business, Columbia University, 2000.

Jordà, Ò., Schularick, M. and Taylor, A. M., 'Macrofinancial history and the new business cycle facts' in M. Eichenbaum and J. A. Parker (eds.), *NBER Macroeconomics Annual 2016*, Vol. XXXI, University of Chicago Press, 2016.

Junner, R. G. *The Practice before the Railway Commissioners under the Regulation of Railways Act 1873*, London: Wildy and Sons, 1874.

Kaldor, N. 'Speculation and economic stability', *Review of Economic Studies*, 7, 1–27, 1939.

Kang, S.W. and Rockoff, H. 'Capitalizing patriotism: the liberty loans of World War I', *Financial History Review*, 22, 45–78, 2015.

Karpoff, J. M., Lee, G. and Masulis, R. W. 'Contracting under asymmetric information: evidence from lockup agreements in seasoned equity offerings', *Journal of Financial Economics*, 110, 607–26, 2013.

Kelley, A. C. 'Demographic change and economic growth: Australia, 1861–1911', *Explorations in Entrepreneurial History*, 5, 207–77, 1968.

Kelly, L. W. and Boyle, R. 'Business on television: continuity, change, and risk in the development of television's business entertainment format', *Television & New Media*, 12, 228–47, 2011.

Kelly, M. 'On the likely extent of falls in Irish house prices', *Quarterly Economic Commentary*, Summer, 42–54, 2007.

Kelly, M. 'The Irish credit bubble', *UCD Geary Institute Discussion Paper Series*, 2009.

Kelly, M. 'What happened to Ireland?', *Irish Pages*, 6, 7–19, 2009.

Kennedy, W. and Delargy, R. 'Explaining Victorian entrepreneurship: a cultural problem? A market problem? No problem?', *London School of Economics Department of Economic History Working Paper*, No. 61, 2000.

Keynes, J. M. *The General Theory of Employment, Interest and Money*, London: Macmillan, 1936.

Killick, J. R. and Thomas, W. A. 'The provincial stock exchanges, 1830–1870', *Economic History Review*, 23, 96–111, 1970.

Kindleberger, C. P. *Manias, Panics and Crashes: A History of Financial Crises*, 3rd edition, London: Macmillan, 1996.

King, W. T. C. *History of the London Discount Market*, London: Frank Cass, 1935.

Kitchin, R., O'Callaghan, C. and Gleeson, J. 'The new ruins of Ireland? Unfinished estates in the post-Celtic Tiger Era', *International Journal of Urban and Regional Research*, 38, 1,069–80, 2014.

Kleer, R. A. 'Riding a wave: the Company's role in the South Sea Bubble', *Economic History Review*, 68, 264–85, 2015.

Kleer, R. A. '"The folly of particulars": the political economy of the South Sea Bubble', *Financial History Review*, 19, 175–97, 2012.

Klein, M. *Rainbow's End: The Crash of 1929*, New York: Oxford University Press, 2001.

Kliesen, K. L. 'The 2001 recession: how was it different and what developments may have caused it?', *Federal Reserve Bank of St. Louis Review*, 85, 2003.

Knoll, K., Schularick, M. and Steger, T. 'No place like home: global house prices, 1870–2012', *American Economic Review*, 107, 331–53, 2017.

Knowledge@Wharton, 'What's behind China's stock market gamble?' https://knowledge.wharton.upenn.edu/article/whats-behind-chinas-stock-market-gamble/, last accessed 19 November 2019.

Knowles, S., Phillips, G. and Lidberg, J. 'Reporting the global financial crisis', *Journalism Studies*, **18**, 322–40, 2017.

Kostal, R.W. *Law and English Railway Capitalism*, Oxford University Press, 1994.

Kynaston, D. T. A. *The London Stock Exchange, 1870–1914: An Institutional History*, PhD thesis, University of London, 1983.

Laeven, L. and Valencia, F. 'Resolution of banking crises: the good, the bad, and the ugly', *IMF Working Paper*, No. WP/10/146, 2010.

Lam, A. 'Government interventions in housing finance markets – an international overview', *U.S. Department of Housing and Urban Development Working Paper*, 2011.

Lambert, R. S. *The Railway King, 1800–1871: A Study of George Hudson and the Business Morals of the Age*, London: G. Allen & Unwin Ltd., 1894.

Lamont, O. A. and Stein, J. C. 'Aggregate short interest and market valuations', *American Economic Review*, **94**, 29–32, 2004.

Lamoreaux, N. 'The future of economic history must be interdisciplinary', *Journal of Economic History*, **75**, 1,251–7, 2015.

Lardner, D. *Railway Economy: A Treatise on the New Art of Transport, Its Management, Prospects and Relations, Commercial, Financial and Social: With an Exposition of the Practical Results of the Railways in Operation in the United Kingdom, On the Continent and in America*, London: Taylor, Walton and Maberly, 1850.

Laurence, H. *Money Rules: The New Politics of Finance in Britain and Japan*, London: Cornell University Press, 2001.

Law, J., *Money and Trade Considered*, Glasgow: R&A Foulis, 1750.

Le Bris, D. and Hautcoeur, P.-C. 'A challenge to triumphant optimists? A blue chips index for the Paris stock exchange, 1854–2007', *Financial History Review*, **17**, 141–83, 2010.

Lee, J. 'The provision of capital for early Irish railways, 1830–53', *Irish Historical Studies*, **16**, 33–63, 1968.

Leunig, T. 'Time is money: a re-assessment of the passenger social savings from Victorian British railways', *Journal of Economic History*, **66**, 635–73, 2006.

Lewin, H. G. *The Railway Mania and its Aftermath*. Newton Abbot: David & Charles, 1968 [1936].

Lewis, M. *The Big Short: A True Story*, London: Penguin, 2011.

Li, Z. 'The emergence of China's 2006–2007 stock market bubble and its burst' in S. Cheng and Z. Li (eds.), *The Chinese Stock Market Volume II*, Basingstoke: Palgrave Macmillan, 2015.

Liao, L., Liu, B. and Wang, H. 'China's secondary privatisation: perspectives from the split-share structure reform', *Journal of Financial Economics*, **113**, 500–18, 2014.

Lincoln, E. J. 'Infrastructural deficiencies, budget policy, and capital flows' in M. Schmiegelow (ed.), *Japan's Response to Crisis and Change in the World Economy*, London: Routledge, 1986.

Ljungvist, A. and Wilhelm, Jr., W. J. 'IPO pricing in the dot-com bubble', *Journal of Finance*, **58**, 723–52, 2003.

Lloyd-Jones, R. and Lewis, M. J., *Raleigh and the British Bicycle Industry: An Economic and Business History, 1870–1960*, Farnham: Ashgate, 2000.

Lowenstein, R. *Origins of the Crash*, New York: Penguin, 2004.

Lu, L. and Lu, L. 'Unveiling China's stock market bubble: margin financing, the leveraged bull and governmental responses', *Journal of International Banking Law and Regulation*, **32**, 146–60, 2017.

Lux, T. 'Herd behaviour, bubbles and crashes', *Economic Journal*, **105**, 881–96, 1995.

Mackay, C. *Memoirs of Extraordinary Popular Delusions and the Madness of Crowds*, 2nd edition, London: Robson, Levey and Franklin, 1852.

Mackay, C. *Memoirs of Extraordinary Popular Delusions and the Madness of Crowds*, 3rd edition, London: Routledge, 1856.

Martin, A. and Ventura, J. 'Economic growth with bubbles', *American Economic Review*, **102**, 3,033–58, 2012.

Martineau, H. *A History of the Thirty Year's Peace, A.D. 1816–1846*, 4 vols. London: George Bell and Sons, 1877.

Marx, K. *Capital: A Critique of Political Economy*, Vol. III, London: Penguin, 1993 [1894].

Mayer, C. 'Housing bubbles: a survey', *Annual Review of Economics*, **3**, 559–77, 2011.

McCarthy, N., Poole, K. T. and Rosenthal, H. *Political Bubbles: Financial Crises and the Failure of American Democracy*, Princeton University Press, 2013.

McCartney, S. and Arnold, A. J. 'Capital clamours for profitable investment, confidence has become eager and may shortly become blind: George Hudson and the railway mania extensions of the York and North Midland Railway', *Journal of Industrial History*, **4**, 94–116, 2001.

McCartney, S. and Arnold, A. J. 'The railway mania of 1845–1847: market irrationality or collusive swindle based on accounting distortions?', *Accounting, Auditing and Accountability Journal*, **16**, 821–52, 2003.

McCulloch, J. R. *A Dictionary, Practical, Theoretical, and Historical of Commerce and Commercial Navigation*, 2nd edition, Philadelphia, PA: Carey and Hart, 1847.

McCullough, B. *How the Internet Happened: From Netscape to the iPhone*, London: W. W. Norton & Company, 2018.

Mercile, J. 'The role of the media in sustaining Ireland's housing boom', *New Political Economy*, **9**, 282–301, 2014.

Merrett, D. T. 'Australian banking practice and the crisis of 1893', *Australian Economic History Review*, **29**, 60–85, 1989.

Merrett, D. T. 'Preventing bank failure: could the Commercial Bank of Australia have been saved by its peers in 1893?', *Victorian Historical Journal*, **65**, 122–42, 1993.

Mian, A. and Sufi, A. 'Credit supply and housing speculation', Princeton University mimeo, 2018.

Mian, A. and Sufi, A. *House of Debt: How They (and You) Caused the Great Recession, and How We Can Prevent It from Happening Again*, University of Chicago Press, 2014.

Mian, A. and Sufi, A. 'The consequences of mortgage credit expansion: evidence from the U.S. mortgage default crisis, *Quarterly Journal of Economics*, **124**, 1,449–96, 2009.

Michie, R. C. *Guilty Money: The City of London in Victorian and Edwardian Culture, 1815–1914*, London: Pickering and Chatto, 2009.

Michie, R. C. *Money, Mania and Markets: Investment, Company Formation and the Stock Exchange in Nineteenth-Century Scotland*, Edinburgh: John Donald Publishers, 1981.

Michie, R. C. *The London Stock Exchange: A History*, Oxford University Press, 2001.

Millward, A. 'The cycle trade in Birmingham 1890–1920' in B. Tilson (ed.), *Made in Birmingham: Design and Industry*, Warwick: Brewin, 1989.

Minsky, H. P. *Stabilizing an Unstable Economy*, 2nd edition, New York: McGraw-Hill, 2008.

Mishkin, F. S. 'Lessons from the Asian crisis', *NBER Working Paper*, No. 7102, 1999.

Mitchell, B. R., *British Historical Statistics*, Cambridge University Press, 1988.

Mitchell, B. R. 'The coming of the railway and United Kingdom economic growth', *Journal of Economic History*, **24**, 315–66, 1964.

Moe, T. G., Solheim, J. A. and Vale, B. 'The Norwegian banking crisis', *Norges Banks Skriftserie Occasional Papers*, No. 33, 2004.

Müller, S. C. 'The real estate bubble in Spain has been pumped up by all of us', *The IEB International Journal of Finance*, **2**, 2–11, 2011.

Munoz, S. F. and Cueto, L. C. 'What has happened in Spain? The real estate bubble, corruption and housing development: a view from the local level', *Geoforum*, **85**, 206–13, 2017.

Murphy, A. E. 'Corporate ownership in France: the importance of history' in R. K. Morck (ed.), *A History of Corporate Governance around the World: Family Business Groups to Professional Managers*, University of Chicago Press, 2005.

Murphy, A. E. *John Law: Economic Theorist and Policy-maker*, Oxford: Clarendon Press, 1997.

Murphy, R. T. *The Real Price of Japanese Money*, London: Weidenfeld and Nicolson, 1996.

Nakaso, H. 'The financial crisis in Japan: how the Bank of Japan responded and the lessons learnt', *BIS Paper*, No. 6, 2001.

Naughton, J. *A Brief History of the Future*, Lymington: Weidenfeld and Nicolson, 1999.

Neal, L. *'I Am Not Master of Events': The Speculations of John Law and Lord Londonderry in the Mississippi and South Sea Bubbles*, New Haven, CT: Yale University Press, 2012.

Neal, L. 'The financial crisis of 1825 and the restructuring of the British financial system', *Federal Reserve Bank of St. Louis Review*, **80**, 53–76, 1998.

Neal, L. *The Rise of Financial Capitalism: International Capital Markets in the Age of Reason*, Cambridge University Press, 1990.

Nehls, H. and Schmidt, T. 'Credit crunch in Germany?', *RWI Discussion Paper*, No. 6, 2003.

Nicholas, T. 'Stock market swings and the value of innovation, 1908–1929' in N. R. Lamoreaux and K. L. Sokoloff (eds.), *Financing Innovation in the United States, 1870 to the Present*, Cambridge, MA: MIT Press.

Noguchi, Y. 'Land prices and house prices in Japan' in Y. Noguchi and J. Poterba (eds.), *Housing Markets in the U.S. and Japan*, University of Chicago Press, 1994.

Noguchi, Y. 'The "bubble" and economic policies in the 1980s', *The Journal of Japanese Studies*, **20**, 291–329, 1994.

Norris, M. and Coates, D. 'How housing killed the Celtic tiger: anatomy and consequences of Ireland's housing boom and bust', *Journal of Housing and the Built Environment*, **29**, 299–315, 2014.

Norris, M. and Coates, D. 'Mortgage availability, qualifications and risks in Ireland, 2000-2009', *Journal of Current Issues in Finance, Business and Economics*, **4**, 191–206, 2011.

Noyes, A. D. *Forty Years of American Finance*, New York: G.P. Putnam's Sons, 1909.

Nyberg, P. 'The Finnish banking crisis and its handling (an update of developments through 1993)', *Bank of Finland Discussion Papers*, No. 7/94, 1994.

Ó Riain, S. 'The crisis of financialisation in Ireland', *Economic and Social Review*, **43**, 497–533, 2010.

O'Hara, M. 'Bubbles: some perspectives (and loose talk) from history', *Review of Financial Studies*, **21**, 11–17, 2008.

O'Sullivan, K. P. V. and Kennedy, T. 'What caused the Irish banking crisis?', *Journal of Financial Regulation and Compliance*, **18**, 224–42, 2010.

Odlyzko, A. 'Charles Mackay's own extraordinary popular delusions and the Railway Mania', University of Minnesota manuscript, 2012.

Odlyzko, A. 'Collective hallucinations and inefficient markets: the British Railway Mania of the 1840s', University of Minnesota manuscript, 2010.

Odlyzko, A. 'Newton's financial misadventures in the South Sea bubble', *Notes and Records*, **73**, 29–59, 2019.

Ofek, E. and Richardson, M. 'DotCom Mania: the rise and fall of internet stock prices', *Journal of Finance*, **58**, 1,113–37, 2003.

Oizumi, E. 'Property finance in Japan: expansion and collapse of the bubble economy', *Environment and Planning*, **26**, 199–213, 1994.

Okina, K., Shirakawa, M. and Shiratsuka, S. 'The asset price bubble and monetary policy: Japan's experience in the late 1980s and the lessons', *Monetary and Economic Studies*, **19**, 395–450, 2001.

Olivier, J. 'Growth-enhancing bubbles', *International Economic Review*, **41**, 133–51, 2000.

Olney, M. L. *Buy Now, Pay Later: Advertising, Credit, and Consumer Durables in the 1920s*, The University of North Carolina Press, 1991.

Opp, K.-D. 'Dump the concept of rationality into the deep ocean' in B. Frey and D. Iselin (eds.), *Economic Ideas You Should Forget*, Cham: Springer, 2017.

Parsons, N. *King Khama, Emperor Joe and the Great White Queen*, University of Chicago Press, 1998.

Pástor, L. and Veronesi, P. 'Technological revolutions and stock prices', *American Economic Review*, **99**, 1,451–83, 2009.

Pástor, L. and Veronesi, P. 'Was there a Nasdaq bubble in the late 1990s?', *Journal of Financial Economics*, **81**, 61–100, 2006.

Paul, H. *The South Sea Bubble: An Economic History of its Origins and Consequences*, Abingdon: Routledge, 2011.

Paul, H. 'The "South Sea Bubble", 1720' in *European History Online (EGO)*, Leibniz Institute of European History, 2015.

Peel, A. G. V. *The Australian Crisis of 1893*, London: HMSO, 1893.

Perez, C. 'The double bubble at the turn of the century: technological roots and structural implications', *Cambridge Journal of Economics*, **33**, 779–805, 2009.

Pope, D. 'Free banking in Australia before World War I', *ANU Working Papers in Economic History*, No. 129, 1989.

Posen, A. S. 'Why central banks should not burst bubbles', *International Finance*, **9**, 109–24, 2006.

Posthumus, N. W. 'The tulip mania in Holland in the years 1636–37', *Journal of Economic and Business History*, **1**, 434–55, 1929.

Postman, N. *Amusing Ourselves to Death: Public Discourse in the Age of Showbusiness*, New York: Penguin. 1985.

Powell, E. T. *The Evolution of the Money Market, 1385–1915*. London: Frank Cass, 1966.

Pressnell, L. S. *Country Banking in the Industrial Revolution*, Oxford: Clarendon Press, 1956.

Purdey, C. 'Housing equity: A market update', *CML Housing Finance*, August, 1–11, 2011.

Purnanandam, A. 'Originate-to-distribute model and the subprime mortgage crisis', *Review of Financial Studies*, **24**, 1,881–915, 2011.

Qian, J. 'The 2015 stock panic of China: a narrative', Shanghai Jiao Tong University mimeo, 2016.

Quinn, W. 'Squeezing the bears: cornering risk and limits on arbitrage during the "British bicycle mania", 1896–898', *Economic History Review*, **72**, 286–311, 2019.

Quinn, W. 'Technological revolutions and speculative finance: evidence from the British Bicycle Mania', *Cambridge Journal of Economics*, **43**, 271–94, 2019.

Radlet, S., Sachs, J. D., Cooper, R. N. and Bosworth, B. P. 'The East Asian financial crisis: diagnosis, remedies, prospects', *Brookings Papers on Economic Activity*, 1–90, 1998.

Rajan, R. G. *Fault Lines: How Hidden Fractures Still Threaten the World Economy*, Princeton University Press, 2010.

Randall, R. W. *Real del Monte: A British Silver Mining Venture in Mexico*, Austin, TX: University of Texas Press, 1972.

Rao, V. 'A new soft technology', *Breaking Smart*. https://breakingsmart.com/en/season-1/a-new-soft-technology/, last accessed 28 August 2017.

Reading, B. *Japan: The Coming Collapse*, New York: HarperCollins, 1992.

Reed, M.C. *Investment in Railways in Britain 1820–1844: A Study in the Development of the Capital Market*, Oxford University Press, 1975.

Regling, K. and Watson, M. *A Preliminary Report on the Sources of Ireland's Banking Crisis*, Dublin: Government Publications, 2010.

Rippy, J. F. 'Latin America and the British investment 'boom' of the 1820s', *Journal of Modern History*, **19**, 122–9, 1947.

Romer, C. D. 'The Great Crash and the onset of the Great Depression', *Quarterly Journal of Economics*, **105**, 597–624, 1990.

Rubinstein, D. 'Cycling in the 1890s', *Victorian Studies*, **21**, 47–71, 1977.

Ruiz, J. F., Stupariu, P. and Vilarino, Á. 'The crisis of Spanish savings banks', *Cambridge Journal of Economics*, **40**, 1,455–77, 2016.

Salidjanova, N. 'China's stock market collapse and government's response', *U.S.-China Economic and Security Review Commission Issue Brief*, 13 July, 2015.

Santos, T. 'Antes del diluvio: the Spanish banking system in the first decade of the euro', Columbia University mimeo, 2014.

Scheinkman, J. A. *Speculation, Trading and Bubbles*, New York: Columbia University Press, 2014.

Scheinkman, J. A. and Xiong, W. 'Overconfidence and speculative bubbles', *Journal of Political Economy*, **111**, 1,183–220, 2003.

Scherbina, A. and Schlusche, B. 'Asset price bubbles: a survey', *Quantitative Finance*, **14**, 589–604, 2014.

Schifferes, S. and Knowles, S. 'The British media and the first crisis of globalisation' in S. Schifferes and R. Roberts (eds.), *The Media and Financial Crises: Comparative and Financial Crises*, London: Routledge, 2015.

Schubert, H. J. P. *Twenty Thousand Transients: A One Year's Sample of Those Who Apply for Aid in a Northern City*, Buffalo, NY: Emergency Relief Bureau, 1935.

Schuermann, T. 'Why were banks better off in the 2001 recession?', *Federal Reserve Bank of New York: Current Issues in Economics and Finance*, **10**, 1–7, 2004.

Schulz, P. 'Downward-sloping demand curves, the supply of shares, and the collapse of internet stock prices', *Journal of Finance*, **63**, 351–78, 2008.

Schumpeter, J. A. *Capitalism, Socialism and Democracy*, Sydney: George Allen and Unwin, 1976.

Schumpeter, J. A. *History of Economic Analysis*, New York: Routledge, 1954.

Shann, E. *An Economic History of Australia*, Cambridge University Press, 1948.

Shiller, R. J. *Irrational Exuberance*, 3rd edition, Princeton University Press, 2015.

Shiller, R. J., Kon-Ya, F. and Tsutsui, Y. 'Why did the Nikkei crash? Expanding the scope of expectations data collection', *Review of Economics and Statistics*, **78**, 156–64, 1996.

Shindo, M. 'Administrative guidance', *Japanese Economic Studies*, **20**, 69–87, 1992.

Shiratori, R. 'The politics of electoral reform in Japan', *International Political Science Review*, **16**, 79–94, 1995.

Shleifer, A. and Vishny, R. W. 'The limits of arbitrage', *Journal of Finance*, **52**, 35–55, 1997.

Silberberg, R. 'Rates of return on Melbourne land investment, 1880–92', *Economic Record*, **51**, 203–17, 1975.

Simmons, J. *The Railway in England and Wales, 1830–1914*, Vol. I, Leicester University Press, 1978.

Simmons, J. *The Victorian Railway*, London: Thames and Hudson, 1991.

Sinai, T. 'House price movements in boom-bust cycle' in E. L. Glaesar and T. Sinai (eds.), *Housing and the Financial Crash*, University of Chicago Press.

Smith, A. *The Bubble of the Age; Or, The Fallacies of Railway Investment, Railway Accounts, and Railway Dividends*, London: Sherwood, Gilbert and Piper, 1848.

Smith, R. C. 'Is China the next Japan?', *The Independent Review*, **21**, 275–98, 2016.

Spencer, H. *Railway Morals and Railway Policy*, London: Longman, Brown, Green and Longmans, 1855.

Stapledon, N. 'Trends and cycles in Sydney and Melbourne house prices from 1880 to 2011', *Australian Economic History Review*, **52**, 293–317, 2012.

Stasavage, D. *Public Debt and the Birth of the Democratic State*, Cambridge University Press, 2003.

Steinfeld, E. S. *Forging Reform in China: The Fate of State-Owned Industry*, Cambridge University Press, 1998.

Stone, D. and Ziemba, W. T. 'Land and stock prices in Japan', *Journal of Economic Perspectives*, **7**, 149–65, 1993.

Stratmann, L. *Fraudsters and Charlatans: A Peek at Some of History's Greatest Rogues*, Gloucestershire: History Press, 2010.

Stuckey, V. 'Thoughts on the improvement of the system of country banking', *The Edinburgh Review*, **63**, 419–41, 1836.

Swift, J. 'The Bubble' in R. B. Emmett (ed.), *Great Bubbles*, Vol. III, London: Pickering and Chatto, 2000.

Sykes, T. *Two Centuries of Panic: A History of Corporate Collapses in Australia*, St Leonards NSW: Allen and Unwin, 1988.

Takagi, S. 'The Japanese equity market: past and present', *Journal of Banking and Finance*, **13**, 537–70, 1989.

Task Force of the Monetary Policy Committee of the European System of Central Banks, 'Housing finance in the Euro area', *Occasional Paper Series*, No. 101, 2009.

Taylor, J. 'Business in pictures: representations of railway enterprise in the satirical press in Britain 1845–1870', *Past and Present*, **189**, 111–46, 2005.

Taylor, J. 'Financial crises and the birth of the financial press, 1825–1880' in S. Schifferes and R. Roberts (eds.), *The Media and Financial Crises: Comparative and Financial Crises*, London: Routledge, 2015.

Taylor, J. *Statements Respecting the Profits of Mining in England Considered in Relation to the Prospects of Mining in Mexico*, London: Longman and Co., 1825.

Taylor, J. B. 'Causes of the financial crisis and the slow recovery' in M. N. Baily and J. B. Taylor (eds.) *Across the Great Divide: New Perspectives on the Financial Crisis*, Stanford, CA: Hoover Institution Press, 2014.

Taylor, J. B. 'The financial crisis and the policy responses: an empirical analysis of what went wrong', Stanford University mimeo, 2009.

Temin, P., and Voth, H.-J. 'Riding the South Sea bubble', *American Economic Review*, **94**, 1,654–68, 2004.

Tesar, L. L. and Werner, I. M. 'Home bias and high turnover', *Journal of International Money and Finance*, **14**, 467–92, 1995.

Tetlock, P. C. 'Giving content to investor sentiment: the role of the media in the stock market', *Journal of Finance*, **62**, 1,139–68, 2007.

Thackeray, W. M. *The Speculators*. www.poemhunter.com/poem/the-speculators, last accessed 30 August 2019.

Thomas, W. A. *The Provincial Stock Exchanges*, London: Frank Cass, 1973.

Thompson, E. A. 'The tulipmania: fact or artifact?', *Public Choice*, **130**, 99–114, 2007.

Tobin, J. 'A proposal for international monetary reform', *Eastern Economic Journal*, **4**, 153–9, 1978.

Tooke, T. *A History of Prices and of the State of the Circulation from 1793 to 1837*, London: Longman, Orme, Brown, Green and Longmans, 1838.

Tooze, A. *Crashed: How a Decade of Financial Crises Changed the World*, London: Allen Lane, 2018.

Totman, C. *A History of Japan*, 2nd edition, Oxford: Blackwell, 2005.

Trichet, J.-C. 'Asset price bubbles and monetary policy', Speech delivered at the Mas lecture, Singapore, June 8, 2005.

Tsuru, S. *Japan's Capitalism*, Cambridge University Press, 1993.

Tuck, H. *The Railway Shareholder's Manual; Or Practical Guide to All the Railways in the World*, 7th edition, London: Effingham Wilson, 1846.

Turner, G. M., *The Florida Land Boom of the 1920s*, Jefferson, NC: McFarland & Company, 2015.

Turner, J. D. *Banking in Crisis: The Rise and Fall of British Banking Stability, 1800 to the Present*, Cambridge University Press, 2014.

Turner, J. D. 'The development of English company law before 1900' in H. Wells (ed.) *History of Corporate and Company Law*, Cheltenham: Edward Elgar, 2018.

Van Helten, J. J. 'Mining share manias and speculation: British investment in overseas mining' in J. J. van Helten and Y. Cassis (eds.), *Capitalism in a Mature Economy: Financial Institutions, Capital, Exports and British Industry, 1870–1939*, Aldershot: Edward Elgar, 1990.

Vanderblue, H. B. 'The Florida land boom', *Journal of Land & Public Utility Economics*, 3, 252–69, 1927.

Velde, F. 'Government equity and money: John Law's system in 1720 France', *Federal Reserve Bank of Chicago Working Paper*, No. 2003–31, 2003.

Velde, F. 'John Law's System and Public Finance in 18th c. France', *Federal Reserve Bank of Chicago*, 2006.

Velde, F. 'Was John Law's system a bubble? The Mississippi Bubble revisited' in J. Atack and L. Neal (eds.), *The Origin and Development of Financial Markets and Institutions From the Seventeenth Century to the Present*, Cambridge University Press, 2009.

Versluysen, E. L. 'Financial deregulation and the globalization of capital markets', *The World Bank Policy, Planning, and Research Working Paper*, No. WPS40, 1998.

Vivanco, L. *Reconsidering the Bicycle: An Anthropological Perspective on a New (Old) Thing*, London: Routledge, 2013.

Voth, H.-J. 'With a bang, not a whimper: pricking Germany's "stock market bubble" in 1927 and the slide into depression', *Journal of Economic History*, 63, 65–99, 2003.

Wallison, P. J. 'Cause and effect: government policies and the financial crisis', *Critical Review*, 21, 365–76, 2009.

Wallison, P. J. 'Government housing policy and the financial crisis', *Cato Journal*, 30, 397–406, 2010.

Walker, C. B. 'Housing booms and media coverage', *Applied Economics*, 46, 3,954–67, 2014.

Walker, C. B. 'The direction of media influence: real-estate news and the stock market', *Journal of Behavioural and Experimental Finance*, 10, 20–31, 2016.

Ward, H. G. *Mexico in 1827*, 2 vols. London: Henry Colburn, 1828.

Ward, J. R. *The Finance of Canal Building in Eighteenth-Century England*, Oxford University Press, 1974.

Weaver, J. C. 'A pathology of insolvents: Melbourne, 1871–1915', *Australian Journal of Legal History*, 8, 109–32, 2004.

Whelan, K. 'Ireland's economic crisis: the good, the bad and the ugly', *Journal of Macroeconomics*, **39**, 424–40, 2014.

White, E. N. 'Lessons from the great American real estate boom and bust of the 1920s', *NBER Working Paper*, No. 15573, 2009.

White, E. N. 'The stock market boom and crash of 1929 revisited', *Journal of Economic Perspectives*, **4**, 67–83, 1990.

White, L. J. 'The credit-rating agencies and the subprime debacle', *Critical Review*, **21**, 389–99, 2009.

Wigmore, B. A. *The Crash and Its Aftermath: A History of Securities Markets in the United States, 1929–1933*, Westport, CT: Greenwood Press, 1985.

Williamson, J. G. 'Earnings inequality in nineteenth-century Britain', *Journal of Economic History*, **40**, 457–75, 1980.

Wilson, C. *Anglo-Dutch Commerce and Finance in the Eighteenth Century*, Cambridge University Press, 1941.

Wood, C. *The Bubble Economy: Japan's Extraordinary Speculative Boom of the '80s and the Dramatic Bust of the '90s*, New York: Atlantic Monthly Press, 1992.

Wood, R. J. *The Commercial Bank of Australia Limited: History of an Australian Institution 1866–1981*, Melbourne: Hargreen, 1990.

Wright, T. *History of the Reigns of George IV and William IV*, London: Jones and Company, 1836.

Xiao, Y. 'French banks amid the global financial crisis', *IMF Working Paper*, No. WP/09/201, 2009.

Xiong, W. and Yu, J. 'The Chinese warrants bubble', *American Economic Review*, **101**, 2,723–53, 2011.

Yamamura, K. 'The Japanese political economy after the "bubble": Plus ca change?', *The Journal of Japanese Studies*, **23**, 291–331, 1997.

Yang, M. and Lim, T. S. 'Why did the Chinese stock market perform so badly in 2008?', *East Asian Institute Background Brief*, No. 247, 2009.

Yao, S. and Luo, D. 'The economic psychology of stock market bubbles in China', *The World Economy*, **32**, 667–91, 2009.

York and North Midland Railway, *Report of the Committee of Investigation, to be Laid before the Meeting of Shareholders, 1st–4th and Final Report*, 4 vols. York: Henry Sotheran, 1849.

Zhan, W. and Turner, J. D. 'Crossing the river by touching stones?: the reform of corporate ownership in China', *Asia-Pacific Financial Markets*, **19**, 233–58, 2012.

Zhu, X. 'Understanding China's growth: past, present, and future', *Journal of Economic Perspectives*, **26**, 103–24, 2012.

Zimmer, B. 'The "bubble" that keeps on bubbling'. Vocubaulary.com Blog, 25 July 2019.

Zimmerman, G. C. 'The growing presence of Japanese banks in California', *Economic Review – Federal Reserve Bank of San Francisco*, **3**, 3–17, 1989.

Zuckoff, M. *Ponzi's Scheme: The True Story of a Financial Legend*, New York: Random House, 2005.

Index